Praise from the Press for *How to Get Rich*

'If this book doesn't get you rich, nothing ever will. Five Stars.'
  — *Mail on Sunday*

'Well-founded advice based on hard-won experience.'
  — *Financial Times*

'Compulsive and hugely entertaining.'
  — *Observer*

'Fearlessly frank and truly inspirational. As good a guide to making it in the business as I have ever read. I strongly recommend this book.'
  — *Sunday Telegraph*

'Startlingly frank and very funny ... crisply delineates the keys to wealth.'
  — *Independent on Sunday*

'Absorbing, provocative and huge fun.'
  — *The Times*

'Absolutely compelling. Provides a unique insight into the mind of the dedicated entrepreneur.'   — *IoM Examiner*

'A warts-and-all guide to riches. Highly recommended.'
  — *The Director Magazine*

'Pacey, funny ... ruthlessly catalogues the author's business failures.'
  — *The Bookseller*

'Chatty, rambling, smart-alec ... Critics Choice.'
  — *Daily Mail*

'Peppered with laugh-out-loud examples of his maverick take on the business world.'
  — *EasyJet Magazine*

'Revealing, sparky and thought-provoking.'
  — *CNBC European Business*

'Well written and full of great advice. Strikes important point after point.'
  — *Seeds of Growth*

'Once you start reading, you will not want to put it down.'
  — *Editor Reviews.com*

'Dennis is wise, fearlessly frank and truly inspirational ... almost every sentence is pure delight.'   — *Mail on Sunday*

'Fantastic, funny and blunt. An immediate entry into my top 10 books about money. It's a classic.'   — *Daily Wealth.com*

Praise from Readers for *How to Get Rich*

HOW TO GET
RICH

HOW TO GET RICH

FELIX DENNIS

EBURY
PRESS

For PETER GODFREY and ROBERT G. BARTNER
who walked with me, shoulder to shoulder, for thirty years

1 3 5 7 9 10 8 6 4 2

This edition published in 2007

First published in Great Britain in 2006 by Ebury Press,
an imprint of Ebury Publishing

A Random House Group Company

The Random House Group Limited Reg. No. 954009

Addresses for companies within the Random House Group
can be found at www.randomhouse.co.uk

A CIP catalogue record for this book is available from the British Library

Mixed Sources
Product group from well-managed
forests and other controlled sources
www.fsc.org Cert no. TT-COC-2139
© 1996 Forest Stewardship Council
FSC

Printed and bound in the UK by Cox & Wyman Ltd, Reading, Berkshire

Cover Design by Mike Dunn
Interior by seagulls.net

ISBN 9780091921668

CONTENTS

Thus spoke al-Kutba, god of the Nabataeans:

'The children of thy children shall
forget Me – and my
Name
it shall vanish from the mouths of men into the dust of the world.
And yet, thy children's children's children shall worship me
unknowing, while thy rich seek after what they need not,
while thy poorest curse at what the rich store up,
and while the cries and lamentations of
Men reach up to the heavens.
All shall be as it was,
from now until
the end of
days.'

How to Get Rich

Good fortune? The fact is
The more that you practise,
The harder you sweat,
The luckier you get.

Ideas? We've had 'em
Since Eve deceived Adam,
But take it from me
Execution's the key.

The money? Just pester
A likely investor.
To get what you need
You toady to greed.

The talent? Go sign it.
But first, wine and dine it.
It's tedious work
With a talented jerk.

Good timing? To win it
You gotta be in it.
Just never be late
To quit or cut bait.

Expansion? It's vanity!
Profit is sanity.
Overhead begs
To walk on two legs.

The first step? Just do it
And bluff your way through it.
Remember to duck!
God speed …

and Good Luck!

PREFACE

CAN THIS BOOK REALLY MAKE ME RICH?

There are few ways that a man can be more
innocently employed than in getting money.
SAMUEL JOHNSON (BOSWELL'S *LIFE OF JOHNSON*)

WHY WOULD A RICH PERSON WASTE TIME WRITING A BOOK TO HELP OTHER PEOPLE GET RICH?

Two reasons. Because I enjoy writing about something I feel I know about. And because I believe that almost anyone of reasonable intelligence can become rich, given sufficient motivation and application.

It also helps that I am writing while sipping a very fine wine indeed (a Chateau d'Yquem 1986 if you really want to know), nibbling on fresh smoked conch tidbits, ensconced by a window with one of the most beautiful views on earth. Across the valley, far, far below me, palm trees fringe the fishing boats and yachts nodding in the harbour. Beyond the bay to the west, a turquoise sea ripples out to a purple and pink horizon, heralding another glorious sunset.

In the words of a Victorian English poet:

How pleasant it is to have money, heigh-ho!
How pleasant it is to have money.

I am in Mustique, a tiny island in the Windward Islands of the Caribbean. More specifically in my 'writer's cottage', a new study-cum-library some distance from the main house, built solely for one purpose – to permit me to write whatever I damn please in peace and quiet. Which is usually poetry, by the way.

And all of this, as if you needed me to remind you, costs money. It's what you get, if you want, when you're rich.

SO YOU AREN'T DOING THIS FOR THE MONEY?

Money is always welcome. But no. Very, very few authors become rich. The odds against it are too steep. Merchandising and 'brand extensions', like movies, games and toys based on fictional books, occasionally do the trick. But nobody is going to buy a toy called 'How to Get Rich' now, are they? (Then again, there's always the board game and the reality TV show … just joking!)

IS THIS SOME KIND OF CON-JOB?
ARE YOU USING A GHOSTWRITER?

Nope and nope. *How to Get Rich* is not a con-job. And it is not being ghost written. I am going to write every word myself in this book, Lord help me.

It will contain no jargon or mumbo-jumbo and it is certainly not one of those messianic 'self-improvement' manuals seeking to spawn a cottage industry of audio-visual tapes, DVDs and dubious hour-long commercials on late-night television. Nor will you have to chant incantations or tie healing crystals round your neck – let's leave that malarkey to footballers' and politicians' wives, shall we?

How to Get Rich sets out to tell you how *I* did it, how I got rich without the benefit of a college education or a penny of capital. It will expose the many errors I made along the way – which will contribute greatly to the length! Finally, it will suggest ways in which you can avoid such errors and start on getting rich.

CAN THIS BOOK *REALLY* MAKE ME RICH? YOU'LL BE SUGGESTING THAT IT WILL IMPROVE MY SEX LIFE NEXT

Possibly, to the first. It depends on your degree of motivation. In the event of that possibility materialising, the answer to your second comment is: 'Yes, it most certainly will!'

I cannot make you happy. I cannot make you healthy. But I'm pretty certain I can improve your *chances* of becoming rich. Which, in turn, will improve your sex life. People who grow rich almost always improve their sex life. More people want to have sex with them. That's just the way human beings work.

Money is power. Power is an aphrodisiac. It even says so in the Bible: 'Wine maketh merry: but money answereth all things' (Ec. 9:10). Money did not make me happy. But it quite definitely improved my sex life.

JUST HOW QUICKLY CAN I BECOME RICH?

Quicker than you probably deserve, but slower than you would like – there are too many variables for a definitive answer.

I have known it done inside five years, but there are very few 'short cuts', either in life or in this book. As the American critic H. L. Mencken once wrote: 'The inferior man's reasons for hating knowledge are not hard to discern. He hates it because it xvi • HOW TO GET RICH

is complex – because it puts an unbearable burden on his meagre capacity for taking in ideas. Thus his search is always for short cuts. All superstitions are such short cuts. Their aim is to make the unintelligible simple, and even obvious.'

Mencken was right. That's why I'm determined to cut any pseudo-scientific drivel and jargon out of this book. It makes for good copy and adds a spurious touch of authority to any debate. But it also leads inevitably to error, being comprised of error itself: the delusion that incomprehensible waffle impresses its audience.

Knowledge learned the hard way combined with the avoidance of error, whenever and wherever possible, is the soundest basis for success in any endeavour.

WHAT WILL I NEED TO DO, APART FROM READING THE BOOK?

All the usual stuff. Just as the brilliant reggae old-timer, Jimmy Cliff, used to sing in his most famous song: 'You can get it if you really want ... ' He succeeded, and so can you. But only if you really *do* want. And only if 'you try ... try and try ... and try again ... ' But we'll get to that later.

The bottom line is that if *I* did it, *you* can do it. I went from being a pauper – a hippy dropout on the dole, living in a crummy room without the proverbial pot to piss in, without even the money to pay the rent, without a clue as to what to do next – to being rich. And I am certainly no business genius, as my rivals will happily and swiftly confirm.

Yet the odd thing is, I've ended up far richer than most of my rivals.

HOW DID YOU DO IT?

Read the book and find out!

DO I HAVE TO READ YOUR BOOK
FROM BEGINNING TO END?

No. Dip in and out as you like. Make notes. Jot down points you think apply, particularly to your situation and your personality. Or make no notes at all – just highlight sentences or examples that catch your fancy.

A book like this is a tool, not an artifact. And you do not have to agree with every point I make – one size does not suit all in the quest for filthy lucre.

WHAT'S THE DIFFERENCE BETWEEN *HOW TO GET RICH* AND ALL THE OTHER BOOKS ABOUT BECOMING INCREDIBLY SUCCESSFUL?

Simple. I am not a charlatan and do not profess to be a miracle worker. *How to Get Rich* is being written for amusement, not just effect or to earn a fortune in the so-called 'self-improvement' industry. And, because I have little left to prove in the field of generating wealth, my book is as truthful and as complete as I can make it.

Lastly, I don't want to *sell* you anything else – like volume II and then volume III or a set of patronising video tapes or DVDs. All you see is all you get with *How to Get Rich*.

I did not become rich by writing manuals telling other people how to get rich. I do not have pearly-white teeth and I do not stride onto TV studio podiums in 'casual' suits costing $10,000 spouting mantras with a cover version of 'Simply the Best' belting out from the loudspeakers in front of a staged audience of adoring 'fans'.

I got rich my way. You might even say the old-fashioned way. By making errors, lots of errors, and learning from them.

Much of what I intend to share with you concerns those errors, rather than my successes. In a nutshell, I'm not a mountebank. I'm just a guy that got rich in the real world, not on the 'self-improvement' happy-clappy merry-go-round, where the only real winner is the weasel with the blow-dried hair.

HOW RICH ARE YOU, ANYWAY?

I don't know. Neither does any rich person know. I haven't cashed in all my assets yet and I'm not certain what they will fetch. Let's say between $400 million (US dollars) and $900 million of net worth before tax. I honestly cannot fix a number any closer than that.

Five homes. Three estates. Fancy cars. Private jets. (The jets are always rented. If it flies, floats or fornicates, *always* rent it – it's cheaper in the long run.) Thousands of acres of land. Art on the walls and libraries stuffed with first editions. Bronze statues littering up the garden. Chauffeurs, housekeepers, financial advisors and other personal staff coming out of my rear end.

Oh, and thousands of bottles of fine wine in the cellars. Never forget the wine.

Less the debt, of course. Around $30 million of debt. Rich people always have a certain degree of debt. Apparently it helps to reduce taxes – but I'm not so hot on the bean-counting side. In fact, I still haven't quite got the hang of a balance sheet. Amortisation always floors me.

But then, I can't fly the jets or drive the Rolls-Royces or Bentleys either. I never had the time or the inclination to learn. My constant refrain when I was bumming rides from friends as a teenager was: 'You don't understand. I was born to *be* driven.' Both my friends and myself thought that was just a smart-aleck remark back then. Now, I kind of wonder if I already knew, or at least suspected.

One or two more questions – then let's move on.

HONESTLY SPEAKING, WHAT KIND OF PEOPLE GET TO BECOME RICH?

An interesting topic. The writer, F. Scott Fitzgerald, once said: 'Let me tell you about the very rich. They are different from you and me.' By which, I suppose, he meant that they appear to have acquired characteristics that set them apart from 'lesser' mortals. Ernest Hemingway's response was: 'Yes, they're different, they have more money.' Typical Hemingway. But his riposte isn't entirely satisfactory.

There is a confidence that radiates from first-born sons and daughters. Not in all the cases I've observed, but in too many for it to be a coincidence. A similar confidence is to be observed, more often than not, in people who are rich, no matter whether they were born with it, inherited it or acquired it through their own efforts.

You can see it in the way they walk into a hotel or restaurant they have never visited before. In the irritating disposition of rich women to haggle in an Oxfam shop over a designer dress – unlike any working-class woman, who would be horrified at the thought of doing any such thing, even though she perhaps needs the discount while the rich woman does not.

You can see it, too, in the way the children of the rich appear to assume that the world was created entirely for their sole benefit. Money brings a kind of insouciance with it. It is among wealth's least attractive characteristics.

Here is Richard Rumbold, an English republican 'conspirator', speaking from the scaffold in 1685:

I never could believe that Providence had sent a few men into the world, ready booted and spurred to ride, and millions ready saddled and bridled to be ridden.

And neither, gentle reader, could I. I never could believe that.

Whatever qualities the rich may have, they can be acquired by anyone with the tenacity to become rich. The key, I think, is confidence. Confidence and an unshakeable belief it *can* be done and that you are the one to do it.

Tunnel vision helps. Being a bit of a shit helps. A thick skin helps. Stamina is crucial, as is a capacity to work so hard that your best friends mock you, your lovers despair and the rest of your acquaintances watch furtively from the sidelines, half in awe and half in contempt. Luck helps – but only if you don't seek it.

The answer to the question, then, is perhaps this: not those who *want* to and not those who *need* to, but those who are utterly *determined* to – whatever the cost.

WHAT ARE THE BIGGEST MYTHS YOU KNOW REGARDING GETTING RICH?

The first is the claim that people did not set out to get rich but became rich by 'accident'. 'Oh, I only did what I love to do and woke up one day to find myself wealthy.' That sort of thing. It may have happened. But very rarely in my experience.

Some people are merely better at disguising desire, that's all. Others, usually not those you would care to spend a vacation with, have a naked lust for money stamped on their features, evident in even their most commonplace conversations. But a capacity for disguise and dissimulation doesn't alter the fact that the vast majority of the self-made rich worked, secretly or openly, like billy-o to acquire their wealth.

The second myth is that people got rich by having a 'great idea'. While this is a more feasible hypothesis than having got rich by accident, it is a trap, because it is a partial truth. All of us have had great ideas from time to time. I have had a great idea for a kind of Spiderman gun that would shoot out a sticky web at a burglar in your house and disable them without harming them. Will it get made? Probably not.

The follow-through, the execution, is a thousand times more important than a 'great idea'. In fact, if the execution is perfect, it sometimes barely matters what the idea is. If you want to get rich, don't sit around waiting for inspiration to strike. Just get busy getting rich.

Thirdly, and lastly, I think that perhaps the most destructive myth about becoming rich lies in remarks like: 'Well, it was OK for *you* starting out in the late 1960s. But times have moved on. You couldn't do it *that* way today.'

Perhaps not, but you can certainly do it *some* way. Times change, but human nature, the lure of wealth and the determination to acquire it remain a shining constant in the world of ambitious men and women. The example of others not even *born* in the 1960s is all around you. They prove such thinking to be false.

If you *think* that it can't be done and *dwell* on that thought too long, then you are likely to remain poor. It's as simple as that.

WHY START A BOOK LIKE THIS WITH A POEM? DID YOU WRITE IT?

Yes I wrote it – but that particular poem is more in the way of a nursery rhyme. And I began this book with a poem to demonstrate that becoming rich has given me the most precious thing in life.

And just what *is* the most precious thing in life that riches can supply? Easy. For me, it's Time.

Time. Time to read and write poetry if I want to. Or to write a book if it takes my fancy. Time to travel on the slightest whim, to walk in the woods, to think, to commission art, to read, to drink, to hang out with friends and loved ones … to do just about anything really, as long as it does not involve day after grinding day making money in an office or a factory for somebody else.

That's what money can do. That's why you picked this book up. To make the money to do what the hell you want. Now I suggest you take a look at the next page and read the poem that follows – even if you do not normally read poetry it's worth a couple of minutes of study. Its subject is the destructive power of a certain type of envy.

Then skip to the Introduction, where we can discuss just how rich you want to be.

What's It Like Then, Being Rich?

What's it like then, being rich,
Knitting gold to warm an itch?
Very much like being poor;
Wealth is just a key, no more.

Why not share this magic key
To luxury – and start with me!
Surely better that you earn it;
Could I trust you to return it?

How does one become your ilk?
Is it bred in mothers' milk?
Many paths can lead to riches,
Few in sunlight, most in ditches.

Wherein lies the difference
From us – this odd ambivalence?
Envy, malice, obligations;
Toadying from poor relations.

Grown far richer than his neighbour,
Why would any rich man labour?
Wealth is salt in wine immersed,
Quaffing but excites the thirst.

Salt my arse! It's filthy greed –
How many homes does one man need?
For some the trick's in trading it;
For others, in parading it.

I've seen. But surely, comfort pales
Perched on padded Chippendales?
When affluence holds no surprise,
Wonders come in others' eyes.

Aye, the eyes of tart and whore!
What might you miss, if you were poor?
Time. The luxury of choices.
First editions. Old Rolls-Royces.

INTRODUCTION

HOW RICH?

What's a thousand dollars?
Mere chicken feed. A poultry matter.
GROUCHO MARX, THE COCONUTS

This is a thin(ish) book with a hefty(ish) price. But a price probably worth paying for those who absolutely, positively – even desperately – wish to be rich.

Not super-rich, mind you. Not filthy, stinking rich. This book cannot assist anyone who aspires to the Bill Gates or Duke of Westminster leagues. No book can do that and that is not our concern here. Bill's vast fortune, I would suggest, did not arise simply from the implementation of good ideas or the fulfilment of any single vision. It derives from deep within Bill Gates – and we'll come on to that later.

The duke, of course, inherited his massive fortune. Today, he is apparently worth the best part of £5 billion. His job is to safeguard that fortune for succeeding generations of dukes, especially from the predations of greedy tax collectors and spendthrift governments. I do not envy him such a task. It must be weary work, labouring for descendants he will never meet.

The duke, then, is massively asset rich and relatively cash poor. *Relatively*, mind. (No pun intended.) We'll come on to that later in this chapter. Relative wealth is a fascinating subject.

No, this book is about becoming one of the common or garden rich – world-class footballer rich; or J. K. Rowling rich; or rich enough to stop looking at the price of almost anything that takes your fancy. Rich enough to retire, or to work eighteen hours a day, or drink yourself into oblivion every night – if that's what you want.

Rich enough to smile sweetly or sneer at bank managers, depending on what you had for breakfast that morning; to turn your relatives green with poorly concealed jealousy while they creep around with their hands out; rich enough to buy a massive yacht (I don't advise it, though) and sail away into the sunset like the Owl and the Pussycat for years on end.

Rich enough to live where you want, to go where you want, to do what you want, to meet who you want. Rich enough to buy the only two things apart from health and love worth fussing about in life. Time. And the option of not having to be in any particular place on any particular day doing any particular thing in order to pay the rent or the mortgage.

And rich enough to begin to worry about taxes. To begin the process of employing that vast army of lawyers, accountants, advisors and estate planners who will descend upon you like uninvited vultures after a battle. A group to whom, even though you pay them tens and tens of thousands of pounds a year, you will be forever in thrall. (That large yacht and the sailing-away plan is looking better by the minute, isn't it!)

Certainly rich enough for people to respect you – but in a peculiar way. Not in the way we respect people who do really tough, worthwhile jobs – those who nurse dying children or teach for a living. And certainly not the respect earned by heroines and heroes like Marie Curie or Nelson Mandela.

Money in sufficient quantities garners a different kind of respect for its owner, a difference rooted in the nature of envy. Few of us have the courage to nurse dying children or to spend decades in prison fighting tyranny. And we do not envy those who *can* do such things, even as we look up to them.

On the other hand, nearly all of us want money. We feel free to envy the rich. And most of us believe, rightly or wrongly, that we would be perfectly able to cope with the pressures associated with acquiring too much money. The more thoughtful among us might conclude that we would be able do a lot of good with it, as well as making ourselves and our families secure.

Ask yourself this: is there a single person of your acquaintance you could be certain would refuse a bequest of £10 million? Personally, I cannot. And I'm willing to bet you can't either.

So how rich is rich?

The value of money changes inexorably over time, even in decades and centuries of low inflation. Economists and historians now have so many methods of evaluating the comparative worth of money over long periods that the exercise has become virtually meaningless to all but specialists. Meaningless because of the changes in the quality and range of goods available, the earning power of immediate and foreign neighbours, the importance (or otherwise) of the preservation of ancestral assets like land and art, and a host of other factors.

So let's ignore all that and plump for 'purchasing power' in the last quarter of a century as a rough-and-ready guide. Since 1980, the purchasing power of $1 million in the US has decreased by more than half. In Britain, the purchasing power of £1 million in 1980 has decreased by over 60 per cent.

To put it another way, £760,000 in hard cash back in 1980 would equate to the spending power of £2 million today. While you might not have been a millionaire technically back then, you would certainly have been the equivalent of one by today's standards.

So how rich is rich in the first decade of the 21st century?

The following table is based on *tax-paid cash-in-hand or assets* that can be swiftly reduced to cash – publicly traded stocks and shares, bank drafts, gold, etc. It takes no account of assets that take time to realise without incurring loss in a 'fire sale' – your home, property, land, shares held in private companies, pension funds or fixed bonds. It also assumes you have low debt and live in a Western democracy.

Table 1: Wealth Measured by Cash-in-hand or Quickly Realisable Assets

£50,000–£200,000	The comfortable poor
£200,000–£500,000	The comfortably off
£500,000–£1 million	The comfortably wealthy
£1 million–£5 million	The lesser rich
£5 million–£15 million	The comfortably rich
£15 million–£35 million	The rich
£35 million–£50 million	The seriously rich
£50 million–£100 million	The truly rich
Over £100 million	The filthy rich and the super rich

Note to Table 1: There are few people in the world who could put their hands on £100 million in cash in a week or even a month, no matter what they are worth. Such people have too much respect for their fortunes to leave that kind of change floating around in quick-release assets or cash. In addition, the reduction of any asset to cash very often leads to the imposition of capital gains tax – the equivalent of the Black Death to the truly rich. If I had to find that kind of money, I would have to borrow it, and then sell assets to repay the debt.

As far as the *total asset value or true net worth* of a person is concerned (as opposed to quickly realisable net worth), the numbers are very different. And different for a variety of reasons. Partly because of capital gains tax and other levies. Partly because death leads to death duties. Partly because of planned inheritance schemes and donations to trusts and charities. And mostly, because few rich people can know their true net worth until all their major assets are sold off.

It sounds crazy, but the richer you are and the more financial advisors you employ, the less likelihood there is that you can ever discover what you are really worth. It's a nice problem to have, but it is still a problem.

This is why so many rich people distrust the 'rich lists' and league tables of wealth published every so often in newspapers and magazines. We know that if *we* cannot calculate our true net worth, and if our paid armies of *accountants* cannot agree upon a figure, then compilers of lists and financial journalists certainly cannot do so with any real accuracy. In the words of the art collector and oil billionaire John Paul Getty: 'If you can actually count your money, you are not really a rich man.'

A final caveat concerning the total asset value of rich individuals is almost as obvious. Above a certain limit, it doesn't really matter to them *how* rich they are – give or take the odd miser and the odd hundred million. That is, it ceases to matter unless you are one of the intended heirs. Then it matters. Boy, does it matter!

You might be surprised at the number of wealthy individuals who die without proper tax-planning, or even intestate – a fancy way of saying that someone has died without a legally enforceable will in place. It is these 'intestate estates' that so please the Chancellor of the Exchequer and his minions. If you die without a legally enforceable will, chances are the taxman will gobble up a great deal of what you left behind.

This next table, then, shows my take on a person's *total net worth*, assuming you are not about to die, that you are prepared to take time to cash out such assets and, again, that you have low debt and live in a Western democracy.

Table 2: Wealth Measured by Total Assets (True Net Worth)

£1 million–£2 million	The comfortable poor
£2 million–£5 million	The comfortably off
£5 million–£15 million	The comfortably wealthy
£15 million–£40 million	The lesser rich
£40 million–£75 million	The comfortably rich
£75 million–£100 million	The rich
£100 million–£200 million	The seriously rich
£200 million–£400 million	The truly rich
£400 million–£999 million	The filthy rich
Over £999 million	The super rich

Note to Table 2: The importance of taxation upon assets in such a table cannot be underestimated. In certain circumstances the true net worth of an individual or family might be reduced by as much as half, if little or no tax-planning has been undertaken.

So how rich do you want to be? The usual answer is 'rich enough to be happy'.

But riches do not confer happiness! I have lost count of the number of friends, lovers and acquaintances I have told this to, especially when I first passed seven noughts of cash in hand. I don't bother any more. The incredulous look on their face is always the same. What they are really thinking is: 'Well, maybe *you* are not happy with all that dough, Felix, but I know that *I* would be. Just try me!'

Still, let me repeat it one more time. Becoming rich does not guarantee happiness. In fact, it is almost certain to impose the opposite condition – if not from the stresses and strains of protecting wealth, then from the guilt that inevitably accompanies its arrival.

Even leaving any moral dimension – heaven, camels and the eyes of needles – out of the equation, consider at least the wise sentiments of the author James Baldwin in his book *Nobody Knows My Name*, in which he concluded:

> *Money, it turned out, was exactly like sex. You thought of nothing else if you didn't have it, and thought of other things if you did.*

But let's face it, you didn't buy this book to be happy. You bought it in the hope it would provide pointers to becoming rich. According to my tables of wealth, 'rich' starts at a total asset value of £15–£40 million (also known as 'the lesser rich').

So that's where we're aiming. For starters, anyway.

At the top end of that range, you might (just *might*, mind!) creep into the last few places on the Sunday Times Rich List, compiled annually by Philip Beresford and his team of researchers. The STRL is the gold standard of league tables of the wealthy in Britain.

Your rank then would be around '999 equal' of the top 1,000 richest individuals and families in the UK. As far as the USA is concerned, your £40 million would place you nowhere on any major list, except, perhaps, somewhat high in the kind of esteem I described earlier among family, friends, partners, gold-diggers, stockbrokers, bankers and estate agents. Well, I did say that £15–£40 million was only a start!

Of course, all measurements are arbitrary. They are just an attempt by humans to make some kind of order out of a chaotic universe. In and of themselves, they are meaningless.

Quite as valid a measurement of money as asset value or cash in the bank might be 'Availability on Request' or 'Lifetime Spending Totals'. If you had no money yourself, but a fairy godmother gave you exactly what you needed whenever you requested it, you would never make the Sunday Times Rich List, but you would be the richest person in the world, even if you gave everything away each night.

And as for Lifetime Spending Totals (LSTs) as a measurement, I would love to know how much various people have spent in the course of their life – including me. Sadly, I know I am never going to be able to figure it out, except for the certainty that I have spent hundreds of millions of dollars. My LST will have been eye-watering.

I also know that because nearly all so-called 'old money' has to be protected from any one generation's carelessness, their family wealth – especially property – is tied up in trust funds and entailments. In effect, many of the children born into this 'old money' are as poor as church mice, simply because they cannot get their hands on the loot. They would have surprisingly low LSTs. Clean fingernails and good manners, certainly; but low lifetime spending totals.

Now, enough waffling about definitions. Let's get down to making some dough.

Let's get rich!

PART ONE

REASONS NOT TO GET RICH

1

POLE POSITIONS

No task is a long one but the task on which
one dare not start. It becomes a nightmare.
CHARLES BAUDELAIRE, *MY HEART LAID BARE*

LADIES AND GENTLEMEN,
START YOUR ENGINES ...

For a great many people, getting started on the road to wealth is the most difficult part. Or so they believe. The nuances of each individual case need not concern us, but the difficulties, as stated by virtually every wannabe I ever listened to on the subject, usually fall into one of three broad categories – often age related.

If **young** and **relatively penniless**, many will argue their **lack of experience** and **capital** (especially capital!) dooms them to decades of wage slavery.

If **slightly better off and on the way up** with a halfway decent job and perhaps the probability of further advancement, the problem is often considered to be **the loss of what they have already achieved**. Plus the lack of capital.

By the time one is a **senior manager** or **professional**, probably with a decent house, a mortgage and children, it is the **risk to the security and happiness** of the latter (and maybe to a spouse), plus the usual lack of capital, which are most often cited as insuperable difficulties to taking the plunge.

All such objections to becoming rich are spurious, no matter how sincerely held. But before dealing with each in turn, let me digress for a moment regarding **upbringing**, **race**, **colour**, **educational qualifications** and **gender**.

I am doing so here because I do not wish to waste anybody's time. We will be touching on some of the circumstances described above shortly, but, in a nutshell, my experience has been that money is colour-blind, race-blind, sex-blind, degree-blind and couldn't care less who brought you up or in what circumstances.

Money is one of the most neutral substances on earth. Others may conspire against you obtaining it through bigotry or prejudice. But they can only succeed if you permit them to.

The object of your goal, in and of itself, is non-sentient. If you truly believe that your race, sex or upbringing can keep you from becoming rich, then you had best give up here. Either return this book to the shelf or, if you have already bought it, return it to the bookstore for a refund or give it to a friend. You may obtain the refund or please your friend.

But you will never get rich.

YOUNG, PENNILESS AND INEXPERIENCED?

> *It's the same the whole world over,*
> *It's the poor wot gets the blame,*
> *It's the rich wot gets the pleasure,*
> *Ain't it all a bleeding shame?*
> VARIETY HALL SONG (C.1915)

Excellent. You stand by far the best chance of becoming as rich as you please. You have an advantage that neither education nor upbringing, nor even money, can buy – you have almost nothing. And therefore you have almost nothing to lose.

Yes, yes, I know you've heard all that before. But consider for a moment: nearly all the great fortunes acquired by entrepreneurs arose because they had nothing to lose. Nobody had bothered to tell them that such and such a thing could not be done or would be likely to fail. Or if they *had* been told, then they weren't listening. They were too busy proving those around them wrong – without even meaning to.

Not knowing that something cannot be done, you are likely to waltz into uncharted minefields where angels before you have feared to dance. Astonishingly, you may be fortunate enough to succeed, to some degree or another. Conventional wisdom will then be revised by those around you and the next generation will be taught that what you did can *always* or *often* be done – only to discover, when they attempt it themselves, that in reality you missed every landmine by pure, dumb luck.

Never trust the vast mountain of conventional wisdom. It contains great nuggets of wisdom, it is true. But they lie alongside rivers of fool's gold. Conventional wisdom daunts initiative and offers far too many convenient reasons for inaction, especially for those with a great deal to lose. Fortunately for you, you do not have anything to lose and can afford to ignore the 'jobsworths' and Jeremiahs who have lived upon the mountain for so long that they have come to worship it.

Nor is a propensity for risk-taking your only advantage. You have stamina far, far beyond those who are twenty or thirty years older – the stamina necessary for long, grinding hours of labour in the cause of getting rich. Stamina enough to party all night and go straight back to work for a twelve- or sixteen-hour day. I remember such stamina fondly.

You have no idea how much the stamina of the young is envied by the rest of us. Along with a degree of callousness and enviable powers of speedy recuperation from reverses, stamina is your secret weapon. Its attributes will see you through a raft of catastrophes that would virtually annihilate older men and women.

In addition, your instinctive knowledge of modern technology gives you another edge. (All those hours spent playing computer or video games might not have been such a waste after all.) At least you know the difference between an iPod and a JPEG. And knowledge is power, at whatever age, whether earned by blood and tears or imbibed at a mother's breast.

Treasure that instinctive knowledge. I still own half of the personal computing magazines in Britain – *PC Pro*, *Computer Shopper*, *Computer Buyer*, *MacUser*, *Custom PC* – in part because of an early addiction to pinball and electronic arcade games. While I knew nothing of computing (and still do not), the instincts honed by countless hours of shoving money into slots forewarned me of their potential. The first few million pounds I ever trousered were a direct result of trusting instincts entirely at odds with conventional wisdom of any sort.

Two immediate examples leap to mind. As we will see in more detail later, I published a series of eight-page full-colour, folded posters (with headlines and articles printed on the back) and charged the same cover price as magazines with ten times that number of pages. The result was dubbed a 'poster-magazine' and sold millions of copies around the world. Nobody had told me it couldn't be done because nobody had done it before.

Similarly, as previously noted, I launched half a dozen magazines about a new fad called 'personal computing' back in the 1980s, even though British magazine retailers and wholesalers at the time were unanimous in their belief that 'nobody will ever buy them'. Those magazines have earned me tens of millions of pounds in the last twenty-five years and are still earning me money today. Conventional wisdom is usually right. But when it is wrong, it can offer quite extraordinary opportunities for those too stubborn or inexperienced to pay attention to well-meaning naysayers.

Perhaps most importantly of all, as a young and penniless and inexperienced person, you are not an 'expert'. Thus you are more willing to learn than those in their thirties, forties or fifties. You are not afraid of making mistakes, admitting them when you do and getting right back on track. (Speaking of tracks, you have no track record to defend, either.)

Here is a pearl beyond price and – Glory Hallelujah! – it cost you nothing to obtain. Anyone not busy learning is busy dying. For as long as you foster a willingness to learn, you will ward off sclerosis of the brain and hardening of the mental arteries. Curiosity has led many a man and women into the valley of serious wealth.

Ambition, fearlessness, self-belief, stamina, a degree of callousness, a willingness to learn. These are your advantages over the middle-aged and the old. 'Gather ye rosebuds while ye may!' Could you turn the clock back for me by forty years, I would willingly swap you every penny and every possession I own in return. And I would have the better of the bargain, too!

So what does the future hold for a young man or woman determined to become far wealthier than their parents? Here is how I see it:

The way will most likely be hard, your failures many. It will be fun and it will get a little hairy, even scary, at times. But the earlier you start and the more risks you are prepared to run, tempered by listening hard and choosing the right mountain (we'll come to that later), the more certain it is that, sooner or later, you will find yourself with a small success on your hands.

And one success, with luck, will lead to another.

If there is a single category of person for whom this book should prove the most useful, it is you: the young, penniless and inexperienced. I know. I've been there.

And if I was lucky enough to find a way through, then so can you.

Stick with me, young brother or sister. You are suffering from nothing more than excusable confusion and a lack of experience, conditions that will pass with time, and whose passing can be expedited by fierce determination and application.

Believe it or not, I envy each and every one of you.

SLIGHTLY BETTER OFF AND ON THE WAY UP?

I have a bone to pick with Fate.
Come here and tell me, girlie,
Do you think my mind is maturing late,
Or simply rotted early?

OGDEN NASH, 'LINES ON FACING FORTY'

This is the point at which many people vaguely wonder about starting their own business, either on their own or with a partner or two. They have enough experience to know how the companies they work for function. Perhaps even how their industry functions. And they see a niche – as yet imperfectly filled. They have 'an idea'. (See Chapter 5: **The Fallacy of the Great Idea**.)

Yet they hesitate. They fear losing what they have already achieved more than they desire to enrich themselves. Personally, I am on more than familiar terms with this syndrome. I meet it every day, because it affects (or afflicts) a great many of the fine men and women who run my own companies. Perhaps even a majority of them.

I employ a great many people smarter than I am. That's not false modesty, that's a stone-cold fact. The only two reasons such geniuses continue to work for me and put money into my pocket are that, on the positive side, they enjoy their work, and on the negative side, they fear losing what they have already gained – challenging work, congenial colleagues, a certain status and the promise of promotion and pay rises.

They know this as well as I do. (They are far from fools, otherwise I would hardly employ them.) But fear holds them back, with the exception of those rare individuals who are content with their lot.

And what is fear? 'Fear is the little death, death by a thousand cuts,' goes the ancient Japanese saying. Nifty, but ultimately unhelpful. Similar to Shakespeare's 'Cowards die many time before their deaths: / The valiant never taste of death but once.'

But is fear really the father of cowardice? Let's leave that to the philosophers. In business, in the accumulation of wealth, it is an impediment, for sure. But then, so is recklessness. No, I believe that it is *the fear of failure* which looms largest here. And fear of failure is definitely something that can be dealt with, and *will* be dealt with at length in this book. (See Chapter 3: **Harnessing the Fear of Failure.**)

Outsiders are sometimes surprised at my reaction when people in this category, the Slightly Better Off and On The Way Up, decide to leave one of my own companies and set up on their own. I always wish them well. Not only outwardly, but in my heart, too. Often I throw a party for them. Or write glowing testimonials. Once or twice I have even underwritten their office lease or introduced them to a banker or a lawyer I trust. Why do I react that way?

Three reasons. Firstly, I'm proud of them. Proud that those who work for me are brave enough, motivated enough and trained sufficiently well to go for it on their own. Boldness attracts applause, as the writer and philosopher Goethe once remarked in doggerel:

> *Whatever you can do, or dream you can, begin it!*
> *Boldness has genius, power and magic in it.*

Secondly, it's win–win. If they fail, they may well return to our company, especially if they remember that my senior colleagues and I sincerely wished them success in their new venture. Thus, if they fail, the company will be enhanced by their return. While if they should succeed – then we will be all richer for having an old alumnus as a friendly rival in the industry, rather than having created a enemy who wishes us anything but well.

Lastly, it's because I fear them. I fear they may have spotted something we have missed, some gap in the market. I fear we may have failed to listen to them. I fear that their new venture will grow at our expense while it poaches our personnel and our market share. And the only way to deal with fear is to cosy up to it. To look it in the eye and pump its hand. To translate its negative energy into adrenaline. To harness it. To laugh *with* it, rather than *at* it.

Perhaps this could be *you* giving your current boss the scare of his or her life? At the very least, providing your idea or venture has serious merit, any sensible company would attempt to buy you off. If they do not, then perhaps they are not a company that deserves to benefit from your talents? It's a thought, isn't it?

As one who has been 'the boss' for longer than many of you have been alive, I can assure you that you enjoy much greater leverage than you might believe. But you will never find that out until you go for it.

For the Slightly Better Off and On The Way Up, *now* is the time to consider whether or not you intend to continue making me (and people like me) even richer, or whether you wish to become rich yourself. You have little time left in which to make up your mind. Your youth and stamina is ebbing away. You are getting too comfortable.

It is not a course for everyone. But I think you can guess what my advice to you would be.

What the hell. Go for it!

SENIOR MANAGER OR PROFESSIONAL?

Pushy young turks are impatient for news –
Young Cinderellas are singing the blues –
Wannabees, just like you used to be ... Choose!
Whose gonna fill this dead man's shoes?
'DEAD MAN'S SHOES'

Welcome! I'm surprised you could bring yourself to read such a book. It's a good sign. It shows you're still curious. Still hungry. Not as hungry as the penniless lad or lass at the beginning of this chapter, of course. But then youth is wasted on the young – and they have so much learning to do, do they not?

You, on the other hand, have learned much. There is little about your company you do not understand. Little, too, about your industry that has escaped you. You have seen a great many fools take the plunge into freelance work or set up in business on their own with such high hopes. And watched nearly all of them come crashing down in flames or creep through the bankruptcy courts hoping nobody would notice.

But I bet *you* noticed. I'd bet my bottom dollar that *you* noticed.

Still, there have been one or two who made it, haven't there? One who even suggested you take the plunge with her and take a *piece of the action*? Was that the one you turned down? The woman who waves when she passes you in her Mercedes-Benz SLR convertible on her way to a golf club you cannot afford to join? From a house on the water with its own dock, apparently. The one who is now far richer than she deserves to be? The one who got lucky? Let's face it, you were, and are, smarter than she is. Or ever will be.

Annoying, isn't it?

But you don't have to give up hope. With luck you'll make the board in four or five years, if you haven't already. So much easier to strike out on your own from such a position, rather than acting precipitately, *non*? The banks will listen more closely to a board director, after all.

And it's true you have responsibilities. The mortgage has some years to go, although the house increases in value every year. The kids aren't through college yet, but they soon will be. It's just a question of waiting. Of recognising 'the realities of the present tempered by the necessities of the past and the possibilities of the future', as the author R. G. Collingwood put it. But then, he was writing about history.

If you detect a trace of cynicism in the above description, then you are correct to do so. And for a simple reason. In nearly forty years of doing business, I know of only six senior managers or professionals between forty and fifty who struck out on their own. And two of those were lawyers.

One did very well indeed with his own law firm. Two of them did *fairly* well. One went belly up and never recovered financially. One threw in the towel and owns a tiny bar on an island in Croatia. (I suspect he is the happiest of the lot.) The remaining one shot himself when his venture collapsed. None of them became *really* rich.

Yet you picked up this book. You're still curious. You're still hungry. Read on, my learned friend. *How to Get Rich* may subvert you yet, though I very much doubt it.

And you know what? The kids and the house and the mortgage and your retired parents and the love of your life (whether a man or a woman) and all your current responsibilities – they are not the real problem. They are either inanimate, or they love you, or they don't love you. They will not love you less (or more) if you decide to surprise everyone around you and seize the time. As you *could* seize it, if you truly wished to. Then you'd show them.

Why not face the unpalatable truth? These are excuses. They are nothing but a smokescreen. An alibi. Convenient camouflage to prevent you from accepting that you will probably never be rich.

Soon, you must choose. Many people would say you have left it too late to choose. But still, *you picked up this book*. You're still curious. You're still hungry. *And you know it can be done*. Even better than the young and penniless and those on their way up, you *know* it can be done. Better still, you know *how* it can be done. You have helped make it happen – for someone else.

The only question is: will you dare to try? If you will, then you are one in a million. Or two million or three. Your chances are slim, but they are not impossible. My earnest advice is to get yourself a young and fearless partner with tons of stamina.

Choose him or her with care. It's your best chance to get rich.

2

A MILLION
TO ONE

There are three kinds of lies.
Lies, damn lies and statistics.
THOMAS CARLYLE, *CHARTISM*

'Dare not' is one thing. 'Cannot' is another. Not everyone can be rich. But anyone can *dare* to. Somebody *has* to. Let's take a look at the arithmetic relating to the odds.

By my earlier definition, only 0.000016 per cent of 60 million British citizens are rich. That's less than 1 per cent of 1 per cent of 1 per cent of 1 per cent of 1 per cent of the total population. If your best friend inherited one million pounds and gave you 0.000016 of their windfall, you would receive a princely sixteen quid. 'Hey! Thanks a bunch, old chum.'

If wealth were decided by lottery, you would have sixteen chances in a million of scraping into the top thousand richest people in the UK. To reach the top fifty, you would have to do better. A lot better. Like one chance in a million, allowing that a fair percentage of the places in those leagues are taken by those who inherited their loot – or a good chunk of it, anyway.

These are not very enticing odds.

Fortunately, less and less wealth is decided by the lottery of inheritance. Only a quarter of the entries now in the Sunday

Times Rich List in Britain find themselves there due solely to inherited wealth. If, indeed, it is that many.

Twenty-five years ago it was different story. Back then, nearly three-quarters of the buggers were force-fed their wealth from golden spoons. (In those days, though, there were only 200 entries on the list.) Low have the mighty fallen! And they'll be falling further yet when another blasted *nouveau riche* like you, dear reader, elbows his or her way into the golden horde.

If you can, that is. Because not all of us are cut out for it. Let us explore factors likely to exclude an individual from becoming rich. This is where we sort the wolves from the does, the prey from the predator and you from a lifetime of wage slavery.

There's health, for a start. People in poor health usually find it difficult, no matter how clever they are, to muster the stamina that becoming rich demands. In any case, when you are *really* poorly, the allure of wealth rapidly recedes – except as far as first-class health care is concerned. (I can attest to this from personal experience. Twice now I have survived life-threatening illnesses. Making money was not big on my list of priorities at that time. In fact, I was so far gone at one point, that I forgot to sue the bastards who were responsible. Looking back, I must have been *very* ill indeed!)

As always, there are exceptions. The theoretical physicist, Stephen Hawking, has been confined to a wheelchair for years with a rare and appalling disease. Yet he made a bundle with a book that very few people have ever read right through to the end. A book that has sold millions of copies, *A Short History of Time*. (And did you know he featured in an edition of *The Simpsons*?) My hat off to you, professor.

We must also factor in disadvantage and age. Not of colour, sex, race, religion, upbringing or lack of education. None of those present insuperable hurdles in a Western democracy. But mental handicap, growing senility and the physical decline of old age – none of which need be life-threatening in the short term –

virtually rule out any serious accumulation of wealth, except by inheritance or winning a lottery.

So that leaves the relatively fit and those not old enough to call themselves old. Close to 40 per cent of the population of the UK are either old enough to have little hope of acquiring real wealth if they have not done so already, or are too young to be able to acquire it in the short term, except by inheritance. If you fall into neither of these groups, you now have only 35,999,000 people to beat.

That equates to twenty-five chances in a million of scraping into the top thousand richest people in the country. Still daunting odds.

But, wait! There are huge chunks of the population around you who either have no desire to be rich or have chosen professions that rule them out of the race. I asked a researcher to estimate for me the total number of people working for the government in Britain. (If you can afford it, always get someone else to do the grunt work. See Chapter 13: **The Joys of Delegation**.) While it is theoretically possible for a civil servant to resign from their job and become a multi-millionaire (especially, apparently, if they worked for the Ministry of Defence), the number of ex-civil servants in the Sunday Times Rich List is tiny – two of them having inherited their wealth while parading in the corridors of power, and one who was rich long before he became a minister.

So what did my researcher discover? Well, the number is astonishing. Over 5 million people work for the government in the UK in one way or another and are unlikely ever to become rich. Your odds now have improved to twenty-eight chances in one million.

And now look around you. How many of the people you work with, the people you socialise with, the people you see in the street, do you think have dedicated themselves to getting rich, or are likely to do so any time soon? Or have the drive or aptitude to attempt to do so? Two per cent? Three per cent? Five per cent? Let's take 3 per cent, which I believe to be a massive overestimate, by the way. Personally I know only five acquaintances who dedicated themselves to achieving success in business in order to make themselves seriously rich. (As opposed to scores of senior managers or professionals known to me who dedicated themselves to success in their business life, but allowed others to reap the main financial rewards of their labours.)

Those five people, I might add, amount to a lot less than 3 per cent of all the people whom I believe *could* have become rich had they wished to do so. Or had they drummed up the confidence to try.

So – 3 per cent of the 30-odd million people still in the race amounts to just under one million rivals. To reach the top thousand earners among them, all other things being equal, you have now shortened the odds to one chance in a thousand. Which is significantly better than the sixteen chances in a million we began with. Now you know what Carlyle meant by lies, damned lies and statistics.

Lastly, in any list of reasons not to get rich, we must come to philosophy and the benefits of hindsight. If I had my time again, knowing what I know today, I would dedicate myself to making just enough to live comfortably (say £30 or £40 million), as quickly as I could – hopefully by the time I was thirty-five years old. I would then cash out immediately and retire to write poetry and plant trees.

Making money was, and still is, fun, but at one time it wreaked chaos upon my private life. It blocked me from beginning to write poetry until my early fifties. It consumed my waking hours. It led me into a lifestyle of narcotics, high-class whores, drink and consolatory debauchery. As a philosopher might have put it – all the usual dreary afflictions of the seeker after wealth. These afflictions, in turn, helped to undermine my health.

But like an old, punch-drunk boxer, I couldn't quit. I always craved just one more massive pay-day. One more appearance under the lights with the roar of the crowd and the stink of the sawdust and leather. One more fight. 'I can take this young punk. I know I can. Just this once, so I can go out as a winner. So I can retire as the champ. Then I'll retire. Just this last one.'

Pathetic. I should have known better. There is no such thing as a permanent champ. After all, I co-wrote the first bestselling biography of Muhammad Ali back in 1974. (You'll find it, republished as *Muhammad Ali: The Glory Years* on Amazon.com.) And there isn't a single fan of Muhammad Ali who does not wish he had quit the ring several years before his failing powers made the decision for him.

It's no excuse, but making money is a drug. Not the money itself. The *making* of the money. This sounds like so much hooplah, but it's true, all the same. Nobody believed that *exercise* could prove addictive until science stepped in and discovered 'endorphins' or whatever the damn things are called. And making money, I assure you, is a hell of a lot more of a rush than jogging.

Up to just seven years ago I was still working twelve to sixteen hours a day making money. With hundreds of millions of dollars in assets I just could *not* let go. Like I said, it was pathetic. Because whoever dies with the most toys *doesn't* win. Real winners are people who know their limits and respect them.

Eventually I found a way out. I handed over day-to-day control of my businesses to younger and mostly smarter boys and girls. I cleaned up my personal life. I began doing what I wanted to do – not what I felt I *had* to do. After all, what did I have to prove? Except, perhaps, to myself.

It is possible that you will avoid such mistakes when you get rich. I hope so. One thing is for sure: 'the usual afflictions' are no reason not to make the attempt. There is no reason on earth why financial success should lead to personal catastrophe. Least of all the odds.

The odds may still appear daunting, but only to those lacking sufficient guts and determination to try. If the odds of getting rich put you off, then you deserve to stay poor. Or, to put it more kindly, whether you *deserve* it or not, you *will* stay poor.

But we're done here with reasons not to get rich. Our ends are not foretold in our beginnings. The poet was wrong there. We're heading for our own version of *The Glory Years*. We're on our way.

It's time to concentrate on getting started. To take the first step on the long road to getting rich.

PART TWO

GETTING STARTED

3

HARNESSING THE FEAR OF FAILURE

Go tell the Spartans, thou who passeth by,
That here, obedient to their laws, we lie.
John Dryden, on the Spartans at Thermopylae

THE EIGHT-HUNDRED-POUND GORILLA

This is the 800lb gorilla. The King Kong of your nightmares. The reason, almost certainly, that you have not already begun to make yourself rich. He's a big bastard, so arm wrestling is out, but he's not quite as scary as you might think. Maybe we can bribe him with a sack of bananas? Or poison him? Or teach him to sit up and beg? Let's see.

'Not begun until half done,' lectured John Keats gloomily in a letter to a relative nearly two hundred years ago. Keats was a sublime poet, who died when just twenty-five years old. Although he would rank well inside my own top twenty favourite writers of verse in English, perhaps in the top ten, he would have made a totally rotten entrepreneur.

I would use, instead: 'Once begun – the job's half done.' Because taking that first, irrevocable step has proved to be the most difficult part of nearly every venture I have been involved in.

In the memorable words of the American philosopher and poet Ralph Waldo Emerson:

No matter how much faculty of idle seeing a man has, the step from knowing to doing is rarely taken.

There are so many reasons not to do anything, many of them highly persuasive, especially in the mouth of a Jeremiah. And the world is full of Jeremiahs. They infest our planet. In the living room, in the pub, in the office, at the boardroom table. Everywhere you look, you will find men and women who appear to take perverse pleasure in pointing out the shriekingly obvious: that if a new venture does not succeed, it may result in failure.

Not that they will say so in so many words. It would be so much easier to overcome the bulk of their objections if they did. Instead, they trot out facts and figures, statistics and trends, charts and graphs, together with endless reminders of failures of the past, with especial emphasis on the failures of those lucky enough not to be in the room at the time. (There is rarely any mention of their own failures, in my experience.)

They will say the company or the individual does not have the resources. That it has all been tried before. That 'the light isn't worth the candle'. That outside advice is required or that an individual should seek further counsel. That the individual or company is uniquely unsuited to such an enterprise. That it is too late, or too early, for such an idea to have any chance of succeeding.

How many millions upon millions of man-hours are wasted annually, I wonder, in all this doom-mongering? Personally, I've had a bellyful of it.

At the last extremity, as far as most company enterprises are concerned, the Jeremiahs will call in the big guns. 'We must form a committee to investigate the possibility of proceeding. That's the answer. A *committee*. Who shall we choose to chair the committee?'

This is the death knell, in nine cases out of ten, for any new venture. What lies behind it is the desire to apportion blame that may accrue later as widely as possible. If a committee is formed and eventually makes its recommendations, then future blame for either action or inaction cannot be laid at any one person's door. In business and political jargon, this nonsense is called 'collective responsibility'. In common parlance, it is 'covering your backside'.

'A committee is a cul-de-sac down which ideas are lured and quietly strangled,' as Sir Barnett Cocks, clerk of the House of Commons, once pointed out. Well, Sir Barnett should certainly have known. He served on enough of them. Or in the words of an anonymous American wit: 'A committee is a group of the unwilling, chosen from the unfit to do the unnecessary.' Just so. And they do it so brilliantly well. Whether in a college dorm, or in the walnut-panelled boardroom of an international conglomerate, or around your own kitchen table.

Of course, there is nothing wrong with robust debate, either with others or with oneself. What *is* undesirable, however, is the pretence that any such debate can resolve the risks involved in advance. It cannot. All debate can do is clarify, support or contest the next step. The risks remain, however much talking is done.

It is for this reason that committees are discouraged on the battlefield. A commander may be proved wrong. He may be proved right. But prompt decisions and orders, right or wrong, are far healthier than endless debate and prevarication. This applies equally to a debate within one's own mind. Fretting is counter-productive at any level.

And so is lack of action. Knowing that fear of failure is holding you back is a step in the right direction. But it isn't enough, because knowing isn't doing.

> *Knowing isn't doing what you need to do, my son;*
> *Telling me you know is only bluffing on the run;*
> *Knowing isn't doing;*
> *Doing isn't knowing;*
> *Nothing but the knowing and the doing gets it done.*

Fear of failure and the avoidance of blame, then, is what drives Jeremiahs and haunts them. To be fair, it haunts all of us. In essence, it comprises two components. The first is our natural desire to avoid letting ourselves or others down, perhaps with calamitous financial repercussions. The second is the exposure of that failure to the outside world.

The majority of you reading this now are mentally nodding in agreement. (Otherwise, why would you be reading a book called *How to Get Rich?*) No shame there.

Believe me, I have sat with colleagues and partners of long standing, many of them highly experienced, and listened in disbelief while they have talked themselves round and round in circles. Or figures of eight. Or any configuration designed to delay the agony of saying:

'OK. Let's do it.'

Or even: 'OK. Let's forget it.'

And looking back, I have to say that I regret the majority of the times I acquiesced in shilly-shallying and a retreat to safety. I would rather have tried and failed, in most cases, than have taken the safer course that so often appears to be wiser in the abstract.

Back in the late 1970s, for example, I had a conversation with a much older man, a senior manager at the high-street retailer, W.H. Smith. W.H. Smith are a power in the magazine and newspaper industry. This old buffer was friendly and helpful towards my little publishing company. I was interested in launching a personal computer magazine. He dissuaded me, warning me over and over that 'nobody would ever pay money to read monthly magazines about dinky little computers'. Several colleagues in my company agreed with him. After weeks of discussions, I abandoned my plans.

Shortly thereafter, another entrepreneur, Angelo Zgorelec, launched just such a title, called *Personal Computer World*. It soon exhibited all the signs of becoming a big success. Fortunately, Angelo did not have sufficient capital to promote it. In the nick of time I was able to purchase a majority stake in the magazine, which I proceeded to sell for a small fortune four years later to a large conglomerate.

So what is the lesson here? Because I had been dissuaded from launching my own title, and did not own the magazine outright, I was forced to pay Angelo a million pounds or so for his remaining share. Well done, Angelo!

Had I launched a similar magazine myself earlier, I would have been £1 million richer in the autumn of 1982. (Around £2.4 million in today's money.) If I had invested that £2.4 million at a low rate of compound interest, I would be £4 million richer than I am today.

That is what that well-meaning old gentleman at W.H. Smith and his long-winded advice cost me. He cost me nearly $8 million in my pocket right *now*. And whose fault was it? It was mine, for prevaricating and listening to a Jeremiah.

Let's return to the two components of fear of failure. Firstly, letting others or yourself down and the consequent financial calamity. My response is: so what? You may let others down if you act. You may let yourself down if you do not act. And just how calamitous will utter failure prove to be, in any case? Which, of course, is what gives the young and penniless such a huge advantage in the race to get rich. They instinctively know what Bob Dylan preached forty years ago: 'When you got nothin', you got nothin' to lose'.

Still, potential loss is always an important consideration. Everything will depend on the degree of desire and belief you bring to an enterprise. What are you willing to sacrifice to achieve it? How great is the sacrifice in reality, as opposed to your nightmarish fears at 3 o'clock in the morning? Does such a venture really risk utter destitution? Or is it (far, far more likely) that you fear the *embarrassment* of failure more than the possible financial penalty.

This nastier, stickier second component, the 'broadcasting' of our misjudgements or errors to the rest of the world, and especially to our peers, is often the nub of the matter. Whether I am sitting around with colleagues at Dennis Publishing trying to figure out if we should invest millions of pounds to launch a new car magazine, or whether a young woman, an only child not long out of college, is considering whether to take over her father's used-car business or invest another two years of her life in obtaining a Ph.D. in bio-engineering – the same factors apply.

Neither decision will involve utter financial ruin, either way. But fear of attempting something, the result of which cannot be easily hidden, weighs heavily in the balance, whether we are aware of it or not. This applies not only to getting rich, but to almost all business and career-related decisions. And, perhaps, to the majority of all important decisions we make in our lives.

The board of directors that runs Dennis Publishing will talk earnestly and sensibly about the effect on morale for the rest of the company (usually forgetting to mention their own morale) in the event our proposed new magazine bombs. (Nobody ever mentions the loss to my personal bank balance or *my* morale.)

In reality, Dennis Publishing staff working, say, on *The Week* or *Maxim* or *Computer Shopper* won't give two hoots if the company's new car magazine is a sensational flop. But by discussing the matter in such terms, in code if you like, the board gives itself the opportunity to weigh their own fears while appearing to weigh the fears of others.

Imputing desires or fears or loss of morale to others probably has a fancy psychological moniker – like auto-displacement activity. And it's not always a bad thing. At least it encourages serious communication, even if it adds little to the decision process. Even so, it is a form of well-disguised cowardice.

On a less corporate level, the young woman mentioned above believes she would like a career in car sales management, especially as a part-owner. She even believes that she might be able to expand her father's business a tad more aggressively than he has done in the past. On the other hand, a Ph.D. would add status to her life and offers the prospect of a fulfilling career in science.

But she must decide. Her father is unwell and cannot wait another two years for her decision. What if she takes over the company and it subsequently goes belly up? What if she shoots for a master's degree and does not achieve it?

A failure to obtain her master's degree could be disguised fairly easily. It is not likely to be broadcast to the rest of the world. After all, she already has a degree. If failure seems likely, she can always quit, claiming she has become bored with bio-engineering. The decision to take over her dad's company, however, will be far more closely monitored – by relatives and neighbours, by the people who work there, by rival car dealerships, by the bank manager, and not least by her father. Should she fail, she will run the risk of becoming a laughing stock or an object of pity.

So what is her best option?

Much will depend on her desires and her goals in life. She is unlikely to get rich as a bio-engineer. But she might well get rich expanding the dealership, especially because she is aware that her father has never invested to the extent that he might have done in marketing and promotion, especially on the internet. There is an opportunity, but is she prepared to exploit it?

Why is she unlikely to get rich in bio-engineering? Because starting up your own bio-engineering firm takes vast quantities of capital and the persuasive abilities of a Richard Branson to obtain it. The car dealership, however, is already capitalised, and although she will have to pay off her father eventually, the repayments can be spread over a number of years. He is hardly likely to foreclose on her.

So what should our young college girl do? Normally, I would hesitate to offer any advice whatever. But I happen to know her. I was half in love with her once. She happens to be real and her name is Julie. All this happened a long time ago.

In the event, she took her degree and her father sold the business to an outsider. She is a highly competent bio-engineer and has enjoyed her career enormously. But on more than one occasion, she has told me she regrets not taking her father up on his offer. The passage of time and a happy marriage have softened that regret. But it's still there. It will always be, I think.

What swung the balance was her fear of failure in such a 'public' endeavour. Or, at least, an endeavour that *felt* rather public at the time. She was young. She was a woman. She was frightened that others (especially the male-dominated community of car sales firms) would laugh at her or criticise her lack of hands-on experience, even though she would have made an excellent sales manager. She was not prepared to grow a carapace or to risk the fear of public humiliation and say:

'To hell with them. Let's go!'

Her decision still haunts her, if only from time to time. And it irks her to know that she will never be rich. It always irks intelligent people like Julie.

And I can give you other examples. One of them is my mother. She will be furious (if she ever reads this) that I have mentioned her in such a book and such a context. But I know my mother well. I know beyond a shadow of a doubt that everything I have achieved I owe not just to care and love, but to her genes.

She could have built herself a fortune had she wished. Her personality combines the resilience, the drive and the restless energy of so many people who become rich. Like her eldest son, for instance. And that resilience and restless energy was always there with my mother. As it was with me. Right from the beginning.

But sixty years ago it was almost unheard of for a woman to act out such ambitions. Her parents would have been scandalised. Neighbours would have viewed such behaviour in the most negative light imaginable. Had she failed, they would have nodded their donkey-like heads.

And had she succeeded, horror of horrors, she would have earned their undying enmity. It just was not 'done' for a woman to earn a fortune for herself – except, somewhat dubiously, as a movie star perhaps. Or a writer of crime novels.

Single or newly married women from respectable families in the 1940s and 50s were actively discouraged from involvement in business except for a little light typing or serving in shops and department stores. Especially if they had children. Especially if they lived in the South of England. (And this after they had helped to win a world war on the home front! But that was considered a vile aberration.)

Never mind that my mother had more brains in her little finger than half the twerps she worked for as an accountant. Why, women were not even allowed to sign a hire-purchase form back then. They had to get their husband or their brother or their father to do it!

There were a hundred obstacles and hurdles in those days, visible and invisible, to keep women in their place – which was firmly believed to be on a pedestal before marriage and in the kitchen and nursery directly afterwards. Fortunately for all of us, society has wised up somewhat; but the change came too late for my mother.

So she didn't become rich. She had a decent career, that's all. She earned enough to support my brother and me and to provide us with more than just the necessities of life. And she married again and became a pillar of the community. But I know that she *could* have done it, had she been prepared for the unpleasantness, the sheer nastiness that would have been unleashed upon her if she had chosen to say:

'To hell with them. Let's go!'

It was not so much a fear of failure on my mother's part, I believe, as a fear of upsetting the whole apple cart of the community in which she lived. Which is why so very few women from her generation – so very, very few – ever *did* do it. They cared very much about what their neighbours thought. And now she is an elderly, if formidable lady who quietly walks her dog along English country lanes.

She knows all this, of course. And she, too, knows that she will never be rich, except through her eldest son. Which is a subtly different thing.

To sum up then, if you wish to be rich, you must grow a carapace. A mental armour. Not so thick as to blind you to well constructed criticism and advice, especially from those you trust. Nor so thick as to cut you off from friends and family.

But thick enough to shrug off the inevitable sniggering and malicious mockery that will follow your inevitable failures, not to mention the poorly hidden envy that will accompany your eventual success. Few things in life are certain except death and being taxed. But sniggering and mockery prior to any attempt to better yourself financially, followed by envy later, or gloating during your initial failures – these are three certainties in life. It hurts. It's mindless. And it doesn't mean anything. But it *will* happen. Be prepared to shrug it off.

The Germans have a superb word for the (secret) pleasure humans obtain from the misfortunes of others. It is *Schadenfreude* – from *schaden* meaning 'harm' (from which we get the word 'shadow'), and *freude* meaning 'joy'. Those of you who are definitely going to be rich will recognise it often enough in the faces and body language of idiots around you. It is the price you must learn to pay for any attempt to raise yourself in the world. And I suspect that was as true ten thousand years ago as it is today.

Now comes the hard part. Before we really get started on getting started, I ask you to consider carefully the short list below. It is by no means comprehensive, nor will it be the last list in this book, but should you find yourself unable to measure up to even *one* of these initial demands (and I mean just *one*), then my suggestion is that you close this book and give it to a friend.

○ If you are unwilling to fail, sometimes publicly, and even catastrophically, you stand very little chance of ever getting rich.

○ If you care what the neighbours think, you will never get rich.

○ If you cannot bear the thought of causing worry to your family, spouse or lover while you plough a lonely, dangerous road rather than taking the safe option of a regular job, you will never get rich.

○ If you have artistic inclinations and fear that the search for wealth will coarsen such talents or degrade them, you will never get rich. (Because your fear, in this instance, is well justified.)

○ If you are not prepared to work longer hours than almost anyone you know, despite the jibes of colleagues and friends, you are unlikely to get rich.

○ If you cannot convince yourself that you are 'good enough' to be rich, you will never get rich.

○ If you cannot treat your quest to get rich as a game, you will never be rich.

○ If you cannot face up to your fear of failure, you will never be rich.

The truth is that getting rich means sacrifice. And the worst of it is, it isn't always *you* that's doing the sacrificing. You must get used to that, or give up the quest. This is not a calling for the faint-hearted. There is no shame in turning away. After all, if everyone was prepared to make the necessary sacrifices, who would be left to work for my *own* companies?

Quite apart from sacrifice, there is a last brutal truth to be confronted. If the fear of failure is holding you back – and it almost certainly is – then what strategies can be devised to set you free? No book, including mine, can do it for you. All I can do is alert you to the problem and suggest a course of action.

Here is my suggestion. Think of this fear not as the King Kong of bogeymen, but as a mare. A nightmare. A mare, after all, is a horse. A horse can be tamed, bridled, saddled, harnessed and (eventually) ridden. Harnessing the power of such a creature adds mightily to your own. Thus the nightmare of prospective failure provides you with the very opportunity you are seeking. Not only does it restrain smarter people than yourself from becoming rich – and there can only be so many rich people in the world – it affords you the chance of increasing your confidence, both when you confront it and when you master it.

For make no mistake, if you will not confront and harness this all-too human emotion in one way or another, then you are doomed to remain relatively poor.

You either get over it, go round it, go at it, mount it, duck under it or cosy up to it. But you cannot surrender to it. That way lies paralysis, prevarication, ignominy and defeat.

After a lifetime of making money and observing better men and women than I fall by the wayside, I am convinced that fear of failing in the eyes of the world is the single biggest impediment to amassing wealth. Trust me on this.

If you shy away for any reason whatever, then the way is blocked. The gate is shut – and will remain shut.

You will never get started. You will never get rich.

4

THE SEARCH

Until one is committed, there is hesitancy; the chance to draw
back; always ineffectiveness concerning all acts of initiative
and creation. There is one elemental truth, the ignorance of
which kills countless ideas and splendid plans: that the
moment one commits oneself, Providence moves all. All sorts
of things occur to help one that would never otherwise have
occurred. A whole stream of events issue from the decision,
raising in one's favour all manner of incidents and meetings
and material assistance which no one could have dreamed
would come his or her way.

JOHANN WOLFGANG VON GOETHE

WAITING FOR GODOT

'What do you want to be when you're grown up?' is the dreaded,
inane cry from well-meaning aunts and uncles to infant children.
This morphs soon enough into anxious queries about examination results. By the time college is on the horizon, many
teenagers are ready to wreak physical violence upon adults who
pester them with thinly veiled questions and tedious advice
concerning their future career.

This probably happened to you, just as it did to most of us.
The best response I ever heard came a few years back from one
of my godchildren, delivered with a serene smile and carefully

articulated irony to a nosy neighbour: 'Oh, I'm going to be rap god, Mrs Milburn, and pimp half your Brownies.'

The Brown Owl who had asked him was anything but amused.

Just at the very time hormonal chaos, acne, drugs, alcohol, sport, fashion, gadgets, cars, music, body piercing, partying and sex are emerging as matters of compelling interest, we find ourselves faced with an eternal mantra about earning a crust. All of this is irritating in the extreme, mostly because it harps upon what is patently obvious – that one day we are going to have to make a living.

And yet, there is a kernel of wisdom buried in the pulp of these parental and family concerns. The truth is that the vast majority of people doing the asking did not choose their own career. Either they stumbled into it or they were pushed.

Knowing this, adults are often subconsciously seeking, however clumsily, to nag the young into confronting as early as possible the biggest decision over which any of us is likely to exercise real control. We do not choose our parents. We do not choose our nationality. We do not choose who we fall in love with. We do not even choose the personality or character of the children we bring into the world or our own personal character-istics – random configurations of DNA do it for us.

But we *do* get to choose, if we are determined enough, what it is we want to do for a living. Most of us flunk this test. Me, for instance. My career as an entrepreneur magazine publisher came about entirely by accident. If you had asked me when I was eight-een years old what I would be doing for the next thirty years, I would have told you I was going to be one of the biggest R&B singers in the world.

That didn't happen, and if I'm honest about it, I'm still a little disgusted with myself that I quit the dream so early. But, hey, I was getting tired of stealing food and bumming other people's cigarettes and not having the rent money. It was no fun shinning down a drainpipe to ensure I avoided meeting my land-lady in the hall.

And in any case, I had an appointment. It wasn't one of my own choosing, but it came along all the same.

> ESTRAGON: Charming spot. Inspiring prospects. Let's go.
> VLADIMIR: We can't.
> ESTRAGON: Why not?
> VLADIMIR: We're waiting for Godot.
> SAMUEL BECKETT, *WAITING FOR GODOT*

Who never arrives. So is it such a terrible thing that the vast majority of us settle for what comes along rather than making a career plan and sticking with it? And how do you get to decide what career you might excel at anyway?

Most parents and teachers reading this are not going to like my answer. It's this: none of it matters a damn if you want to get rich.

This is not to say that 'the Search' is not important to young people. It's important and it's scary and it's fun and infuriatingly confusing. For most people, it occurs in their twenties or very early thirties. For a small number, the Search is over by their teens, either because they have a shriekingly obvious talent or because they have already spent too many hours hanging out in the wrong company.

For the rest of us, though, the Search is a lot scarier than we usually care to acknowledge. And this arises, ironically, from the success of Western Democracies, those with a capital 'W' and a capital 'D'. They have provided too much choice for younger citizens. Nobody but an idiot would deny this is a good thing – even a wonderful thing. But choices are confusing. They take time to consider, to sample, spit out and reject. And too many of them provide a ready-made excuse for procrastination and shilly-shallying.

Not to mention fantasising. It came as a shock to me to read in *The Week* that 20 per cent of British teenagers in school claim they would abandon their education if they could just get themselves on television. In any capacity whatever. Just to be a 'celebrity'. Which probably explains the queues clamouring to be humiliated on 'reality TV', a modern equivalent to ancient Rome's gladiator circuses. That is, it came as a shock until I remembered my own certainty at seventeen that I would knock The Rolling Stones flat on their ass.

All of us have our dreams. And these are not to be despised or mocked. They are a part of us, whatever they are.

If you want to serve your fellow man, then go do it (and God bless you). If you want the status of being a professional – a professor or a lawyer or an economist, then go do it. If you want to be secure so that you can marry and raise kids, then choose the civil service, because bureaucrats never go out of style and pensions for senior civil servants these days appear to be gold-plated. If you want to be a world-class writer, musician or athlete or movie producer, then go do it – it won't be that long before you discover whether you have the talent to hack it or not.

In other words, if you feel absolutely moved towards a particular vocation, then that's exactly where you should head. But be aware that if you want to make huge sums of money, then earning a living by slowly swarming up the greasy pole is rarely the way to do it.

For a start, the salary begins to have an attraction and addictiveness all of its own. A regular paycheck and crack cocaine have that in common. In addition, and more to the point, working too long for other people can blunt your desire to take risks. This last factor is crucial, because the ability to live with and embrace risk is what sets apart the financial winners and losers in the world.

If you want to be rich, you are not looking for a 'career', except as a launch pad or as a chance to infiltrate and understand a particular industry. A job for the rich-in-training is merely something to keep you ticking over, to put food on your plate and wine in your glass.

Additionally, it will provide excellent training in man-management and negotiation skills; it will supply inside market information; above all, it will act as a salutary reminder of what happens to 99.99 per cent of your colleagues – the ones who buy lottery tickets and dream of becoming rich but who haven't a hope in hell of achieving any such thing.

Sounds pretty arrogant and selfish, doesn't it? Not exactly 'playing the game' or exhibiting what a human resources manager would call 'a constructive team attitude'. But then, who ever heard of a rich human resources manager? Right. Neither have I. And, in any case, if you do the thing right, there is no reason why such a manager need ever know. Or care.

So if you want to be rich and you are in the Search phase of your life, then get used to one thing. You are *not* part of a team – although you may have to pretend you are. To put it more politely, you may have to adopt the *idea* of teamwork, for the time being, to help yourself understand better how individuals, departments, companies or industries function.

You should certainly do so enthusiastically and conscientiously. But in your secret heart, however hard you work (and if you want to be rich, working a damn sight harder than the punk next to you is the only sensible option), you must not be deceived.

Working for others is a reconnaissance expedition; a means and not an end in itself. It is an apprenticeship and not a goal.

You should have no long-term, or even medium-term, requirements of the first two or three companies you work for. Promotion is always welcome and brings with it the opportunity to learn more, but you are there to ensure that you take every opportunity to suck out the marrow of what you need to know, to understand it and place it within a greater context for a future purpose. The purpose of getting rich.

Team spirit is for losers, financially speaking. It's the glue that binds the losers together. It's the methodology employers use to shackle useful employees to their desk without having to pay them too much. While lives may depend on it in a few professions, like soldiering or fire-fighting, in commerce it acts as a subtle handicap and a brake to ambitious individuals. Which, in a way, is what it's designed to do.

Here's an example. Back in the early 1980s, I launched *Star Hits* magazine in the USA. It was based on the highly successful pop-music rag *Smash Hits* in Britain.

I negotiated a deal with EMAP, the owners of *Smash Hits*, to pay them a small royalty on each copy we sold in America. In return, they helped me to hire a couple of their *Smash Hits* staff who were willing to relocate to New York City and work for me there. One of these guys was an editor called Neil Tennant, a young man with a wry smile and the look of eagles about him.

Launching a magazine is an exhausting process. Most magazines fail within two years, and although it lasted a little longer than that, *Star Hits* was destined for a short, if spectacular, existence. But we didn't know that in 1984. British pop groups were popular at that time in America – especially a group called Duran Duran. Being associated with the mighty *Smash Hits* in England gave us an edge in obtaining photographs and interviews. *Star Hits* took off like a rocket in America.

In no time at all we were selling hundreds of thousands of copies each month. Letters from readers arrived in their thousands from every corner of the country and the sacks piled up in the hall of our pokey New York City midtown offices. The staff of *Star Hits* worked all hours of the day and night and were fiercely determined the magazine should succeed. Nearly all of them were young, and for some of them this was only their second or third job.

My small company's financial resources were limited, which meant that people on the magazine were often promoted quickly.

Neil Tennant quickly found himself the editor of one of the hottest magazines in America. New York City lay at his feet. His desk was entirely swamped by tottering piles of promotional material sent by record companies. He could get backstage at any gig, from huge arenas like Madison Square Garden to hip, crowded nightclubs downtown. Managers and PR agents vied for his attention. He flew anywhere he wanted and interviewed whoever took his fancy. This was a dream job and Neil was on top of the world.

Morale and team spirit in the office were high, too. Staff were not required to wear suits or ties and as long as the job got done, nobody cared what anyone looked like or bothered them with corporate rules or red tape. Neil and the staff of *Star Hits* were having a whale of a time. I was kind of enjoying it myself.

Late one afternoon he sauntered into my office. He was holding a cassette tape which he tapped with his fingernail as he slumped on a battered chair and stared at me, half sheepishly, half defiantly. 'Felix, I'm going to leave *Star Hits*,' he said. 'I've been working on some numbers and I think I have a real chance of making a go of it. Listen to these and tell me what you think.' Later that evening I played the tape (which I still have in my archives). It was not my kind of music, but one particular song, 'West End Girls', I think, was a stand-out. I had vaguely known of Neil's personal interest in recording, but had never dreamed he would risk such a fantastic job for the vagaries of becoming a pop star.

I went to work on him the next day. How I would be happy to pay him more money. How *Star Hits* was poised on the brink of greatness. How he would be certain to be offered even more glamorous editorial jobs by my competitors if he stuck it out. Above all, I pointed out how disappointed and let down his editorial team would be.

No dice. Neil was right. The Pet Shop Boys became huge stars. On his last day, at a small office leaving party, he told me that within a year he would make the front cover of *Star Hits* in his own right. And he did, too!

When it comes right down to it, 'team spirit' and not letting your colleagues down is a feeble reason for procrastination when opportunity comes knocking. Nearly always, it is an excuse to avoid the possibility of humiliating failure. If one of the team *you* work with inherited ten million quid tomorrow, do you really believe they would be checking in to keep up morale? Of course not. Neither would you, or anyone in their right mind.

Which leads us to a note of caution. Those who can never be rich may not want *you* to become rich. That's an ugly thing to say, but unless you realise and accept that you cannot be 'one of the boys', that your bosses and you are not 'in this thing together', that only those who refuse to be conned by the idea of 'team spirit' in the workplace can succeed – unless you come to fully comprehend and understand all this, then you will only make other people rich. You will receive their heartfelt thanks and maybe a gold watch when you retire. But you will not get the money!

It's the same with close friends and family members. Consciously and outwardly they may want you to succeed beyond your wildest dreams. But subconsciously, often without being aware of it themselves, they might be far happier if you failed or only succeeded to a limited degree.

It's a selfish world out there. But, hey! when you've piled up your first few million in the bank, you can salve your conscience by giving generously to your relatives. Or by promoting young managers and waffling on to them about 'team spirit' in your own business. Not that the brightest of them will believe you for a moment. (They're the ones you promote fastest, by the way.)

What else is there to consider during the Search? Some industries are more enticing and glamorous than others. Some require huge investment to get off the ground and some can be made to work in an attic or a garage. And some are growing while others are in decline. Should you choose only to work in glamorous, growing industries? Where is the most opportunity to be found?

First off, forget glamorous. One of the richest self-made men I know digs holes in the ground to dispose of household waste. That's not how his company describes itself in its annual report, but essentially that is what it does, along with building incineration plants.

Glamorous? No. But in a good year he puts £20–£30 million on the bottom line and earns a gross margin of over 20 per cent. That's a sensational result for a small, wholly owned private company. Not to mention that the relentless growth of the packaged-goods industry ensures that his business will grow and grow virtually by default – providing he can find enough places to dig holes, that is.

While you may not necessarily want to be in a glamorous sector of any market, and they are often very crowded sectors, it helps to be in a *growing* one. Swimming with the tide rather than against it, so to speak. A swelling tide raises all boats, including yours.

On the other side of the 'glamorous' coin, very few of those who want their picture on the front cover of *Vogue*, or wish to become a movie director or to run the coolest PR company in the world, get to achieve anything. The reason is obvious. The laws of supply and demand are absolute – and they apply not only to commodities, but to people. Too many people want to make a blockbuster movie and live in Beverly Hills. Not enough people want to dig holes.

New or rapidly developing industries, whether glamorous or not, very often provide more opportunities to get rich than established sectors. The three reasons for this are availability of risk capital, ignorance and the power of a rising tide.

Investors are drawn to emerging industries in the hope of making a fast buck. To get rich, you will need capital, and to acquire capital you need to be where loose capital is searching for a home. In addition, the combination of ignorance and misconception that surrounds any new market or technology works in your favour. If you are quick at grasping concepts and jargon, you become an 'instant expert'. The owners of capital love 'experts'.

Finally, the power of a rising tide masks many start-up difficulties, putting individuals and small companies on a more even footing with conglomerates and established operators; for a while, at least.

I've had personal experience of this craziness. Back in the late 1970s I knew nothing of personal computers. And I mean, literally, nothing. The only PC I had ever seen was built by a nerd from a kit. It appeared to allow the nerd and his fellow nerds to play a pathetic video game called 'Pong'. On top of that, it permitted like-minded nerds to converse with each other in a jargon beyond the understanding of non-nerd mortals. To sum up, PCs were for trainspotters.

This was not exactly promising ground for an entrepreneurial publishing company. Even so, the enthusiasm of these nerds and of science journalists in the mainstream press concerning the potential of personal computers was growing. To cut a long story short (and a story which has still not ended thirty years later), my tiny little company became 'instant experts' on personal computing. We launched magazine after magazine on the subject, both trade and consumer based, and established several exhibitions.

Our acquisition of apparent 'expert' knowledge, together with all our new launches, bred respect among our vendors, primarily paper merchants and printers. They vied to offer us far better credit terms than they would normally have considered offering. This provided me with desperately needed capital to expand.

As magazine publishers, we could not hold a candle to our bigger rivals, and no one knew this better than they. But at least we *appeared* to know what we were doing, which in turn attracted editorial talent who really *did* know. Better still, the tide of personal computing technology rose high – higher than anyone could have predicted, and it rose quicker than anyone had thought possible.

Here was the power of a new market at work. By the time our bigger rivals were comfortable enough to launch against us (a hesitation resulting from ignorance), the tide had carried us beyond the reach of their big guns. New capital, ignorance and a rising tide had done the trick. In this instance, the Search had paid off in spades.

As a general rule of thumb, then, growing industries with relatively low start-up costs offer more opportunities for those who want to get rich than declining industries, or those that require huge start-up investment. This is not an iron-clad rule, however. While magazine and newspaper sales have been in slow decline in the Western world for decades, this 'declining' industry is where I made a great deal of my own money.

More important than any particular industry are the sectors within each industry. A sizeable fish in a growing sector, however small, is more attractive to prospective purchasers and investors than the same size fish in a diminishing or static pond.

This is one of the factors in stock-market bubbles – all growth is good (as far as investors are concerned), while all decline is fatal. I happen to believe that such sentiments are flawed. But what I believe is immaterial. It's what the providers of capital believe that counts, no matter how illogical. After all, what are banks and venture capitalists but usurers who offer you an umbrella when the sun is shining and snatch it away the instant a few rain clouds appear? (Ah, the old jokes are the best jokes.)

I do know of a few examples of self-made multi-millionaires from static industries, especially in commodities, publishing and precious metals, who were lucky enough to persuade banks and venture capitalists to back them with millions of dollars. Of course, this means that they rarely remain in control of their own destiny.

Capitalism demands that whoever takes the most financial risk calls the piper's tune. The biggest rewards go not to those individuals who came up with the idea, nor to those individuals who built the empire. They go to those entities or individuals who funded the enterprise and own the most stock. Always bear this in mind during the Search.

This is the system you are pledged to both join and beat. To join because you need to get rich. And to beat because you have insufficient capital. Either by appearing to join those who will financially back you (while holding on grimly to every piece of stock you can), or by piecing together just enough success to borrow enough money to grow without disposing of your sacred shares. (See Chapter 12: **Ownership! Ownership! Ownership!**)

Depressingly, the only way for a start-up entrepreneur to succeed is often to part with equity in return for an infusion of capital. But never forget that no matter what promises or verbal guarantees you receive from investors during the Search, the issue will eventually come down to control. And control, even by a single per cent of the shares of a business, the fabled 51–49 per cent split, is often the be-all and end-all of the game. (See Chapter 6: **Obtaining Capital**.)

Whoever controls a business can force its sale. Whoever controls a business can implement a merger. Whoever controls a business can fire you. Whoever controls a business, even by a pitiful 1 per cent, is likely to take a great deal more money out of it than the minority shareholders. Remember, too, that in both private *and* public companies, not all shares are necessarily equal, either in voting power or financial value. Choosing a growing industy, or growing sector of a static industry, can free you from such financial control freaks.

To gain control of a company, investors often pay well over the odds. However, those still clinging to the residue, even though they are protected from 'oppression' by the majority shareholder in law, rarely see equal value when all is said and done. For a minority shareholder who helped found a company, this can be a bitter pill to swallow. They may even have sold some of their shares to ensure the company's viability, only to discover that having won such a battle, they have lost the war.

This is especially true in start-ups, and even more true in start-ups that do not require substantial capital investment. While engaged in the Search yourself, spare a thought for the software giants of today, most of which were founded in basements, spare bedrooms and garages a quarter of a century ago. They went through the Search themselves. The search for a niche. The search for funding.

Once upon a time, the chance was there, for those who could see it, to get in on the ground floor of this potentially huge industry. To most of the geeks and nerds who slaved away creating primitive operating systems and applications (for which there were no known uses), one or two percentage points of their tiny companies appeared to them to be, literally, neither here nor there. Few inventors or 'creative types' make very good managers or businessmen, in case you hadn't noticed.

But today, those one or two percentage points would be worth hundreds of millions of dollars in hard cash. Inch by inch, share by share, the nerds diluted to gain capital to expand and survive. Eventually, the majority of them lost control of their tiny companies. Many became salaried employees of the company they had helped to found. Much depended on whether they lost control prior to or after a public stock offering, but we needn't go into that here.

Just a few, a very few, held on to enough stock to become immensely wealthy. Ownership is power. Ask Bill Gates of Microsoft or Larry Ellison of Oracle. But don't ask the guy who claims to have invented the world's first computerised spreadsheet. Last time I heard, he was living on welfare in a crummy district of San Francisco.

But we are getting ahead of ourselves. The division of spoils comes only when there are spoils to divide. So how to choose the arena in which you intend to carve yourself a fortune? There are usually three factors involved in the Search: inclination, aptitude and fate.

We all have inclinations of one sort or another. To me, spending an afternoon inside the bonnet of a classic car with an oily rag for company is my idea of hell. Yet a retired friend of mine works on the two classic Rolls-Royces I own whenever he gets the chance – and enjoys it so much he refuses to accept payment. On the other hand, how many other people would consider working eighteen hours straight on a complicated poem as a way to 'enjoy' themselves? There's 'nowt as strange as folk', as my Yorkshire friends never tire of reminding me.

Your inclinations really do count. You have to pay attention to them. If, like me for example, you abhor television, then it probably isn't a good idea to move into that industry, unless you have a yen to *direct* or *write* for the small screen. A different thing entirely than *watching* TV night after night.

If you love art, but cannot paint or sculpt to save your life, then perhaps you can still make your millions in the art world – providing you possess not only a natural affinity and sense of aesthetic, but the wit to spot and winkle out talent in young artists. Plus the ability to sell, which is usually nothing more than a talent for hype and keeping a straight face as you demand a fifty times mark-up from potential buyers who wouldn't know a Damien Hirst from a pickled sardine.

An understanding and passionate affinity with any subject, in combination with effective management, sales and marketing techniques, could well provide a tailor-made solution to the Search. Cherish your inclinations and affinities. Though not infallible, they may well lead you in the right direction. But do not fall into the error of making a *fetish* of your passion. You're reading this book to get rich. Not to confirm your own prejudices regarding those talents or inclinations you may have.

Because aptitude is a very different kettle of fish. Few of us are lucky enough to be born with a talent so obvious that the Search is never an obstacle to progress. Yet even here, inclination may prove a stumbling block to real wealth. One of the best sales people I ever employed, and one who was so conscious of her ability that I was forced to pay her nearly twice the salary and bonus of her immediate boss, now lives in Cornwall and paints watercolours.

They are not very good watercolours, in my opinion. But neither my opinion, nor the promise that she would be a multi-millionaire before she was thirty-five, proved a sufficient inducement to keep her nose to the grindstone. The aptitude for selling advertising was obvious, and was the envy of all her colleagues. But her inclinations led elsewhere. She is happy as far as I know and I wish her all the luck in the world. But she will never be rich. Fortunately, she says she has no wish to be.

So how do you judge your own aptitudes? Trial and error is the only way I ever heard of. The problem is that we create an image of ourselves in our childhood and youth (often at the urging of parents, siblings or friends), and subsequently attempt to graft reality onto this image. More often than not, the graft doesn't take and the result is bewilderment and disappointment. Far better to ruthlessly analyse what your particular aptitudes are and act upon them rather than attempt to graft an oak tree onto a dandelion.

If you are still young, here is where the advice of a godparent, a trusted teacher or lecturer, or even a career counsellor can prove useful, bearing in mind that impartiality is a better guide than parental pride. Your parents, likely as not, will be of little use here. Their love for you may well blind them to the harsher realities of your true abilities and potential. There are a great many doctors and lawyers who apprenticed themselves to their profession solely to please an ambitious parent – only later to regret their acquiescence at leisure.

If you *do* decide to ask for advice concerning your true aptitudes, then preparation shows you are serious and will be more likely to effect a serious response. As a godparent, I am always willing to discuss the matter, but only if my godchild has prepared a list of questions and suggestions, and only in private. Casual conversations around a family living room, with others sticking their oar in or trying to show off with banter and smart remarks, are tedious and counter-productive. For ambitious young people this is a serious matter and deserves to be taken seriously.

Of course, such discussions cannot make you rich. But they can really help in the Search. They can build confidence, a key element in risk taking, and the only way I know of to get rich from a standing start. And they can inform you, too, of your weaknesses, which in turn can protect you from spending your working life making other people rich – the probable fate of nearly everyone you currently know.

If you are older, and by older I mean in your thirties, then the matter becomes far more difficult. I would say almost impossible, as far as advice is concerned.

How many of us at that age know somebody to whom we can say: 'What do you truly believe my strong points to be?' and expect a meaningful answer? And even if we *can* find someone we feel comfortable discussing such a subject with, how many of us know anyone whose opinion is worth the potential embarrassment? Blind faith and trial and error are just about all that's left unfortunately. There *ought* to be a better way, but no one I know has ever stumbled across it.

Inclinations are easy to list. Aptitude is far less so. Trial and error, combined with fierce determination and a willingness to discard cherished perceptions about ourselves, is the best that I can suggest.

It is highly unsatisfactory and frustrating that the most important decision we are likely to *consciously* make leaves so very much to chance. A small success, though – even a tiny success – can provide a clue. It was my own success at selling magazines on the street that led me to begin to publish them eventually.

Which leads to fate. To chance. To serendipity. And, to a lesser extent, to the shared social delusion of the supernatural. I do not believe myself to be any more superstitious than the next person, although it is true that I find myself knocking on an actual piece of wood just a little too often for comfort. Even so, as a history and biography buff, it always amazes me how the self-made rich appear irresistibly drawn toward the mines in which they will excavate their fortunes. What led them there? How did they know where to turn?

It is the instinct to seize an opportunity when it presents itself that perhaps sets apart the self-made filthy rich from the comfortably poor, the willingness to ignore conventional wisdom and risk everything on what others consider to be folly. One could even argue that it hardly mattered that young Henry Ford was drawn to automobiles, or that Ruben Rausing chose packaging, or that Bill Gates gravitated to software to create those vast fortunes. I would be open to persuasion that had their roles, and the century in which they lived, been reversed, they would have done just as well and raised themselves every inch as high from the common herd financially.

Their ability to take chances and to subsequently exploit initial success counted more than their inclination towards a particular industry. Their execution of a strategy trumped the subject of their obsession.

Luck? Fate? Chance? Although I am reluctant to even write these words, without them, it appears, nothing can be done. (See Chapter 10: **A Few Words About Luck.**) While it infuriates me to admit it, there are just too many people I am acquainted with who appear to draw bad luck to them for this not to be so. If the influence of luck is a delusion, then all I can say is that the delusion is virtually universal.

The filthy rich are not gods. They are men and women who put on their underwear in the morning pretty much as you do. It is true that they were in the right place at the right time and did the right thing. The difference is that in some way they placed themselves in fate's way, then grasped her by the forelock as she sprinted past. ('Lady Luck is bald behind', says the old proverb.)

To put it less fancifully, they were lucky in the Search and skilful in their follow-up. Boldness helped. Conquering fear of failure helped. Persistence helped. But, without some luck, no one can get anywhere in the search to discover the exact arena in which to do battle, the arena that suits an individual's aptitudes and inclinations.

Boldness? The most successful generals or admirals in military history shared one characteristic: they were willing to ignore orders and risk utter disgrace in order to exploit rapidly changing circumstances. When the chance came, they recognised an opportunity, weighed the odds swiftly, and placed their lives and careers on the line to snatch a victory. (Not to mention the lives and careers of those around them.)

The three great quotes concerning 'luck' for me are these:

> *'Luck is preparation multiplied by opportunity.'*
> SENECA, ROMAN PHILOSOPHER

> *'The harder I practised, the luckier I got.'*
> GARY PLAYER, GOLF CHAMPION

> *'Luck is a dividend of sweat.'*
> RAY KROC, MCDONALD'S FOUNDER

Fortune favours not just the brave but the *bold*. Boldness has a kind of genius in it, as Goethe pointed out. It can lead to complete failure and defeat, because conventional wisdom often proves to be at least wisdom of a kind. But should boldness succeed, should the chance be seized and sufficiently well executed, then success will surely lead to glory.

All around us, every day, opportunities to get rich are popping up. The more alert you are, the more chance you have of spotting them. The more preparation you have done, the more chance you have of succeeding. The more bold you are, the better chance you have of getting in on the ground floor and confounding the odds. The more self-belief you can muster, the more certain will be your aim and your timing. And the less you care what the neighbours think, the more likely you are to take the plunge and exploit an opportunity.

Here is the key, then, in the Search. Whatever your inclinations, your aptitude, your abilities or your preferences, never shrink when opportunities arrive. If you have weighed the odds and find yourself convinced, ignore the protestations of sensible people and their conventional caution.

Seize Lady Luck by the forelock and hang on for your life. More men and women have become rich by this single tactic than all 'the best-laid plans of mice and men' guided by plodding strategy.

Chances come to everyone in life, in all shapes and sizes, often disguised, and more often radiating risk and potential humiliation. Those who are prepared to analyse the risk, to bear the humiliation and to *act* in deadly earnest – these are the 'lucky' ones who will find themselves, when the music stops, holding a potful of money.

But then, in reality, they made their own luck. They never stopped searching. Perhaps they spent months or even years searching in the wrong place. Or possibly they hit upon the object of their search at the first attempt. No matter.

Having found what they needed where they needed it, and having done what they judged needed doing, their search is over. And it is *they* who will become rich.

5

THE FALLACY OF
THE GREAT IDEA

Between the idea
And the reality
Between the motion
And the act
Falls the shadow
T. S. ELIOT, 'THE HOLLOW MEN'

'I'VE JUST HAD THIS GREAT IDEA ...'

The novelist and poet Vladimir Nabokov may have been coming it
a bit high when he told an interviewer in the mid-1960s that 'great
ideas are hogwash' and that 'style and structure are the essence of
a book'. In the real world, at least, ideas are not hogwash. But they
are very unlikely to make you rich on their own.

More importantly, it really does not matter who gives birth
to any particular idea. This is borne out by the laws relating to
patents and inventions. You cannot patent an idea. You can only
patent your own method for implementing an idea. It is for this
reason that so many people have become rich despite never
having had a single great idea in their lives. As it happens, I count
myself among them.

It is good to have a goal. True believers in a 'great idea' are often obsessed with achieving a particular goal. Such an obsession, properly harnessed, can produce wealth. Sadly, that wealth rarely finds its way into the pockets of the person whose obsession created it. As far as this book is concerned, their goal was flawed even though their aim was true.

Take a small example. Decades ago, my old friend Tony Elliott was determined to force British television and broadcasting companies to permit him to publish their forthcoming programme schedules in his London weekly magazine, *Time Out*. The BBC and ITV, among others, were aghast. They were making a fortune by licensing their schedules for the week ahead exclusively to *Radio Times* and *TV Times*.

Tony's great idea was simple. He wanted to break that cosy monopoly and force the broadcasters to release their schedules to any publisher who requested them. Alongside *Time Out's* reviews and listings of movies, plays, concerts, restaurants and all the rest, he planned to include a comprehensive television-viewing guide. This was certainly a laudable goal and not a bad idea.

But the goal, in and of itself, could only produce so many extra readers. In addition, should he succeed, this would mean that a great many *other* publishers would obtain access to these television schedules and publish them in their own magazines. Many of these publishers were rivals, at least on the newsstand, to *Time Out*. In addition, taking on the television broadcasters in a long drawn-out legal battle was likely to be an expensive undertaking. To sum up, was the light worth the candle?

Tony thought so. He sought allies and found them. He spent real money in legal fees on his campaign. He became obsessed with this goal for a while, or at least, it seemed that way to me, ignoring even his own staff's concerns that there might be more important battles to fight and more pressing issues to address.

Eventually, after a long and gruelling battle, Tony won a victory. But only a victory of sorts. Television broadcasting schedules, to a degree, moved into the public domain. Many magazines could now publish them.

And what happened? I expect *Time Out*'s sales went up, briefly, when its fully fledged television listings appeared. But I would bet considerable money they did not go up anything like enough to repay the legal costs and lost management time Tony must have incurred.

Worse still, it was mostly other magazine publishers in Britain who reaped the real harvest, and continue to do so. Today, UK retail shelves are groaning with magazines that carry television listings. Tony's great idea *was* a great idea. But it proved to be an even better idea for other publishers.

Fortunately, *Time Out* has since gained a large UK subscriber base and has stabilised newsstand sales in Britain. Better still, it has established several foreign editions, most notably in New York City, which have done vastly more to improve Tony's fortunes than his noble battle with the emperors of television all those years ago.

Having a great idea is simply not enough. The eventual goal is vastly more important than any idea. It is how ideas are *implemented* that counts in the long run.

Good ideas are like Nike sports shoes. They may facilitate an athlete who possesses them, but on their own they are nothing but an over-priced pair of plimsolls. Specially adapted plimsolls may be a good idea. But the goal is still to win, and sports shoes don't win. Athletes do.

And yet I have lost count of the number of men and women who have approached me with their 'great idea', as if this, in and of itself, was some passport to instant wealth. The idea is *not* a passport. At most, it is the means of obtaining one.

Ray Kroc, of McDonald's fame, did not *invent* the idea of 'fast food'. Humans have been stuffing their face 'on the run' since the dawn of history. His genius was merely to recognise this fact and implement a simple five-point plan: standardise the food and prices, franchise the outlets, produce the food swiftly in clean surroundings, offer value for money and market the whole shebang relentlessly.

Easy to state; hard to implement. And it flew in the face of all conventional wisdom concerning the sale of fast food at the time.

But it was the *implementation* of this plan that turned a 52-year-old milkshake-mixer salesman with diabetes and asthma into a billionaire. Every element of his plan had been 'discovered' years before. There were thousands of 'fast food' outlets in the USA at the time, including a few owned by the McDonald brothers, from whom he purchased his own outlets.

Yet it was Kroc's McDonald's that emerged as the ultimate market leader, not just because of a 'great idea' but through unremitting sweat and adherence to core principles. Personally, I despise fast food, and consume it only when there is no alternative. But Ray Kroc's story remains a testimony to the ability of an entrepreneur to change the face of an industry – and make himself very rich in the process.

There is another side to the subject of ideas in commerce. Stealing them. Or to put it more pleasantly, emulating them. The error of failing to emulate a winning idea pervades every industry at all levels. Mainly this is due either to indolence or to folly. Of indolence, no more need be said. The folly, on the other hand, often takes the shape of a peculiar affliction, known colloquially as the 'it wasn't invented here' syndrome. I would place this affliction very high on the list of reasons preventing individuals and companies from achieving major success.

Why people should be loath to emulate success is a matter for psychologists. The fact that they do is a matter of fact. The result of such ostrich-like behaviour can be catastrophic. As I discovered to my cost.

Dennis Publishing had been involved in magazines featuring computer and electronic games from their beginnings in the 1980s. We had competitors, of course, but we were certainly a big part of the UK market. What we didn't know was that we were about to take a massive pasting from a smallish rival.

Enter Chris Anderson, who founded Future Publishing. Chris had two great ideas, which he executed perfectly. Firstly, he was prepared to pay the likes of Sony a king's ransom to secure the publishing rights to magazines such as *The Official Sony Playstation Magazine*. Secondly, he put his magazines in a bag and also popped into the bag a playable electronic game.

All this meant that Future's magazines were more expensive to produce than their competitors' and more expensive on the newsstand. It also meant that Future Publishing did not own such magazines themselves. The intellectual property rights were licensed from the hardware manufacturers. In the end, *The Official Sony Playstation Magazine* did not belong to Chris. He was just the publisher.

The thought of publishing a magazine I did not own was offputting to me. Nor was I that keen on handing over millions of dollars in advance to huge companies like Sony or Sega. Thus Dennis Publishing stuck to producing 'unofficial' magazines in the games market. Sounds smart, right?

Our costs were less, although we were forced to scrabble around constantly, attempting to locate second-rate games to include in our bagged issues. Future's games were top of the line, because they were 'official'. (By now, most readers had come to expect a 'free' game with every electronic games magazine they bought.)

The result was predictable. Future Publishing wiped the floor with Dennis Publishing in the computer and electronic games magazine market. Readers didn't *care* about the magazine. They cared about the free game in the bag. Manufacturers of games were reluctant to allow us to buy their games to put in our bags, because we published only 'unofficial' titles. In essence, the market was a monopoly and Dennis Publishing had backed the pirates and lost.

In the end, we sold those few Dennis Publishing games magazines that we had not already folded to Future at 'fire-sale' prices. (Well, maybe not fire-sale prices, but nothing like as much as I would have wished to receive!) They had pasted us; and we deserved to be pasted.

And yet, this process took years. Year after year, we plugged away attempting the impossible. We invested heavily on the internet and produced a successful games portal – which we also sold to Future. The Dennis internet games portal was more successful than our magazines. Why? For the simple reason that we were not fighting with one hand tied behind our back, as we were on the newsstands with the 'official' versus 'non-official' branding. On the internet, at least, we were not perceived as 'pirates'.

It wasn't that Dennis wouldn't fight, or that we lost heart. But we were not prepared to emulate Future and invest the money to acquire 'official' licences ourselves. Even when we *did* try with a later games platform, Microsoft's X-Box, our rivals were smart enough to pay way above the odds to shut us out of the market.

Future's template was there. Their success was obvious. Dennis had the financial resources, or could have borrowed them at a pinch. But we hated to admit that we were wrong, and by the time we had come to grips with our idiocy, Future had signed up virtually all the 'official' games magazine publishing rights that mattered. Even today, I shudder at the thought of the wasted blood, sweat and treasure we expended on our games magazines.

Dennis Publishing failed in the electronic games market because we would not (and later, could not) emulate a winning idea. My managers argued, both at the time and in hindsight, that the licences themselves were immensely difficult to obtain and that Sony's dominance precluded success once Future had obtained it. All this may be true, but why then did we continue battling what amounted to a monopoly for so long in the same old way? The answer is that we found it repugnant to admit that

Future had hit upon the right idea and that we had refused to emulate it.

What I should have done was to take my best men and women in the company and send them to Japan, Europe or America. Or anywhere where Sega, Sony and Microsoft and the rest would agree to meet with us. We should have wined, dined and cosied up to them. We should have searched for another vehicle via which the popularity of such games could be exploited.

If no other vehicle could be found, we should have tried trumping Future's offers worldwide. Cash is a great persuader. If this wouldn't fly, we should have exited the market. We did none of these things, in any meaningful way, and we paid the price. We were pasted because we refused to emulate.

On a less painful note, let's take a look at what happens when you *are* prepared to emulate an idea and execute it brilliantly. In May 1994, Britain's largest magazine publishing company, IPC, launched a magazine for young men called *Loaded*. This was the brainchild of its editor, James Brown. How Brown had persuaded the 'suits' at IPC to permit this stroke of genius remains a mystery, although I can personally testify to James's powers of charm and persuasion in a clinch.

Loaded was the first of the so-called 'lads' magazines and its success created a new genre, simultaneously threatening old-guard titles like *Esquire* and *GQ* while racking up colossal newsstand sales. *Loaded* was a breath of fresh air in the men's magazine market: irreverent, funny, subversive and addictive. James's timing was impeccable. This was the ink-on-paper version of the BBC sitcom *Men Behaving Badly* or the sports quiz *They Think It's All Over*. Every other consumer magazine publisher in England was consumed with envy.

IPC's deadly rival, EMAP, immediately set about revamping a tiny men's fashion title they had acquired called *FHM* (For Him Monthly), possibly the worst-named magazine in history.

But names don't count, as pop groups like the Rolling Stones or the Beatles demonstrate.

FHM became a copy of *Loaded*, with a twist of its own. It avoided madcap elements, for which the latter was infamous, and had a slightly sexier, more sophisticated image. Right from the start, *FHM* courted advertisers as hard as they courted readers. EMAP correctly identified that the top brass at IPC were somewhat embarrassed by *Loaded*'s brash tone, and had consequently skimped on the title's advertising sales and marketing resources.

In addition, *FHM* forged links with tabloid newspapers like the *Sun*, providing them with exclusive use of their photoshoots of female celebrities in bikinis in exchange for publicity. Within a very short time, *FHM* had established an unassailable lead in the British 'lads' publishing market, a lead which neither *Loaded* nor *Maxim* (Dennis Publishing's launch in 1995) has ever been able to rival.

The success of *FHM* in the UK demonstrates the power of emulation, especially when executed with verve and confidence. I am told that the British edition of *FHM* put £12 million on the bottom line the year before last. EMAP deserves it. (Of course, that wasn't quite the case in the *Maxim* vs *FHM* battles abroad – but that's a story for another day.)

The lesson is clear. Despite the words of the old rock 'n' roll song, the original is *not* the greatest. Not always. If you want to be rich, then watch your rivals closely and never be ashamed to emulate a winning strategy. They may josh you a little for doing it, but that's a price well worth paying.

The problem with the great idea is that it concentrates the mind on the idea itself. This is fine as far as it goes. But unless the idea is executed efficiently and with panache and originality, then it doesn't matter how great the idea is, the enterprise will fail. Ideas are certainly of immense importance, but I have seen so many people attempting to create a start-up company become obsessed with proving that their idea is 'right' rather than obsessed with making money. And I have watched them wasting years doing it.

Nobody really cares if an idea is 'right', except the person who came up with it. Apple (on whose computer I am typing these words) is a case in point. Begun by two 'nerds' in a garage, Steve Jobs and Steve Wozniak, Apple took off with its Apple II computer more than a quarter of a century ago and, after a difficult period with the ill-fated 'Lisa' model, hit pay dirt with the Macintosh computer in the mid-1980s. More recently, its iPod music storage device has transformed the consumer technology landscape.

Let me make it clear that I am a loyal customer and great fan of Apple. I bought a Lisa back in 1983 or thereabouts. I bought the first Mac the next year and have proceeded to buy nearly every new model since. For twenty years, my company has also published the world's finest Macintosh computer magazine, *MacUser*. I know the company and their products well, at least from an historical perspective.

But Apple have a problem. They have always had a problem. His name is Steve Jobs. Steve has been a victim of the fallacy of the great idea over and over again. Back in 1984, Apple were poised to take over the world of personal computing. All their larger rivals, including IBM, were in disarray. They just didn't *get* the personal computer revolution. Jobs and Wozniak *did* get it.

Apple's products were innovative, slick, cool and far, far superior in every way to any other personal computer available at that time. In fact, they were so cool their users often spent a great deal of time proselytising for the Apple cause. Users like me, for instance. So why is Apple such a small part of the personal computer market today? The answer is Steve Jobs.

Steve comes up with or encourages brilliant ideas. He has the guts to back them and to see them through. He is smart, passionate and a great man. But he will not admit he is wrong and he would, apparently, rather go broke than make such an admission. It was Steve, I am told, who insisted that the early

Macintosh computers should be 'closed boxes' and that the Mac operating system would never be shared or licensed to other manufacturers.

A description used by Apple marketeers at the time was that the Mac was like a Cuisinart – a food blender – and did not need to connect to the rest of the world. A Mac could do for you whatever you wanted to do with a computer. It would not compromise itself by sharing the opportunity to communicate with lesser machines or devices.

The hardware would be Apple, the accessories would be Apple, the software would be Apple. No open architecture. No compromise with the 'jerks' running the big old-style computing companies who were flexing their muscles and salivating at this burgeoning new market. Steve Jobs would not share his operating system, as IBM and others subsequently did. His attitude towards all rivals (and I have witnessed this at first hand) was astonishingly arrogant. I'll bet it still is.

There is a story from the early days of Apple, which I like to believe is true, of Jobs being invited to the CEO's office of a huge rival computer corporation. Steve parked his bum on the corner of the great man's massive desk, leaned over and told him: 'I am going to bury you. Apple is going to bury your company.' No he didn't. *They* buried *him*.

This arrogance, and belief that only *his* (or his company's) ideas are right, is the dark side of the fire that has driven Apple up and down a financial roller-coaster for nearly thirty years. Jobs is the saviour of the company. Jobs is also a man who appears to be in thrall to what he sees in a mirror.

It is not true that there is a large sign on Steve Jobs's desk at Apple which reads, 'My Way or the Highway' – but the fact that so many people believe there *is* such a sign tells its own story. Apple's innovations and ideas (as well as its corporate arrogance) are a legend in the computer industry. Those ideas, and their eventual execution, are often world-beaters.

But an idea is not enough. It is never enough. And even its successful execution as a piece of technology is not enough if the company refuses to join with the rest of the world and its own customers in cooperative exploitation.

Even Apple's iPod, a stunning technological and marketing achievement, is designed to keep the rest of the world at bay. To get songs downloaded onto an iPod, you *have* to go to the Apple music store on the internet. No other source of music (officially) connects with an iPod. Why? Because it is 'My Way or the Highway'. It is classic Steve Jobs.

Just as he did two decades ago, I predict that Steve Jobs will take his company to the top of the share-price mountain and then race downhill with them under an avalanche of 'lesser' rivals and mortals who will conspire to connect with each other and thieve Apple's customers. If it wasn't so tragic, it would be hilarious.

The story of Apple is a morality tale, a tale of the great idea wrapped in the passion of one man (once Steve Wozniak had departed), wrapped in a ball of arrogance, wrapped again in a shell of marketing genius. It's great theatre. It makes for wonderful stories in financial newspapers and technology websites. It is a joy to behold for those who know the historical context. But it is *not* smart business, except in the short term, before 'lesser' men have caught up. And except for Steve Jobs.

Without Jobs, Apple could never have risen from obscurity to become a world-class brand. But *with* Steve Jobs, Apple will always attempt to mould the universe to fit Steve's vision of Apple, and will pay the price again and again and again. 'Lesser' companies and men will filch their ideas, connect, connect, connect, and beat Apple at its own game.

Steve Jobs is not a monster. He is an all-American maverick and a world-class marketing genius. But until a man or woman as powerful as he is arrives at Apple (over his dead body), who is determined to break the cycle he has indulged in for so many years, Apple will remain merely an icon of awe. It will not become a company of the size that truly could (and *should*) 'bury' monsters like IBM.

So if I believe all this, why do I use Apple computers? I use them because they are better computers. Far better than any other personal computer available on the planet. And because I was in at the beginning and still feel in myself the incredible excitement that Wozniak and Jobs stirred in what they called 'the rest of us'. I am still one of 'the rest of us' and will remain loyal to Apple products. In my heart of hearts, too, I wish Steve Jobs and Steve Wozniak *had* buried their corporate rivals. But then, I was always a sucker for the underdog.

As for Mr Jobs himself, you should understand that the 'character flaws' I have harped on about in the preceding paragraphs, if flaws they are, have made him an insanely rich man. Far, far richer than I could ever hope to be. His Pixar film animation company has been extraordinarily successful and has now been purchased for nearly $7 billion, yes seven *billion* dollars, by Disney.

Steve is the majority shareholder in Pixar. He has now become the biggest stockholder in Walt Disney's old media monster. Not bad for a guy with 'character flaws' who started in a garage, eh! Let us hope he helps revive the fortunes of that venerable old beast.

Even so, beware of the great idea. You must encourage great ideas and search for them diligently. But either you control and develop such ideas or the ideas will come to dominate your waking thoughts. And that would not be such a great thing. Not unless you are Steve Jobs.

I just took a break and went down to a local bar to watch the sunset and sink a few beers. There, I was foolish enough to mention this chapter, The Fallacy of the Great Idea. A wise gentleman on the barstool next to me, who has stewardship of more money than I will ever think about, reminded me of the phrase attributed to the American philosopher and poet, Ralph Waldo Emerson:

If a man write a better book, preach a better sermon, or make a better mouse-trap than his neighbour, tho' he build his house in the woods, the world will make a beaten path to his door.

'There's the power of a great idea, Felix,' he smiled.

'Not so,' I countered. The operative verb is 'make'. It is not 'think up', or 'dream up'. It is *'make'*. The idea would be worthless, no one would beat a path to any door, unless they heard that *the mouse-trap had been made.*

I read that Google, the tremendously successful internet search engine in America, encourages certain staff to spend 20 per cent of their working time developing their own pet ideas. It will be interesting to see how this plays out. Google raised so much money upon its flotation on the stock market that many Google employees became millionaires overnight. Will such millionaires, with a Ph.D. in computer engineering, be content to make Google even more money? Or will they strike out on their own? Will there be lawsuits relating to exactly where a particularly successful idea was developed? It will be fascinating to see.

If you never have a single great idea in your life, but become skilled in executing the great ideas of others, you can succeed beyond your wildest dreams. Seek them out and make them work. They do not have to be your ideas. Execution is all in this regard.

If, on the other hand, you spend your days thinking up and developing in your mind this great idea or that, you are unlikely to get rich. Although you *are* likely to make many others rich. That is usually the way of it. Ideas don't make you rich. The correct execution of ideas does.

6

OBTAINING CAPITAL

No one would remember the Good Samaritan
if he'd only had good intentions.
He had money as well.
MARGARET THATCHER

DOLPHINS, SHARKS AND FISHES

There are only six ways of obtaining capital. You can be given or inherit it; you can steal it; you can win it; you can marry it; you can earn it; you can borrow it.

The first four of these are beyond the compass of this book. All I will say about 'winning it', presumably by gambling, is that the odds are very bad indeed. It's no way to get rich.

It is true that certain people exhibit incredible ability in games of skill like poker. But in the end, the losing streaks always seem to become longer and the winning streaks shorter. Gambling, even for those at near genius level, is time-consuming and totally exhausting. As for games of chance, I will not insult your intelligence by discussing them. The Lottery is merely a pleasant name for organised racketeering.

As to theft, leaving aside the morality of it, I do not believe the light to be worth the candle. The downside is too high and the upside too uncertain. Should you succeed in stealing a great deal of money, you will then spend many years looking over your shoulder in fear of discovery. As Shakespeare put it:

> *Suspicion always haunts the guilty mind;*
> *The thief doth fear each bush an officer.*

Marrying into money has a nice ring to it. But rich in-laws often know very well – very much better than your innocent spouse, in fact – why it was you married. That's not to say it doesn't work. I knew a KGB colonel who is now an arms dealer based on his divorce settlement. And I know a therapist who married into an old-money pile. But I wouldn't exactly describe their road to riches as uneventful. Apart from jealous spouses extracting their pound of flesh, both men appear restless and are quick to take offence if they think others are sneering at them. (Which, of course, we sometimes are).

The French socialist Pierre Proudhon had the right of it: 'Property is theft!' he thundered. Aye, so it is. But it is *legalised* theft, the main pillar of Western capitalism, a rotten and debased system of managing human affairs, and yet the only system that has survived the demise of all rivals.

However we may feel about it, capitalism is the only system under which readers of this book are likely to labour. And as its name implies, it requires capital for those who wish to play the game and succeed.

As to the fifth method of acquiring capital – earning it – this is a long-term game plan, although it is true that if you can demonstrate the ability to earn money early on, it does become somewhat easier to borrow from others successfully later.

For the majority of people who start with nothing and seek to be rich, borrowing money in one form or another becomes a necessity sooner or later. Let's explore the various options on the borrowing front.

Firstly, avoid sharks like the plague. Perhaps you have read stories about people who launched a small company by taking out a dozen credit cards and juggling their cash limits for a few months to obtain capital?

It makes for heroic reading, but it isn't smart. Your credit rating is extremely precious. The interest rates on credit cards or similar instruments are beyond the capacity of nearly any legal business to sustain, and while bankruptcy laws have become more generous to creditors in recent years, a history of bankruptcy will plague and hinder you when you seek to return to the fray.

There are other predators in the sea, too, but nearly all of them demand punitive rates of interest. Anyone who has borne the burden of a loan that sucks the lifeblood from you week after week, month after month, leaving you exhausted and no further forward than when you started, will tell you what a terrible price such borrowings exact from the human spirit. Better to labour as a wage slave than as a beast of burden to a loan shark.

It's not all doom and gloom, though. While it may not look like it to you, there is simply too much money in the world; too much capital seeking too few investment opportunities.

That, at any rate, is what you'll read in the financial press from the mouths of investment bankers, venture capitalists, mutual fund managers and from a new breed of gunslingers on the block, hedge fund managers. (Hedge funds, according to *Fortune* magazine, by the way, are mutual funds with the 'ability to short stocks and deploy exotic financial instruments'. Well, bully for them.)

If you wouldn't know a hedge fund from an asparagus bed, welcome aboard. I can assure you though, based on decades of owner/manager experience in both private and public companies, that asparagus beds do have *one* thing in common with hedge funds. Manure. Tons and tons of manure. The only people I ever met who got insanely rich from a hedge fund operation were (you guessed it!) the managers of hedge funds.

So how come it's so difficult to locate capital if there's so much of it about?

The simple answer is that the amounts of money you probably have in mind are way too small. And 'small' can work on many levels. In 2004 my company did the rounds of New York City banks and institutions. We were looking for a measly $20 million at a reasonable rate of interest spread over five or six years for a specific purpose. No dice. We were offered $100 million dollars, no sweat – but only if the providers could cut themselves in for 'a piece of the action'.

This seemed crazy to me. I had plenty of security and was merely looking to borrow a little money, not lumber my company with an 'end-game partner'. Eventually, we found what we needed, but we had to come back to Europe to do it.

So what had happened? Many US providers of capital of any stripe now only wish to play ball in return for 'a piece of the action' – not to mention the guaranteed return of the capital and interest if no action materialises! (In that sense, we were probably the victims of recent low interest rates, which have forced traditional bankers into a game of Darwinian evolution. If interest rates won't bring home the bacon, then maybe 'a piece of the action' will. Banks, like everyone else, have to evolve or die.)

This, of course, is the premise upon which venture capitalists have always operated. Venture capital companies are one way to raise capital, for sure. But the price they demand is nearly always that you hand over a huge chunk of equity. More often than not, they also insist on a date by which your new venture must be sold, either back to yourself or to outsiders.

Why? Because their own funds usually come from wealthy individuals who demand a high return within a limited time frame. This, in turn, leads many venture capitalists to move from an advisory to an operational role in any business in which they invest, cramping your style and scaring the pants out of everyone who works for you. Those wealthy investors in their own funds are unforgiving and merciless, and venture capitalists will therefore do anything it takes to protect and maximise short-term returns from your business.

They aren't so much sharks as dolphins – a nickname deriving from their frantic desire to 'flip' every deal as quickly as possible. By 'flipping', I mean a sale. They do not care who the venture is sold to (yourself or an outside party), but the return of their investment, with a massive bonus for the risk and skill they have invested, is mandatory.

Venture capital money, dolphin money, is not for the faint-hearted. Too often, it is only for the desperate – unless building a business for a quick(ish) return and a small piece of the action is your goal. And there is nothing wrong with such a goal in the short term.

If that is the case, then it's worth remembering that the best of the dolphins can certainly boast a ton of managerial talent and experience. They tend to know what they are talking about in the abstract, if not in your particular niche. Dolphins can afford to hire such talent for the simple reason that they absolutely *have* to. Your successful venture-capital-funded business must also pay for the failures that the same venture capitalist invested in last year.

In the glorious lines of Jonathan Swift:

> *So, naturalists observe, a flea*
> *Hath smaller fleas that on him prey;*
> *And these have smaller fleas to bite 'em,*
> *And so proceed **ad infinitum**.*

And from a later poet, Augustus de Morgan:

> *Great fleas have little fleas upon their backs to bite 'em,*
> *And little fleas have lesser fleas, and so **ad infinitum**.*
> *And the great fleas themselves, in turn, have greater fleas to go on;*
> *While those again have greater still, and greater still, and so on.*

Ad infinitum indeed! Ah, the wonders of capitalism! Adam Smith, you old rogue, what have you to say now?

Time and again I have watched existing companies wishing to expand, or new ventures anxious to get started, mire themselves with the slippery dolphins. A few of them succeed, and succeed gloriously, it has to be said. But a great many other original owners or creators are squeezed out long before the fabled 'big pay day'.

If you fail to grow your businesses swiftly enough, then flipper becomes agitated and noses in. His very survival (or at least his annual bonus) depends upon your performance *that year*. Flipper doesn't care about long-term prospects. He doesn't even care about long-term shareholder value. He only cares about growth – and he cares about it *now*.

As with his co-denizen of the deep, the shark, he either keeps moving forward or he drowns – and you have no choice but to move forward or drown with him. Except it will not be *his* corpse spiralling down into the depths if things go wrong. He will live to fight another day. You, on the other hand, will be shark bait.

Venture capitalist short-termism, with its eye firmly glued to the sale of an enterprise within three or four years, is the hallmark of nearly all venture capital activity. As is their insistence on a massive stake, often a controlling one, in any business they provide capital for. Experience has shown them that this control, combined with growth at almost any price, is the course most likely to return the profits they need to satisfy their own investors – the great fleas on *their* back.

Believe me, they are hard taskmasters. But they may be the only way for you to really get started. More often, you will start up underfunded, on your own or with the fishes (we are coming to that), and only turn to the dolphins for the injection of capital you believe will propel you to the next level. That is usually the way of it. You will need a degree of success to exhibit to them. And you will need to be somewhat humble – except in your financial projections.

I have been approached by venture capitalists on many occasions. They are not evil men and women; far from it. They are mostly smart, well connected, persuasive and passionate about success. But their first loyalty is to the quick buck. You do business with them at your peril. Be warned: with them, you may have a better than even chance of making your first million. But you will make *them* many, many more millions in order to do so. And you are unlikely to stay in control of your own destiny with any business they invest heavily in.

Should you decide to approach venture capitalists, and by some miracle should they agree to back you, then I urge you to seek the finest legal advice that your money can buy for the ensuing negotiations. Just one sentence, even a phrase, within the initial contract can make all the difference in the world to the outcome a few years down the road.

The dolphins are consummate professionals – to them you are just another amateur in the sea trying to stay afloat, to grow, to make his or her financial dreams come true. Amateurs are easy meat. (Real life dolphins, by the way, are not the gentle creatures children believe them to be. They can be dangerous and their beaks are as hard as bone. They can, and do, batter sharks to death in massed attacks if they have to. And their appetite is prodigious.)

Having avoided the sharks and perhaps swum with the dolphins, we turn to the fishes. How I love the fishes! How you will learn to love them, too!

It was via the fishes that I made my own first money – the seed capital which ensured that I retained control and ownership of my own business back in the early days of Dennis Publishing. Fishes come in all shapes and sizes. Friends, acquaintances, relatives, business colleagues, small investors, friendly bank managers of the old school, professional advisors, ex-employers, suppliers and vendors are among them. But how can they be of any use?

Let me illustrate by my own example. In 1972 I persuaded a jolly young lawyer I had met to act for me. His name was Bernie Simons. I had no money to pay him, but perhaps my chutzpah amused him. He helped me to register my £100 limited-liability company and provided me with at least a figleaf of respectability. I think I paid him £20 for his services. The company was called H. Bunch Associates and I intended to publish a series of comic books.

Next, I persuaded a close friend, Dick Pountain, to join me as co-director and production manager. There wasn't much in the way of a salary on offer, but Dick came all the same. We 'liberated' a few sticks of office furniture, two electric typewriters and a floor camera from the offices of OZ magazine (where Dick and I had met), which was then in the process of winding up.

Another friend, Lemmy, later to become famous with the heavy-metal band Motörhead, mentioned that an acquaintance of his was vacating a garret in the West End – perhaps we could move in there? (Lemmy used occasionally to sleep under the OZ design table while recovering from excessive ingestion of alcohol and other substances.)

Lemmy was right about the empty flat. Three rooms at the top of the most rickety stairs I had ever climbed. The building had been badly damaged in the Blitz and never properly rebuilt. The last tenants had been breeding puppies there in straw pens. It took a long time to get rid of the stink of puppy shit.

The place was a total dump, but at least we had an 'office'. I reluctantly sold one of the electric typewriters and produced a deposit for the landlord. He was anxious only that we should never mention we were using the garret as an 'office'. The local council had designated it as a 'residence'. A 'residence' with no kitchen, no bathroom and no ceiling. In one room you could look straight through the rafters into the gaps between the roof tiles and see the sky.

Next, a close friend and colleague, Richard Adams, designed some smart headed notepaper for us free of charge, suspecting (rightly) that we might be able to provide him with work if our venture succeeded. A small printer I had come to know while working for *OZ* magazine agreed to print this notepaper, knowing full well I could not pay him for it right then.

A semi-friendly, amused bank manager at Barclays Bank in Tottenham Court Road opened an account for the company, into which I deposited the mighty sum of £50. A magazine distributor, Moore-Harness, with whom *OZ* had done business, agreed to distribute my product, although I had nothing to show them. All we needed now was content for our comic, and a printer to print it.

The content was not a problem. We knew plenty of comic illustrators and they would not expect to be paid in advance. Indeed, some of them would not expect to be paid at all, and were surprised when we eventually managed to do so. The printing was the big stumbling block, of course. Somehow, I had to persuade a printer to provide machine time and paper to produce the comic we were busy preparing in the garret. The bill would come to a few thousand pounds.

I had written a great many record reviews when I worked for *OZ* magazine. The record companies would send albums directly to my flat in the hope of soliciting a review and they never asked for the LPs back. I sorted out all the albums I could bear to part with and sold them to a local record shop. This brought in just sufficient funds to at least get a few printers to talk to me while Dick and I lived on £10 a week. But unless I could guarantee that the printers got paid, not one of them, very sensibly, would budge.

Then I had an idea. I asked Brian Moore and Charlie Harness, the owners of my potential distributors for the comic, to write to a particular printer, promising that he would be the first to receive money from Moore-Harness when the comic came out. Brian and Charlie did not *guarantee* the money; they were not exactly idiots. But they made it sound, as a matter of common sense, that at least enough money was likely to be generated by sales of the comic to pay the print and paper bill.

And they stressed that their client, my little company, would only receive any residue when and if the printer had been paid in full. This was the key. Brian and Charlie turned out to be the most effective fishes in the pond of my ambition.

Business must have been slow, because the printer agreed to Moore-Harness's proposal. I secretly suspect that he did so as much to keep me from constantly badgering him as anything else. Persistence is a powerful tool in the hands of a hungry young hustler on the make. And he probably did not wish to offend a powerful distributor like Moore-Harness. Distributors sometimes have a say in who gets to print what.

Thus it was that the first issue of *Cozmic Comics* was unleashed upon an unsuspecting world. It barely made a cent, but it provided the framework for yet more publishing ventures. Within two years I had sixty thousand pounds in the bank. (That is the equivalent of half a million pounds today.) The printers were paid. The contributors were paid. The designers were paid. The landlord was paid. Bernie Simons got paid. Even Dick and I were paid.

Above all, I retained control of the company. A company I still own 100 per cent of thirty years later. I had created capital by swimming with the fishes.

Without Dick's expertise, or the kindness of a lawyer, or the trust of contributors and designers, or the amused tolerance of my distributors, or any of a hundred other encouragements from those around me, it simply could not have been done. I have read, in articles written about me since in newspapers and magazines, that fierce loyalty to old friends and colleagues is my best characteristic. I believe that to be so. But having read all of the above, can anyone wonder why?

Some will argue that what I did back in 1972 could not be emulated today. But human nature does not change and, at bottom, we are cooperative animals. Many people are indulgent towards the young – after all, we were all once young ourselves. Those who wish to start a company and get rich cannot expect a free ride. But they might be surprised at the number of fishes in their particular pond willing to help them to some degree or another.

And look at the consequences in my own case:

○ Moore-Harness continued to distribute my magazines. When Brian and Charlie were forced to sell their company years later, I fought hard to ensure fair treatment for its two founders. By that time, I was in a position to return their original favour.

○ Dick Pountain is still a director of Dennis Publishing and the company has put food on his table for more than thirty years.

○ Our landlord was happy to sell me the building in which our garret was located decades later when he retired.

○ The printer went on printing for us until the day he sold up. As far as Dick and I were concerned, we owed him.

○ I continued to bank with Barclays for far longer than I should have done, solely from a sense of misplaced loyalty.

○ Richard Adams still designs projects for me.

○ And guess what? My legal advisors in the UK today are a firm named Simons, Muirhead & Burton, founded by none other than one Bernie Simons, a young lawyer who helped a kid on the make register his first company.

○ Lastly, to this day, I always do my best to encourage, or to be of some practical help, to others who wish to strike out on their own.

Venture capitalists, major investors and bankers all have their part to play in providing capital for individuals and start-up companies. But if it is at all possible, give me the fish over the sharks and dolphins every time. It may take a mite longer to get there, but you'll be far richer, or at the very least, happier, in the long run.

One last word on obtaining capital. It's the worst part of the whole business of getting rich. Nothing is more humiliating or debilitating than trudging the rounds with your hand out, no matter how good your project or fierce your determination. Everyone has to do it and everyone hates it. For a self-made man or woman there is no avoiding it. Beware of anyone who tells you that there are short cuts to obtaining even a small amount of capital. Outside of family and friends, there are none that I ever heard of.

Look on the bright side. Those lazy bastards who turn away from this odious task are going to be your employees. They are going to make you rich. In a sense, this exhausting and miserable search is what separates the wannabes from the gonnabes. The only way through it is to keep trudging. 'When going through, hell,' Winston Churchill once remarked, 'keep going.'

If you cannot bear the thought of prostrating yourself to obtain the seed corn, then you will almost certainly never own the farm. 'To get what you need / You toady to greed.'

Or else, you ask; very, very nicely indeed.

7
NEVER GIVE IN

Never give in! Never give in! Never, never,
never, never – in nothing great or small, large
or petty. Never give in, except to convictions
of honour and good sense.
WINSTON CHURCHILL

HANDSTANDS ON THE RIM OF HELL

Some years ago, I bought up part of the library of the novelist
J.B. Priestley. In the pages of one of his books, *Up Hill and
Down Dale*, by a virtually unknown poet, Kenneth H. Ashley,
published in 1924, I found a slip of paper where Priestley had
marked a particular poem:

Out of Work

Alone at the shut of the day was I,
With a star or two in a frost cleared sky,
And the byre smell in the air.

I'd tramped the length and breadth o' the fen;
But never a farmer wanted men;
Naught doing anywhere.

> *A great calm moon rose back o' the mill,*
> *And I told myself it was God's will*
> *Who went hungry and who went fed.*

> *I tried to whistle; I tried to be brave;*
> *But the new ploughed fields smelt dank as the grave;*
> *And I wished I were dead.*

I know that feeling, and if you are set on creating your own business from scratch, then so will you. Despite all my brave words earlier in the previous chapter, I never knew a worse few months than when I was bashing my head against a brick wall attempting to start my own outfit in the early 1970s. The whole process was pure misery.

Looking back through the prismed eyes of a champagne flute, I suppose I could argue that perhaps it was my finest moment. Not that it felt like it at the time. To be honest, it nearly broke me.

But I would not give in.

That was the secret ingredient. I *would not* be a wage slave. I *would not* take 'no' for an answer. I *would not give in*. I was going to be rich. Some how. Some way. Some day soon. And I would not retreat to the safety of a decent job until I was starved out of house and home.

I would not give in.

Not that I cared, to be honest I barely noticed, but Britain appeared to be in terminal financial decline at the time. Interest rates had sky-rocketed and strikes were so commonplace it was difficult to recall a landscape not riven by demonstrations, lock-outs and industrial disputes. The banks and the markets weren't just skittish, they were downright terrified. Property values either soared or collapsed. Politicians were jittery. IRA bombs were exploding left, right and centre. The UK had been railroaded into what was then the European Community. They were not good times.

No one appeared very interested in loaning money to an unemployed, long-haired south London lad who called himself a publisher. And frankly, who could blame them?

What fuelled me was the desperation of knowing that unless I found a way round my lack of capital, unless I could pour my energy into a venture of my own, I would be condemned to a life of wage slavery. There is absolutely nothing more likely to dampen the prospects of becoming rich than a nice, fat, regular salary cheque.

Many of my friends were in the same boat, and not a few of them were better educated and smarter than I was. The cleverest of them had chosen careers in advertising agencies or with record companies or in television or radio.

It was depressing meeting with them, listening to stories of their latest promotion, never able to buy a round in the pub as they were so generously willing and able to do. Month after month I soldiered on, while 'the new ploughed fields smelt dank as the grave; and I wished I were dead'.

But I would not give in.

I had had offers. One or two of them decent offers. There were people who believed I could make them money. And I could have done. It was tempting.

My years working at *OZ* magazine had served as a fine apprenticeship (an apprenticeship I shall always be grateful for) and, as a result, I had met many people in the arts, the media and in politics. In addition, the owner of *OZ*, Richard Neville, had once asked me to spend a few weeks at a poster company with the bizarre name of ECAL, which stood for Effective Communications Arts Limited. ECAL owed *OZ* money for advertising. Rather a lot of money. It was my job to get it back.

I had arrived at ECAL's Covent Garden offices one fine summer morning. It was a shambles. They had a fantastic stock of posters in the basement, but there were far too many layabouts on the payroll and precious little in the way of organisation or sales and accounts staff. I astonished those present by firing one or two people.

This was unspeakable. Hippies did not 'fire' each other. I was hauled in front of one of the directors, Bill Butler. What nobody knew was that Barry Miles *and* Bill Butler, two of the founders of ECAL, had already agreed to me running their ship for a while. They were growing as tired of unpaid bills as their customers and vendors were. The firings stood.

I was ostracised. Which worried me not a whit. For a few weeks I hurled myself into the business. I was abrupt, obnoxious, full of myself and spectacularly successful. When I discovered a particular poster was selling like hot cakes (Frank Zappa sitting on the loo), I ordered more. We would have to wait, I was told. The printer was busy. So I printed it on crappy paper at another printer. Who cared? They still sold.

More horror from staffers. ECAL was an *art* business, I was primly informed. No it wasn't. It was a basement with a lot of idle tossers in it scrounging a living.

The net result of my work in the basement at Covent Garden was that *OZ* got repaid and ECAL became more profitable. For a while, anyway. But they soon slipped back into their comfortable ways and shut up shop.

So I knew I could run a business. I knew I could turn one around, if I had to. What I didn't know was how the hell I was going to find the money to get started. In fact all I knew was – you guessed it – I would not give in.

I remember a bitter winter night in my West End flat at the back of a Savile Row sweat shop. Edward Heath's three-day week was in operation, or at least a precursor to it, and some daft minister had suggested that the citizens of the UK should learn 'to shave in the dark' to save electricity. That was nothing new to me. The electricity had been turned off in my flat weeks ago. So had the gas. I couldn't afford to pay the bill.

I sat by an open fire, feeding broken furniture I had scavenged from a skip into my living-room fireplace, watching scorched veneer bubble and peel from the sawn-off leg of a chair. My girlfriend sat beside me on a battered old beanbag. The food we had just cooked had been bought by her. So had the cigarettes we were smoking. She worked in a boutique round the corner in Carnaby Street.

Softly, cautiously, insistently, she set out to persuade me to take the job I had been offered as a result of yet another attempt to raise money. She reminded me that at twenty-five years old, I was still a young man. That I could always give up the job and then start my own company later. That this was not the time. That she hated to see me so bad tempered, doing little but making plans and spinning wheels in a hopeless quest to raise capital to start my own business.

I nearly cracked. I loved her as only the young can love, and I knew I would lose her if I refused. Not that she ever said as much, she wasn't a greedy or a cruel lass, but even so, I knew. Perhaps she was right. Maybe I should take the job and try to launch my own company in a year or so's time. Why not, if it would make her happy? It was only a job, after all. Not like joining the army – I could always leave in a few weeks – or months – or years.

If I had promised her then, sitting by that fire, promised that I would 'earn a crust like a normal human being', then my life would have taken a different course, I think. Yet, like the poet Robert Frost: 'Knowing how way leads on to way / I doubted that I should ever come back.' There was the rub. It was now or it was never.

How close did I come? Did I open my mouth to speak? Memory plays tricks when you're older, and I cannot be sure. I am sure of one thing, though. That promise never came out of my mouth.

I did not give in.

Then the phone rang. (I would have walked naked in the

street before I allowed them to cut off my phone.) It was a pal of mine; somebody I was later to employ for many years. He had some good news.

He had bought a second-hand car with his salary from his advertising sales job and was parked downstairs by the telephone box. I let him up and he produced some bottles of beer and a spliff. He drove my girlfriend home later. You can guess the rest. Money talks. Bullshit walks.

The next day, I went straight back to knocking on doors and punishing the phone, pestering people for capital. Learning how to swim with the fishes. No way was I going to spend my life making other people rich. No way was I going to become a token hippy in some record company. No way was I going to do any damn thing except get on the merry-go-round of making dosh. Real dosh. My dosh.

I would not give in.

That is what it is like in the beginning. Always. It is desperate and it is humiliating. As you will find, in your own way, unless you were born with a rich mummy or daddy or uncle. For the rest of us, if you want to be rich, then you must walk a narrow, lonely road to get the capital to make it so.

Off in the wings, there are always the gentle, siren voices of friends, parents and employers, of reasonable and sensible people, torn between concern for your welfare and the secret fear that you might succeed. A harsh reading of such concerns, I admit. But a true one.

If you happen to read biographies, as I do (scores of them every year), you will find a thread that runs through almost any story of success against the odds. Whether money comes into it or not. Whether the person succeeded or failed. Or even, most sadly of all, when they *did* succeed, but did not live long enough to learn of their success.

In one of the finest such books in the world, *Letters to My Brother* by the artist Vincent van Gogh, collected and published long after his death, you will find unbearable heartbreak, madness, rejection, hunger, passion, nightmare terrors and a tale of a man who never gave in. Who would not give in, though it cost him his life.

Van Gogh's obsessions and talents drove him mad. And he knew it. They goaded and scourged him. He said himself that he had given his life and half his sanity to his art. There was only one shining star of kindliness in his universe. His brother, Theo.

Theo, despite the sensible entreaties of his sensible wife (who could scarcely abide, let alone understand, her husband's wastrel brother), kept sending what little he could afford for Vincent to purchase brushes, canvas and paint. These acts of charity, which Theo could not easily afford and which grieved Vincent to receive, changed the course of the history of art.

Because Vincent often had no money. None at all. He would sell his paintings to peasants or inn-keepers in exchange for food and board. Canvases that would later sell for tens of millions of dollars were exchanged for the roof of a barn and a breakfast or lunch. (I wonder if any of those canvases are still lying, undiscovered, in a dusty old Dutch attic?)

His clothes were worn out. He wandered the countryside like a tramp. He knew himself to be a disappointment to his family and to those few friends who remembered his existence. He had been a disappointment to the only woman he ever lived with. He was certainly a disappointment to himself. Nothing went right, except, very occasionally, a particular painting. Above all, it grieved him to be a burden to his brother.

But he would not give in.

He would die first. He would kill himself first. And that's what he did. To our eternal shame, he did just that. He died having written: 'I cannot help it that my pictures do not sell. Nevertheless, the time will come when people will see that they are worth more than the price of the paint.'

Aye, they were, Vincent. They were worth more than that.

Go buy yourself a copy of Vincent's letters. If his paintings had been judged to be daubs fit only to kindle a fire, his letters would still shine like diamonds in the mud of everyday life. Go buy a copy, and when the going gets rough, my friend, or appears to be rough to you at the time, think of Vincent van Gogh, tramping his way across a nightmare landscape of destitution and rejection for what he believed in. A man who believed he had failed.

But a man who never gave in.

You must choose. Life is comfortable enough in the Western world for most people. In most parts of Europe there are the safety nets of the social services and of government-subsidised medical care. There are decent jobs at decent salaries with decent colleagues and a decent retirement; and all without the heart-stopping fear of bankruptcy, of years of risk amid fears of ignominious failure.

Why do handstands on the rim of hell? Why bother to punish yourself in such a way? Nobody else does it – why should you? Go on, make everyone around you happy.

Why not give in?

If you are merely a wannabe, then the siren voices will prevail, and they will be right to prevail. If you are a gonnabe, then they will not prevail. Like Odysseus you will stop your ears with wax or bind yourself to the mast. You will learn to walk your narrow, lonely road – and to hell with the siren voices.

You will not give in.

And you will be rich.

8

THE FIVE
MOST COMMON
START-UP ERRORS

The history of all human ideas is a history of
irresponsible dreams, of obstinacy, and of error.
SIR KARL POPPER, *CONJECTURES AND REFUTATIONS*

THE FIRST ERROR:
MISTAKING DESIRE FOR COMPULSION

All error springs from flawed assumptions. If there are no
assumptions, there can be no error.

I am told that during the Vietnam War, a sign was kept nailed
on a wall above a particular marine commander's desk which
said: 'Assumption is the mother of all f***-ups'. Those seven
words should be carved into the heart of every entrepreneur, the
wealthy or the wannabe, the gonnabe or the been-there-done-
that. A shame they weren't nailed above the desk of the president
of the United States at the time.

As far as getting rich is concerned, the cardinal error is to
begin such a quest in the vague belief that you would *like* to
be rich. Wishing or desiring to be rich is perhaps the most

commonplace of human desires, other than sexual fantasy. Yet few people ever succeed in achieving it.

Such desire is a fleeting thing, a will-of-the-wisp floating across the surface of the mind as you pass the front window of a chic boutique: 'I wish I was rich. If only I could afford it, I would march straight inside and buy that beautiful handbag.' Then the No. 43 bus comes along, and all such thoughts are abandoned on the pavement.

Wishes are fishes that swim in the nets
Of castaways' souls by the shores of the dead,
Where coins are as rare as a ferryman's debts,
And nobody cares what you did, or you said.

Wishes come skipping and eager to play
In the ravenous dreams of childless wives;
Wishes are thoroughbreds feasting on hay
While rickety mendicants limp all their lives.

Wishing for or desiring something is futile without an inner compulsion to achieve it. Such lack of compulsion, if not frankly acknowledged, can lead to great personal unhappiness. We have all met deeply unhappy souls muddling along in professions or careers for which they are patently unsuited.

Worse still, by continually wishing and never delivering, you risk denting your confidence, beginning a vicious downward spiral that appears to draw misfortune like a magnet. The assumption that you *might* be able to achieve some goal if you only wished *hard* enough is not just a f***-up. It's a potential personal tragedy.

Life is not some kind of rehearsal. Why, then, do so many people punish themselves in this way? The answer, in almost every case, is that they were 'persuaded' or hectored into becoming a banker or a lawyer when, in reality, they would have preferred to do something else entirely. Their misery is made all the worse by the realisation that had they acknowledged their lack of enthusiasm early on and stuck to their guns, their lives might well have taken a far more congenial course.

It is my hope that this book will cause you to consider very carefully whether you are truly driven by inner demons to be rich. If you are not, then my earnest and heartfelt advice to you is: *do not on any account make the attempt.* What are riches anyway, compared to health or the peace of mind that even a modicum of contentment brings in its wake? In and of itself, great wealth very rarely, if ever, breeds contentment.

Believe me, I know. I am both an entrepreneur and a poet. Perhaps it is the poet typing these words now and not the entrepreneur. But no condescension is intended whatever when I ask you to quietly turn over in your mind whether or not you are fit to be rich. Whether the sacrifices involved – not only your own, but those you will ask of your family, present or future – are worth the tyranny that such ambition, by its very nature, exacts.

Never yet have I met a self-made rich man or woman whose family or personal relationships were not plagued by the burden of creating a fortune, even a small fortune. A rocky marriage; lack of time spent with their children; the substitution of expensive gifts to repress guilt created by their frequent absences from home; the concern that their children have grown used to privilege and are consequently slacking in their education or lacking in ambition – all of these come as part and parcel of self-made wealth.

There is no escape, although each of us believes we can be the exception that proves the rule. Is this a price you are prepared to pay?

And there is worse yet. Such an attempt, without the conviction to sustain it, can bring the worst of all worlds, for if a person *does* achieve wealth, at great personal sacrifice, they will have at least acquired a vast fortune in assets or in cash. But to make the attempt without sufficient passion and commitment, knowing in your heart of hearts that you lack the conviction to succeed, risks the suffering of a self-inflicted plague without even the consolations the loot may bring.

Do not mistake desire for compulsion. Only you can know the song of your inner demons. Only you can know if you are willing to tread the narrow, lonely road to riches. No one else can know. No one else can tell you either to do it or to refrain from the attempt. When the going gets tough, when all seems lost, when partners and luck desert you, when bankruptcy and failure are staring you in the face, all that can sustain you is a fierce compulsion to succeed *at any price*.

Somewhere in the invisible heart of all self-made wealthy men and women is a sliver of razored ice. The love of another, or of family (or of their God, if they have one), can help to contain it. Seeking great wealth will release that sliver to grow. It is in the nature of the beast. If you do not wish it to grow, then quit any dreams of becoming wealthy now.

This all sounds rather melodramatic. But then I have an advantage. Not only have I grown that sliver myself, to kill my enemies with, to slay demons in the night and to harden myself against the losses to others my victories have engendered – not only that – but I have watched it grow in others who have become wealthy. It is always there and will swell into a protective carapace as you seek to grow rich.

'Better to have tried and failed than not to have tried at all,' drones the old saw. But in this instance, the cliché is wrong, utterly wrong.

Better to have chosen a different life, a quite different path, than have placed yourself and those you love in harm's way when early reflection and thought could have advised you differently. I repeat: do not mistake desire for compulsion. Those that do nearly always fail, at great cost to themselves and those around them.

THE SECOND ERROR:
OVEROPTIMISM CONCERNING CASH FLOW

Any trained accountant or auditor reading this book has just nodded their head. The last four words of the subheading above are the source of the vast majority of business failures. But why should they concern somebody who is determined to get rich? Isn't cash flow a bean-counter topic? The concern of accountants?

The answer is that not only does lack of cash flow eventually doom any enterprise, it just as surely prises control of any entity from its owner or majority shareholder. And it is *control* and *ownership* of a business entity which brings with it the promise of future wealth.

Lose control of a business by running out of cash and you are relegated to the status of minority investor or salaried employee. Once you lose control of a business, then no bank, white knight, investor or new owner is likely to permit you to gain control again, if for no other reason than that of your original sin, your overoptimism concerning the venture's cash flow in the first place.

All new ventures (and established ones, too, come to that) require positive cash flow if they are to grow and to succeed. This is an elementary point, which would scarcely need reiterating if it were not for the number of times I have seen a promising venture snatched away from its founder when cash flow faltered.

Cash is a serious matter. Its management is utterly vital in any enterprise. If, like me, you have no head for figures whatever, then this is no cause for concern. You simply employ somebody who does and listen to them carefully. Lord knows, there are enough qualified bean-counters in the world and forecasting cash flow is hardly rocket science.

It was only when a venture I was involved in became a publicly listed company that I bothered to ask a senior accountant to explain to me what a balance sheet really was. He was astonished.

How could I have become a multi-millionaire many times over without truly understanding a balance sheet?

In point of fact, he did not believe it possible at first. I explained to him that I had always left all that stuff to my finance directors and accountants – I was too busy *making* (and spending!) money, and had always begrudged the time it might take to grasp the finer points of formally recording its movement or current resting place.

Today, I have at least a rudimentary understanding of depreciation and suchlike on a balance sheet. But as far as cash flow is concerned, I have little to learn from any qualified accountant. Cash flow is something that any entrepreneur must fully comprehend from the get-go. Balance sheets are a matter for accountants, banks and auditors. But cash flow is the heartbeat of your company.

If cash flow is good, then no matter how badly run or poorly managed a company is, there is always a decent chance of turning its fortunes around. At the very least, there is time enough to be able to do so. But if a business's cash flow is weak or failing, then the chances are that it must shut down or be sold in the not-too-distant future and its assets disposed of to satisfy creditors.

Why is it that cash flow is so often the cause of business failure? Most often, either the business is not a viable one, or it has expanded beyond its capacity to support its rate of expansion.

Undercapitalisation is a frequent culprit. So is the 'ostrich syndrome', where inexperienced managers or owners focus only on new business coming in the door while neglecting to attend to mundane tasks like meeting payroll, rent and tax demands. Or, and this is far worse, and more common, they have refused to listen to whoever is in charge of cash flow. Perhaps customers are refusing to pay? Perhaps bad debt has crept up to unacceptable levels? Perhaps there *are* no customers left except for the new ones?

Like Dickens's Mr Micawber, instead of doing something to

stem the tide, such owners are always certain that 'something will turn up'. So it does, often in the form of a writ for bankruptcy or a bailiff's court order.

In the early days of my first UK company, desperately under-capitalised and without the funds to grow as quickly as I wished, I realised to my horror that I would run out of cash in a few weeks unless I acted. I went to see a friend who owned his own small company, who must remain nameless here. He, too, was concerned about his cash flow. Both of us had already turned to our respective banks for an overdraft, but our companies were too young to elicit any such benevolence.

Between us we hatched a plot. (I can think of no other word for what we did.) I invoiced my friend's company and he invoiced mine, not just once, but several times over the course of the next few months. Each paid the other using a company cheque. In Britain, unlike in America, it is not a federal offence to issue a cheque without the funds in your account at that time to cover payment, providing you *intend* to pay. Turnover at both our little companies increased substantially. We timed our payments precisely, so that our accounts were just in funds to meet each other's demands. This meant we both had to pay special attention to our respective cash flows.

I went back to the bank. They were delighted that business was booming. They were even *more* delighted that I was moni-toring my cash flow so adroitly. My friend did the same. Eventually, both banks issued each of our companies an overdraft facility. That facility permitted me to grow at a much faster rate than I could have done otherwise, and eventually produced the profits necessary to grow further and to pay off the overdraft.

I have no idea if what my friend and I did was illegal, though I doubt it was. Without question it was not very ethical, although it certainly proved effective. What I *am* sure of is that the bank appeared more impressed with my ability to *control* cash flow than they were with my company's 'growth'. That keen-eyed control was the key to unlocking yet more capital, via an overdraft with which to expand. It bred confidence.

And now we come to a difficult topic. Factoring debt. I feel like a hypocrite as I type this. But then, I have been called worse things in my life and I have broad shoulders. Factoring debt is like smoking cigarettes. You know perfectly well that smoking leads to death – but that death, however appalling, is some way off. And you need a cigarette *now*!

When you do business with a company that factors debt, you make over your debts to them. They charge a fee and percentage of the debt. A swingeing percentage. Bingo! You have solved your cash-flow crisis.

Except you haven't. Not in the long run. Factoring is a deal with the devil, and just like Faust, you will have the worst of the bargain. You should only factor in absolute extremity. You should be careful in your deal to ensure you can release your company from the factoring contract without forking out a massive penalty. Ideally, you should never do it at all. And that's all I have to say about smoking cigarettes or factoring. Both deeply unpleasant, unhealthy and pernicious activities.

Facing up to cash-flow demands and refusing to succumb to the 'ostrich syndrome' is a paramount concern in any start-up. You can delegate many tasks when creating a new business, but monitoring and forecasting cash flow is not one of them. It's *your* responsibility and *your* task. Nobody else's.

You can improve cash flow by observing the following suggestions in a start-up's early days:

○ Keep payroll down to an absolute minimum. *Overhead walks on two legs.*

○ Never sign long-term rent agreements or take upmarket office space.

○ Never indulge in fancy office or reception furniture, unless your particular business *demands* that you make such an impression on clients.

○ Never buy a business meal if the other side offers to. You can show off later.

○ Pay yourself just enough to eat.

○ Do not be shy to call customers who owe you money *personally*. It works.

○ In a city, walk everywhere you can. It's healthy and sets a good example.

○ Check all staff travel and entertainment claims with an eagle eye.

○ If you're going to be late paying, call the vendor's boss. Give a date. Stick to it.

○ Always meet payroll, even at the expense of starving yourself that week.

○ Issuing staff credit cards, company mobile phones or cars is the road to ruin.

○ Leaving lights, computers, printers and copiers on overnight is just stupid.

○ A vase of beautiful flowers in reception every week creates a better impression than £100,000 worth of fancy Italian furniture.

○ Get used to grovelling. Grovelling is an effective tool in a start-up's cash flow.

○ They want your business. Play one supplier off against another. Ruthlessly.

○ Only enter a factoring deal in absolute extremity. Exit it fast.

○ Keep your chin up. It could be worse. *You* could be working for *them*.

Cash flow is the lifeblood of any business. But just as presidents and prime ministers learn to plan for war and hope for peace, you must plan for the worst and hope for the best in all matters relating to the cash flowing in and out of your start-up company.

Regular, even obsessive, monitoring is the key. I hated every minute of doing it in those early days, but if a bean-counting klutz like me could do it, then you can too.

THE THIRD ERROR: REINFORCING FAILURE

Probably the two easiest words to write and the hardest error to avoid in this entire book. We all do it. Even the best of us. And we never stop doing it all our business lives. This is a disease curable only by iron willpower or 20/20 hindsight.

Reinforcing failure sounds so easy to avoid. If something fails, stop doing it and start doing something else, right? Er, right. Except, just *when* do you decide that you have a 'failure' on your hands? Too late, is the answer – always too late.

Let's examine the nature of success and failure for a moment. We know that success has a thousand fathers while failure is famously always an orphan. Not to mention a bastard. Then again, success has been described as the ability to go from one failure to another, unrepentant and with no loss of enthusiasm. All very well. But how the devil can we judge when a failure has occurred so that we can safely cease to reinforce it and move on.

On this matter, all prophets, wits and gurus are silent. My own suspicion is that many failures are merely a matter of timing. What used to fail now succeeds. What once was a sure thing now no longer works.

Take the invention of the fax. Fax technology existed for decades before fax machines were universally adopted. One day my office manager in the US walked me out in the hall to show me how to use our shiny new fax machine.

'Why do we need one?'

'Because everyone is getting one.'

'OK, but why is everyone getting one?'

'I don't know. They just are.'

As far as I could see, the technology had not improved much from the prototype I'd inspected a few years back. But now 'everyone' was getting one. Failure had transmogrified into success. The fax had reached critical mass.

Take another example. In 1977 (after years of arm wrestling with the powers that be), Sir Freddie Laker launched his transatlantic Skytrain service, an airline offering a no-frills service at about one third of the prices of his competitors – notably British Airways. It was a huge success for a while, then failed, collapsing into bankruptcy in 1982 with debts of over £250 million. Conventional wisdom in the City and on Wall Street labelled cheap airlines a flop.

All of a sudden, here in the first decade of the 21st century, bingo! Cheap airlines are all the rage again and turning over billions of dollars of business around the globe. A failure one minute, a success the next. It was just a question of timing.

What has all this to do with reinforcing failure? It is this *possibility*, the chance that we are onto a slow-burn *winner*, rather than being stuck with an out-and-out *loser*, that persuades so many of us (who should know better) to hang in there with a product or service in financial trouble.

Now settle down, children, and I'll tell you a real sob story. Ten years or so ago, I invested heavily in a new project, an interactive CD-ROM disc called *Blender*, based in New York City. *Blender* contained interactive reviews of new movies and albums, electronic games, animated cartoons, video interviews with celebrities and a host of other features. You stuck it in your computer to play it. Or view it. Or watch it. Or listen to it.

It was a pioneering project that made a huge splash in the media world. The idea was to publish this CD-ROM every month, just like a magazine. We had a great marketing line for it, too. 'Stay Cool: Stick Your Head in a *Blender*'.

I loved it. So did the rest of the media. We won a zillion awards. The designers and editors were fêted and rivals began to prowl around the corridors wondering if *Blender* meant the death of ink-on-paper magazines. They needn't have worried.

Blender wouldn't sell. Whenever we took it to focus groups or gave it away, kids and techies alike whooped and hollered and told us it was 'so cool'. I upped the ante. We began advertising it and marketing it. We paid stores to carry it. We worked days and we worked nights. Sometimes I had to order the young men and women working on *Blender* to go home to bed, they were having so much fun.

In our heart of hearts, we believed we were inventing a new media. We made plans for specialist *Blenders*, just like you have specialist magazines: *Blender* for cars; *Blender* for fashion; *Blender* for new movie releases. My tiny company was on fire with ideas.

Some pop stars were so keen on *Blender* they let us have unreleased music videos and tracks from their forthcoming albums to include on our CD-ROM that month. The publishing trade press wrote nice things. I took the concept back to Britain and tried it there, too. Distributors, retailers, publishing rivals – *everyone* was supportive and applauded this new concept. Everyone except the bloody customers, that is. And every issue sold worse than the last.

A very great retailer once said: 'There is no victory over customers.' Oh boy, did he get that right. But I was convinced that if only people would sample *Blender* they would become addicted. Who was I kidding?

Did I quit at $1 million loss? No. Did I quit at $3 million loss? No. Only when I had lost over $5 million did I come to my senses. Five million dollars was a lot of chump change for an individual entrepreneur back in the 1990s. Come to think of it, it still is. *Blender* wasn't even a part of my core publishing business. That meant I was investing money personally. My five million had come from *after*-tax dollars! Just how dumb can one guy be? I had forgotten John Dryden's advice.

> *Errors, like straws, upon the surface flow;*
> *He who would search for pearls must dive below.*
> JOHN DRYDEN, *ALL FOR LOVE OR THE WORLD WELL LOST*

I had forgotten to 'dive below'. I was in awe at the pretty patterns the straw made on the surface. And because I would not give in, my stubbornness turned into a jujitsu master and slammed me to the mat again and again.

Why did I continue to reinforce failure, week after week, month after month, year after year? It's a question I have often asked myself – with no satisfactory answer. The best I can give you is that I came to believe too much in the concept of a regularly published CD-ROM disc and was seduced by the technology. In addition, the *Blender* staff, headed by David Cherry and Jason Pearson, were a great group of people, hard working, talented, innovative, and fun to be around.

In short, I fell in love with the project. I did not listen to my financial advisors or my long-time partners in other companies. I just stuck in there and got myself killed for my pains. Nobody would have thought any the less of *Blender* (or my company) if I had pulled the plug at $2 million of loss after a couple of years. That would have made sense.

So right now, with the interest that would have accrued in eight years, I could have four million extra dollars sitting around in a bank account.

Four million dollars. Think about it. That's the price of reinforcing failure. Good luck in your own attempts at avoiding it. It's obvious that *I* don't know how to!

(NB: One good thing came out of *Blender*. I had registered the name and trademark worldwide in my enthusiasm, an expensive undertaking. When we launched a music magazine a few years later in America, I called it *Blender* and re-registered it – a far less expensive procedure. Today, *Blender* is a success, the only music magazine to come anywhere close to giving the venerable *Rolling Stone* a run for its money. It would be nice to have an extra $4 million to promote it though!)

THE FOURTH ERROR:
THINKING SMALL AND ACTING BIG

Here comes the painful bit. The bit I really do not want to write. The bit that will exhibit yours truly in the worst possible light.

Ah well, dear reader, you have paid money for this book and you deserve the straight goods. I will comfort myself while composing it (though it's not much comfort, to be honest) with the knowledge that my behaviour was far from unique. Others were there long before me and many are in training right now to take my place in the endless queue of idiots who succumb each year. At least I made it out alive.

Indeed, for a while, I got it the right way round. But then the thinking-small-and-acting-big syndrome kicked in and I nearly lost it all – and not just the money. What a cock-up I made of it. But let's start at the beginning.

When I had my first real financial success in 1974 publishing *Kung-Fu Monthly*, a one-shot poster-magazine about the martial-artist film star Bruce Lee, I had already begun thinking big. There's nothing wrong with thinking big.

The fact that this teeny-weeny one-shot had *Monthly* in the title caused a certain amount of mirth in the British magazine business. One-shots are not unknown by any means, but calling them monthlies is coming it a trifle high. Anyway, just how much could hippy journalists who knew nothing about kung-fu publish about one man twelve times a year? Even my friendly distributors only gave *KFM* a year before it folded.

To everyone's surprise, not least my own, *KFM* continued to be published for *ten* years, and each issue was dedicated almost exclusively to extolling the virtues of Bruce Lee. It has to be said that we had one or two things in our favour.

Firstly, Bruce Lee had lived fast and died young, always a great career move for any movie star. Secondly, it is impossible to libel a dead man, legally speaking. Thirdly, he was popular in virtually every country in the world, including the Third World. Fourthly, I had obtained a huge stash of Bruce Lee photographs by sending my friend, Don Atyeo, to Hong Kong at the time of Bruce Lee's funeral. Don is a great journalist. He set about interviewing everyone who had ever known Bruce Lee. Those interviews served as the basis for my magazine for more than a decade.

How else was I thinking big? As soon as *Kung-Fu Monthly* No. 1 was published (it sold over 100,000 copies right off the bat), I got on aeroplanes. Dozens of aeroplanes. In country after country after country, together with an Australian lawyer friend, Andrew Fisher, I licensed *Kung-Fu Monthly* to numerous foreign publishing companies. Eventually, there was even a Chinese edition of *Kung-Fu Monthly*, along with German, French, Italian, Swedish, Dutch, Spanish and Arabic editions.

Then I flew to America. Economy class. I will never forget the two weeks I spent trudging the streets of the Big Apple looking for a partner to publish *Kung-Fu Monthly* in the States. My hair was still halfway down my back. My high-heeled snakeskin boots, Mr Fish tie and Tommy Nutter knock-off suit were not exactly what American businessmen were used to.

One of my heroes was Stan Lee and his Marvel comic empire, which published *The Incredible Hulk*, *Spiderman* and my personal favourite *The Silver Surfer*. To cut a painful ten minutes short, Mr Lee had me tossed out of their Midtown offices. One publisher after another took one look at me and my puny little product and showed me the door. Nobody was even remotely interested.

In desperation I went to visit a British ex-pat whose name had been given to me by my friend Tony Elliott of *Time Out* magazine in London. His name was Peter. Together with his partner, Bob, Peter was just starting up his own magazine company in New York City. His office was shared, more of a cubicle really, but respectable. His demeanour inscrutable. But he had two things going for him – he had capital and he had the contacts to make publishing *KFM* possible over there.

Slowly and methodically Peter examined my sample issues of *Kung-Fu Monthly* and began asking me questions relating to costs, sales and the unusual format of a poster-magazine. 'Let me get this straight,' he said. 'This thing is really an uncut sixteen-page signature from a normal magazine and yet you charge the price of a whole magazines to the reader.'

'You've got it,' I replied. 'You can charge that kind of money,' I went on breathlessly, 'because when they finish reading it, kids can hang it on the wall as a cheap poster.'

Peter looked up at me and smiled. 'I'll try it. I have to try it. What can we lose?' Peter and Robert are still my American partners thirty years later. *KFM* was a success in America. And one magazine led to another. Over the years, Peter, Bob and I have risked hundreds of millions of dollars together. We have created jobs for thousands of Americans. We have become rich.

Thinking big. That's the secret. Of the dozens of independent magazine publishers in Britain back in the 1970s, hardly one of them dared to think big enough to get on an aeroplane and hawk their wares in the biggest market in the world. Those few that did so, *licensed* their magazines in America. They never thought to create a partnership and risk their own capital. Not even the largest British magazine publishers, conglomerates like IPC thought to risk it. Perhaps they had too much to lose?

But the corollary of thinking big is to act small. Just because you have a success or two under your belt doesn't mean you have it made. 'Success is never permanent; failure is never fatal. The only thing that really counts is to never, never, never give up.' That's that old windbag Winston Churchill again. But he was bang on the money there.

Once you begin to believe that you are infallible, that success will automatically lead to more success, and that you have 'got it made', reality will be sure to give you a rude wake-up call. Believing your own bullshit is always a perilous activity, but never more fatal than for the owner of a start-up venture.

By acting small, I mean remaining in touch. Remaining flexible. Constantly examining how your company could do better. Keeping a sense of proportion and humility. Not throwing your weight around playing the great 'I Am'. Remembering that much of your success so far has been achieved by dumb luck.

Acting small in the early days of your business sets an example to those around you. If staff see you indulging in long lunch hours and purchasing yourself a fancy company car, then they are either going to resent it or they are going to emulate you. This is not a good thing. You can do all that stuff later, when you've made your first fifty million.

Most of the worst errors I have made in my life came from forgetting to act small. It's hard to do when you're rolling around in coin and everything is going your way. But acting big leads to complacency, and complacency is the reason that many successful start-ups falter.

Every day you have to hit the ground running, putting in more hours than even your most dedicated member of staff. You have to stay flexible. You have to be willing to listen and to learn and to emulate success elsewhere. If you don't, if you think you have already made the cut, if you're thinking 'game over: time to party', then bad stuff begins to happen very quickly.

I know all this because in the late 1980s and early 1990s I forgot to remember to act small. I spent millions of dollars on drinking, taking drugs and running around with whores. I lost all respect for money and for the blood, sweat and treasure I had expended to acquire it. I was acting big.

In a single decade I got through more than a hundred million dollars living high on the hog. At one time, there were no less than fourteen 'mistresses' depending on a regular stipend from my personal bank account. A single evening's entertainment could come to thirty or forty thousand in the Big Apple, London or Hong Kong. There was nothing I could not do – I was king of the world. Acting big.

Even though I was not so foolish as to use company money for this idiocy, my business still suffered and my health suffered. Some good people I trusted stopped working with me. It was absolutely the stupidest thing I have ever done. And it very nearly killed me.

Eventually, I was hospitalised. When the doctors there heard how much cocaine and booze I had been imbibing over the past few years, they went ballistic. In brutal words of one syllable at a time, they warned me that either I was through with drugs and booze or they were through with me. One of them, a young doctor with a stutter, summed it all up: 'M-M-Mr Dennis, you are ac-ac-acting as if you ha-ha-have a one-way ticket to ga-ga-gaol or the mo-mor-morgue. Wh-wh-which do you wa-wa-want it to be?'

He'd got that right. Acting big.

Eventually I wised up and began to straighten out my life. I escaped by the skin of my teeth from the consequences of acting big. Almost as if by magic, the business began to make progress again. I hurled myself back into the fray, gave up all narcotics (probably the hardest thing I have ever done), stuck to wine as far as the booze went and told the whores to take a hike.

And I have been a far, far happier man ever since. And probably a nicer man. The scars are still there and the damage is done, no getting away from that. But with every passing year it all feels more like it happened to someone else.

Think big, *act* small. It's a recipe that never goes out of style. While especially important for start-ups, it will serve you faithfully long after you have established yourself as a serious player. A successful and *naturally* modest entrepreneur is an object of reverence and respect in the business world. Even if such a fabulous beast is rarer than hens' teeth.

And all in all, it's a lot more fun than strutting around like some obnoxious mini-mogul. Even today, I blush at the thought of the loot I wasted and the shenanigans I got up to when I forgot to act small.

Never again, brothers and sisters. Never again. End of sermon.

THE FIFTH ERROR: SKIMPING ON TALENT

If you are determined to be rich, there is only one talent you require. Can you think what it is before your eyes skim down to the next paragraph?

Right. You need the talent to identify, hire and nurture others with talent. 'There is no substitute for talent. Industry and all the virtues are of no avail,' wrote the novelist Aldous Huxley. I have never been much of a fan of his as far as literature is concerned, but in this Huxley is correct.

Any company managed and run by plodders and jobsworths will be lucky to survive, let alone prosper. Talent is the key to sustained growth, and growth is the key to early wealth. You have to identify and hire talent. You can't skimp on it.

Sometimes, to ensure that a talented individual will work for you, or will stay working with you, you need to be flexible. Money is not always the great motivator here. Talented people want a good salary, of course, but surprisingly often they are more attracted to new opportunities and challenges.

Stephen Colvin, my CEO at Dennis Publishing in New York City, is a good case in point. A Belfast lad who came to London and made a name for himself selling advertising for Dennis, his obvious talent acted as a magnet for my rivals. In secret (this is not as unusual as it sounds), one particular rival flew him and his wife, Pippa, to the west coast of America and tempted him with a senior management position.

Stephen and Pippa were delighted with America and they decided to take the chance to live and work there. Who could blame them? The USA is a long way from the streets of Belfast.

As soon as I had heard the news, I acted. Stephen is not a greedy chap. Putting his salary up in the UK would not be enough to hold him. So what did he want? He wanted to live and work in America.

At that time, I was busy losing money on my *Blender* CD-ROM in the States and working with Peter and Bob on MicroWarehouse, a publicly quoted catalogue reseller of hardware and software we had founded some years before. MicroWarehouse was a two-billion-dollar corporation and my publishing activities in the USA were more or less a sideshow.

What could I offer Stephen Colvin to ensure that I preserved his talent from being poached? I asked Stephen to fly and meet me at my lakeside cottage in Connecticut. He wasn't too keen on the idea. He knew perfectly well that I was going to try to 'turn' him. And he knew, too, that I did not have a Dennis operation in the States that would interest him. Nevertheless he came.

When Stephen arrived, I took him down to the dock and we boarded my boat. A few beers and a high-speed ride later, I cut the engine and we sat looking at each other while the boat bobbed gently on the surface of Candlewood lake. I was careful not to break the delicious silence. Finally, Stephen spoke: 'Felix, I'm not going to stay at Dennis. It's a great company but I want to move on and Pippa and I want to come to America.'

I nodded. And I swear to God, it was only at that moment that I realised what I might be able to do.

'What is the position they're offering you?'

'Vice president,' he replied.

'How would you like to be president of an American company?'

'What company?'

'Dennis Publishing, Inc.'

'There *is* no Dennis Publishing, Inc, Felix. Just *Blender* and a few bits and bobs.'

'Ah, but there *will* be a Dennis Publishing, Inc, Stephen. And soon.'

'What is it going to publish?'

'What would you *like* it to publish, Stephen? You're the bloody president!'

He couldn't refuse. This was the chance he had always wanted. I was going to keep my talent and Stephen was going to come to America. As a last added bonus, I told him that he, Pippa and his children could use my lake cottage whenever they wanted.

A few years later he won an industry award as 'most valued young CEO in media' or some such nonsense. More importantly he built Dennis Publishing, Inc for me brick by brick. And built his own reputation in the process.

When you come across real talent, it is sometimes worth allowing them to create the structure in which they choose to labour. In nine cases out of ten, by inviting them to take responsibility and control for a new venture, you will motivate them to do great things. It is possible that I would have succeeded in rebuilding Dennis in America without Steve's help. But I doubt that it would have been as much fun. And I doubt, too, that we would have succeeded to the degree we did.

Talent is usually conscious of its own value. But the currency of that value is not necessarily a million-dollar salary. The opportunity to prove themselves, and sometimes the chance to run the show on a day-to-day basis, will often do the trick just as well. This holds true even if talent is placed in the driver's seat of a small division within an existing operation. What talent seeks, as often as not, is the chance to prove itself and the opportunity to excel.

My advice on this subject was contained in the second paragraph of this section. You must identify talent. Then you must move heaven and earth to hire it. You must nurture it, reward it properly and protect it from being poached. If necessary, dream up a new project. Better still, get the talent to dream it up.

Youth is a further factor. By the time talent is in its mid-to-late forties or early fifties, it will have become very, very expensive. Young talent can be found and underpaid for a short while, providing the work is challenging enough. Then it will be paid at the market rate. Finally, it will reach a stage where it is being paid based on past reputation alone. That is when you must part company with it.

The French impressionist Degas once said: 'Everybody has talent at twenty-five. The difficult thing is to have it at fifty.' True enough. Most talent does not survive undiminished through its middle forties, although there are some stunning exceptions to this rule of thumb.

Anybody wishing to become rich cannot do so without talent. Either their own, or far more likely, on the back of the talent of others. Talent is indispensable, although it is *always* replaceable. Just remember the simple rules concerning talent: identify it, hire it, nurture it, reward it, protect it. And, when the time comes, fire it.

If you can do all these things with talent in the context of building your own company, I would be truly astonished if you did not become rich. Because the truth is, talent does most of the work for you. Just as it has done since the beginning of recorded history.

After all, who built the pyramids? The pharaohs or the engineers?

Think about it.

Then go hire some talent – just like they did.

PART THREE
GETTING
RICH

9

CARDINAL VIRTUES

And slowly answered Arthur from the barge:
'The old order changeth, yielding place to new,
And God fulfils Himself in many ways,
Lest one good custom should corrupt the world.
Comfort thyself: what comfort is in me?'
ALFRED, LORD TENNYSON, *MORTE D'ARTHUR*

In this chapter, I intend to deal with the cardinal virtues of getting rich. I intend, too, to deal with some common misconceptions that have cropped up on those occasions when people have taxed me about how a guy like me (to misquote John Lennon) got richer than they did.

One thing is certain, it has little to do with merit or fairness. After all, was Pete Best, the 'Fifth Beatle' that Brian Epstein forced to resign from the original group, really *that* much less of a drummer than Ringo Starr? Probably not. Who would want to end up a Fifth Beatle?

PERSISTENCE

If at first you don't succeed, try, try, try again.
Then quit. No use being a damn fool about it.
W.C. FIELDS, AMERICAN HUMORIST (ATTR.)

You will find in the pages of most so-called 'self-improvement' books by quacks (defined as those who have never done it themselves but feel justified in pontificating about it), a great deal of drivel concerning the importance of persistence. In such books, this word is usually spelt with a capital 'P' and is treated as an object of idolatry and reverence.

Fortunately, this is not a 'self-improvement' book. I do not believe anyone can be 'improved' by buying and reading a book. They can only be 'improved', if that is the word, by their own actions.

If anything, *How to Get Rich* is something ever-so-slightly new in the world, or at least I have tried to make it so. It is an '*anti*-self-improvement' book – because it admits openly that the chances of anyone reading it and then becoming rich are minuscule. The vast majority of you are far too nice. And comfortable. And sensible.

My book points out, in harsh detail, the damage to your present contentment and the risk to future and existing relationships that you run by seeking to get rich. It also deals with the coarsening of your nature that will accompany the rough and tumble of acquiring a piece of the pie from another's table. It points out, too, that avarice is tremendously time-consuming and that time is in somewhat short supply – our lives are way too short.

To return to our subject, persistence is important, no doubt about it, and requires a concerted effort of will and stamina to maintain. But it is not an end in itself.

Persistence spelt with a capital 'P' (except at the beginning of a sentence) represents the same old error that one discovers in nearly all 'self-improvement' books, not to mention in the men and women who write them.

They see a rich person with their finger pointing at the sky and, like the saps they are, they stare at the finger. Then they write about the finger and call their books: 'Become A Millionaire By Pointing Your Finger At The Sky', not realising that their subject was merely attempting to draw their attention to a glorious sunset. No matter; such authors will stubbornly persist in their error. As do most of their readers.

Stubbornness is not persistence. Stubbornness implies you intend to persist despite plentiful evidence that you should not. A stubborn person fears to be shown he or she is wrong. A persistent person is convinced that he or she has been right all along, and that the proof lies just around the corner. That with just a little further effort, the veil of failure will be torn away to reveal success. And the difference is ... ?

The difference between the two is as crucial and as intangible as the dotted line on a map across a desert separating one country from another. These lines appear to be of little importance. They *are* of no importance to the living creatures that inhabit the landscape. A desert gerbil does not think to itself, 'So now I am crossing from the United Arab Emirates into Saudi Arabia.'

But at some time in the future, that dotted line that looked so pitiful to us a moment ago compared with the harsh realities of nature, may become terribly important. It may represent billions of dollars in oil revenues. It may mean the difference between wealth and mere subsistence.

'Never give in' is a useful catchphrase. But don't take it too literally. We must all surrender at some time, to love or desire or death. You will be forced into the last of these, and a fool if you never surrender to the first. But never give in *easily*. If you can, attempt one step further along the road than appears sensible before giving in.

So-called 'persistence' is a vital attribute for those who wish to become rich, or who wish to achieve anything worthwhile for that matter. As is the ability to acknowledge that one has made a mistake and that a new plan of action must now be made. Any such acknowledgement is not a weakness, it is a sign of clear thinking. In its way, it is a kind of persistence in itself. Try, try,

try again, does not mean doing what has already failed, over and over again.

Quitting is not dishonourable. Quitting when you believe you can still succeed *is*. You must keep the faith. Belief in yourself and faith in your project can move mountains. But not if you insist on trying to scale the mountain by an impossible route which has already failed.

History is full of examples of success stories that very nearly had an unhappy ending – because it all seemed so hard, because of discouragement and the feeling that the gods were laughing up their sleeve at those involved. And often, because of a sneaking, horrible suspicion that while the destination was right, the road map was badly flawed.

Years ago, my American partners and I went into a new business, a mail-order business for personal computer software and hardware. Who was to be in charge of creating and designing our new mail-order catalogue? I was the natural choice for this task. My experience in publishing so many personal computer magazines made it obvious.

My colleagues and I worked hard on this project. My chief designer was even sleeping in our New York offices to meet the deadline for a few weeks. It was painstaking and exhausting work with no room for error. When we had all the basic designs in place, I reviewed them carefully.

They were a flop. They didn't work. Something was wrong and we all knew it. I was beside myself with worry. This was such an important project and my partners, Peter and Bob, were relying on me to get it right. I almost called them and told them to give the project to someone else – which would not have done much to foster friendly partnership relations. There was simply no time in the launch deadline.

But what else could I do? The damn thing was just not right. I was on the wrong track and found it difficult even to articulate what was wrong. Wrong it was. But why?

An associate who had worked with me for some years, Susan Freeman, made the crucial observation. She was neither a designer nor particularly knowledgeable about computers. But she had a keen eye and was involved in the project up to her neck. 'It looks rather like a magazine,' she said. 'It doesn't look like a catalogue. That can't be right.'

Of course! I had been urging my team, subconsciously, to create yet another magazine. But mail-order catalogues do not have 'readers'. They have potential buyers of goods. We had fallen into the trap of doing what we were trained to do. We were in such a rush that, instead of starting out with a blank sheet, we had moved onto automatic pilot. Every person on the team was a magazine professional of some kind. Dumb, dumb, dumb.

Armed with this insight we went back to a collection of successful catalogues of all shapes and sizes that Susan had gathered together at the beginning of the project. Using these as a template, we persevered. Within days, we had come up with a new catalogue design that worked so well it was still in use years later. Not to mention that many of the original elements we incorporated were later 'borrowed' by our rivals.

Persistence had done the trick – but only with Susan's insight. Do not be afraid to change tack, alter course or make new plans with whatever you are attempting to achieve. Especially if you sense that you are on the *wrong* track.

Above all, avoid banging your head against the same piece of wall. The wall will not get any softer. And don't give up – if you want to be rich.

SELF-BELIEF

No one can make you feel inferior without your consent.
ELEANOR ROOSEVELT

This is the core of it. Persistence is not quite as important as self-belief. I have known people who believed in themselves, who acted on that belief, got lucky quickly and got rich. Persistence merely offers a second or third bite at the cherry. Your belief in yourself brought you to the cherry bowl in the first place.

Self-belief is a priceless asset. We may detest arrogance, yet isn't it true that we *admire* it a little, too? Even though arrogance is a poor, shabby thing compared with rooted self-belief. It is an imitation of the real thing.

Why do we covertly admire such attributes? Because such people often have what the ancients called 'the look of eagles' about them, which has little to do with their appearance. Single-handedly, individuals with ingrained self-belief (and, usually, a dollop of arrogance) have changed the destiny of nations.

We have had one such in the past century in England. Perhaps he was a warmonger. Perhaps he was an incompetent strategist and a jingoist and an empire builder and a silly old buffoon, especially about the rights of women. But Winston Churchill's sense of his own destiny – his unshakeable self-belief – was, for a while, all that Britain contained in its arsenal after Dunkirk.

There were few tanks and less artillery in England in 1940. The British Expeditionary Force had left them behind on the fields and beaches of Belgium and France. All that stood between a democratic, frightened people suing for peace with a treacherous madman intent on his dream of absolute European domination, was a tired old man with a microphone – along with a few hundred Spitfires and the remnants of the mightiest navy the world had ever known.

Within the British Cabinet and the British aristocracy there lay a hidden yearning for peace. Even an admiration for Fascism as a bulwark against the Communist hordes. Peace at any price. Peace to save the world that had supported and enriched Britain's aristocrats for countless generations. Peace, even though they knew full well what Hitler had already done in those countries now swarming with what Churchill described as 'the odious apparatus of the Gestapo'.

His Cabinet colleague, Lord Halifax, would have made peace with Nazi Germany in an instant. As would Neville Chamberlain, the previous prime minister, known as 'the apostle of appeasement'.

And if we *had* made peace, which would have meant disarming ourselves and handing over our air force and, perhaps, our navy to the Nazis, where would Europe be now? And what language would we all be speaking? What would our beliefs be? Which gods would we worship? How many millions upon millions of those among us would have 'disappeared'? And how many would never have been born?

Ignore his politics, and even his principles, by all means. But to read Winston Churchill's speeches today, and, better still, to hear his recordings of them, is to understand the astonishing power and mesmeric quality of self-belief.

Younger men and women may mock all they wish but the iron determination and self-belief of this one old man, this old man with a BBC microphone, meant more to Britain at that moment than all the kings and queens in her long history.

For just one moment, a democratic people were saved from fear of failure, and from the fear of fear itself; from the shame of capitulation to evil – by what? By one old man's belief in his own destiny, by his insane, unprincipled self-belief, and the belief in the destiny of his country and of freedom in Western Europe.

I am not asking you to be Winston Churchill. None of us could be, or would necessarily want to be. He was a child of his time. But I do ask that you begin, right now, right at this very moment, to ask yourself whether you believe in yourself.

Truly. *Do* you believe in yourself? *Do* you? If you do not, and, worse still, if you believe you never can believe, then by all means go on reading this book. But take it from me, your only chance of getting rich will come from the lottery or inheritance. If you will not *believe in yourself*, then *why should anyone else*?

Without self-belief nothing can be accomplished. With it,

nothing is impossible. It is as brutal and as black and white as that. If you take no other memory from this book, then take that single thought. It was worth a damn sight more than the price you paid for it.

Which does not mean that you should trample on doubt. Doubts are like pain. If pain was to be eliminated from humankind, how would we receive warning that something was happening to our body requiring urgent attention? In many situations, pain must be ameliorated – during surgical operations, recovery from serious injury or in the throes of dying, for instance. But to eliminate pain entirely from our lives would not be a sensible objective or in our best interests.

Doubt, too, is a warning system and plays its part in reaching decisions. An important part. Without doubt, as was the case with Hitler's Youth Brigades, there is only naked ego and the kind of certainty that leads to untrammelled arrogance, and worse. Sometimes far, far worse. There is nothing wrong with doubt, or with fear. They are immensely useful tools. But you either learn to incorporate them into your thinking and your life, or you will be ruled by them. There is no 'middle way'.

It is doubt multiplied by the fear of failure, unconfronted, which leads to the creation of a vicious cycle where self-belief is eroded and nothing is achieved. Doubts *can* and *should* be confronted, as should fear. This is best done in daylight, under rigorous examination. (Three o'clock in the morning is a difficult time to confront any such messengers.) Write down your doubts and fears. Examine them. Hold them up to the light. Suck the wisdom out of them and discard their husks in the trash.

Are there things that can be done to bolster self-belief? I believe there are, but they are mostly beyond the remit of this little book. This book deals only with the getting of wealth. I will leave you with two thoughts on the subject.

Firstly, if you have ever escaped from very serious trouble indeed, or have been at the point of death, then you will know that one of two things happens. Either you become cautious to an absurd degree, or you are liberated from many ordinary fears. With liberation comes the knowledge that nothing is really very important in the lives of men; nothing is as terrifying as the fear itself. And from that, paradoxically, comes self-belief – a belief that anything is possible.

Secondly, you should remember that you are unique. Any scientist will tell you so. No other human was ever born, or will ever be born, with the same combination of upbringing, flaws and qualities that you possess. Why should you *not* believe in yourself?

Even the fact of your existence, that you were created by the swiftest sperm of the millions let loose upon the luckiest of eggs that day, is a miracle. What were the odds that it would be *you* who would result? Yes, *you*, sitting in your chair reading these words right now. How then, could you *not* believe in yourself? Nature did. Destiny did. Or, if you wish, your God did.

This business of piling up wealth is an easy business. Easy, that is, compared with giving birth, or raising children, or pressing on a parent's doorbell at midnight to tell them their child has died in an accident. Or nursing children you know will never grow to adulthood, or pulling rocks on rollers under the lash of brutal overseers to build a monument to a deranged pharaoh. How easy do they sound?

If you will only believe that you *can* do it and give it your best shot, then whether or not you succeed, you will perhaps dislodge a pebble that will ricochet down the very small mountain of your life, creating an avalanche that other fools will stand in awe of. You will not find me among them clapping, but you will certainly find enough applause to repay you for the effort. You may even grow to enjoy the process.

If you want to be rich you must work for it. But you must believe in it, too. You must believe in yourself, if only to armour yourself against the laughter of the gods in your quest. Your mad quest to be rich.

TRUST YOUR INSTINCTS

Come to the edge.
We might fall.
Come to the edge.
It's too high!
COME TO THE EDGE!
And they came
and he pushed
and they flew ...

CHRISTOPHER LOGUE, 'COME TO THE EDGE'

Ten years ago, somebody (I never did discover who) popped a copy of a new magazine into the bag I leave in the reception lobby of Dennis Publishing's London headquarters. I'd never heard of it. It was slim. Very slim, indeed. Not usually a good sign for a magazine. And it was printed on low-grade paper with barely any advertisements. The design was basic, to say the least. It even felt a bit grubby.

But I liked it. It was an old idea remodelled. When Henry Luce co-founded *Time* magazine back in 1923, his first instinct had been to create a news digest, culled from news sources around the world. In the end, he took a more expansive editorial route and built one of the greatest magazines ever published in any language.

This one was called *The Week*. I read it twice through, slowly, on my journey back to Warwickshire that night. I doubt it took me an hour. The idea was simple – though, as I found out later, not at all simple to execute. Excerpts and snippets from scores of newspapers and other sources, all carefully credited, were grouped together in sections. The columns had witty headlines like 'Boring But Important' and 'It Must Be True, I Read It in the Tabloids'.

There were precis of articles from newspapers and magazines in Britain, Europe, America and Asia. (How had the editor translated some of them, I wondered?) There was a collection of maps with arrows pointing at cities and countries in the news that week. There were book, music and art reviews and sections on health, travel, technology and property. I especially liked the little box marked 'Health Scare of the Week' and the tiny 200-word 'Editor's Letter'.

It was cute. Clever. But it didn't stand a chance. It had no ads. No distribution clout. No marketing – or, surely, I would have heard of it? Not a chance in the world for *The Week*, then.

So of course I wrote a letter to its founder, Jolyon Connell, who, it turned out, was an ex-Fleet Street journalist and editor, congratulating him on his idea. I suggested he drop by my private office any time he was passing. Then I forgot about it, although a couple more editions found their way into my hands in the months that passed.

Jolyon eventually did drop by. He was looking for investors. He already had a ton of them, many of them his friends, but the amounts they had invested were not large.

Everyone liked the *idea* of *The Week*, and nearly everyone liked Jolyon, but nobody was about to pony up hundreds of thousands of pounds to support it. He had sold his house in London to kickstart the project and had moved his family to the country. Brave chap. It showed guts. I liked him, although we could not have come from more different backgrounds, or sported more different personalities.

Hindsight is a perfect science, and Jolyon may disagree with this version of history, but my recollection is that the writing was on the wall for *The Week*. Without question its accounts were an absolute mess – not so unusual with underfunded start-ups.

Several large publishers have since implied that *they* would have invested if I had not. My answer to that is: why didn't they, then? After all, as Jolyon was the first to point out, he had never heard of me, or Dennis Publishing. The truth is that nobody else offered to invest big money in *The Week* because nobody else believed it could ever work financially. Not as a major title, anyway.

My board of directors at Dennis Publishing certainly didn't. They were dead against my investing in such a weekly. Weeklies eat up cash, especially weeklies with debts, no advertising, a pitiful number of subscribers, no newsstand sales and a bundle of small investors. Voices were raised in that boardroom. Loud voices.

What I hadn't the courage to tell my fellow directors at that meeting, or, for a day or two, even my financial guru, Ian Leggett, was that I had *already* invested. I loved the concept. I was going to own a piece of *The Week*. And to hell with naysayers.

That's easy to say. But it's not good business. It's rude and arrogant to invest in a company you intend to bring into your stable without a thorough and honest discussion of the pros and cons with senior colleagues. Like I said, it's not good business. *But it is the only business an entrepreneur has any right to be doing.*

I am not a manager. I am not even a businessman. I'm an *entrepreneur* and I go with my gut. After that, managers and bean-counters and financial advisors take over. But only *afterwards*.

I had the money and I had the 'feeling'. The 'feeling' is when the hair rises slightly on the back of your arms and neck and you know you are on the scent of something you shouldn't be doing – but you're going to do anyway. It's called commercial instinct. You develop it over the years. You certainly aren't born with it. I had it with *The Week*.

Watching an experienced entrepreneur come into contact with a potential pot of money is like watching a prone lioness raise her nose and sniff. She cuffs her cubs away. Then she sniffs some more. Then she rises and pads away to hunt. Alone. She can't see it. She can't hear it. But she can *scent* it. She knows prey is close. It means food. Prey is her business. It's mine, too.

So I invested heavily in *The Week*. It lost money. What did you expect? Ian Leggett was desperately concerned that I had bitten off more than I could chew. He had a right to be concerned.

I asked some talented people to help out from Dennis Publishing, careful myself not to interfere with the creation of the editorial product. They already had that right. It did not need messing with. *The Week* promptly lost more money, so I bought out all of the minority investors, except for Jolyon Connell, the founder, and the editor, Jeremy O'Grady.

Slowly, almost imperceptibly, *The Week* began to take off. I remember the thrill one evening when I heard a person I did not know at a dinner party quote straight out of my magazine. Even more unbelievably, readers began to proselytise. No, I mean it. Not just express satisfaction, but *proselytise* like religious fundamentalists. Like true believers. In thirty years of publishing, I had never seen anything like it.

Strangers would buttonhole me at gatherings and tell me how many subscriptions to *The Week* they were responsible for amongst their friends. Then they would demand that I did not change a *thing* in the magazine. I was to *leave the editorial alone*, did I hear? I heard. I never had any intention of messing with it, although I did ask Jolyon and Jeremy to introduce obituaries and the weather into its pages, which they did. Imagine that: a magazine which reports on last week's weather!

I met famous people, I mean *really* famous people: prime ministers and presidents and movie producers and A-list movie stars, who were only interested in talking to me because I owned *The Week*. Week by week with every issue the magazine gained more readers, a hundred extra a week, then two hundred, then three hundred. And to all appearances nobody ever cancelled their subscription.

You can guess the result. *The Week* is now the most profitable magazine I own in the UK. Pound for pound (revenues divided by cost), it is the most profitable magazine I have *ever* owned. Its margin is terrific. Today, it has more paid subscribers in Britain than one of the most venerable magazines in the world, *The Economist*.

The Week has launched in the USA and is busy becoming a huge success there, as well, under its editor-in-chief, William Falk, though it cost me $50 million to get it to break even. Justin Smith, its general manager, approached a legend in the newspaper business, Sir Harold Evans, who swiftly perceived its potential. Harry is now editor-at-large for *The Week* in the USA – he was never slow to spot a winner.

Trust your instincts. Do not be a slave to them, but when your instincts are screaming, *Go! Go! Go!* then it's time for you to decide whether you *really* want to be rich or not. You cannot do this in a deliberate, considered manner. You can't get rich painting by numbers. You can only do it by becoming a predator, by waiting patiently, by remaining alert and constantly sniffing the air and by bringing massive, murderous force to bear upon your prey when you pounce.

You can share the kill later, by all means. But if you want to get rich, trust your own judgement when it calls – and leave those whose job it is to manage your business to pick up the pieces. They can have the scraggy bits.

But the heart and liver are yours.

MAKE MORE BASKETS: DIVERSIFY!

As it will be in the future, it was at the birth of Man—
There are only four things certain since Social Progress began—
That the Dog returns to his Vomit and the
Sow returns to her Mire,
And the burnt Fool's bandaged finger
goes wabbling back to the Fire ...

RUDYARD KIPLING, 'THE GODS OF THE COPYBOOK HEADINGS'

Eggs being what they are and the world being what it is, they will sometimes break. No matter how good your idea, how fierce your resolve and how lucky you are in the early days, you must prepare for that eventuality. It will come. It always comes.

I am one of the richest self-made men in Britain for two reasons. I own my company outright, and I began to make more baskets the minute the first had a few eggs in it. Let's get down to how and why.

Forget the magazine business. Take any business and any idea. You need focused, tunnel vision to get it on the road and to begin making some money. You can expand it, maybe franchise it or take it to other cities or even other countries. But, in reality, it is still the same basket with a lot more eggs in it.

If you had created a chain of fast-food stores, then it would be unwise to leave matters there. Public tastes change and customers are fickle. To protect your investment, you would need to create new baskets. You would need to consider, perhaps, the creation of or the acquisition of a soft-drink operation. Or of a branded coffee. And you don't have to be such a massively successful chain to do it. Because, sometimes, the new basket will be worth more than the old.

Take *Chock full o'Nuts*. (Please!) This is probably the stupidest name ever given to a first-rate coffee. (It's still hugely popular in New York City, where I buy it myself at the local supermarket.) And why has it got such a dumb name? Because Mr William Black, who in 1923 founded a single store selling shelled nuts on Broadway and 43rd Street, built himself another basket. When he reached eighteen shelled-nut stores, he started to sell coffee.

The first basket paid the rent. But the second basket made a mint. His coffee was good and his crazy advertising jingle on the radio was even better. 'Better coffee a billionaire's money can't buy.' I can still hum it if you want.

Today, *Chock full o'Nuts* is owned by a large corporation.

They dare not change the weird name, but they have begun opening what they call Chock stores. I believe this is an error. Once a brand is established, any attempt to mess with the name reminds the world just how weird the name is. Not good marketing.

The *Chock full o'Nuts* story contains another germ of truth, too. By concentrating on selling coffee, its founder presumably ran down his shelled-nuts business. If you want to buy shelled nuts (why?) today in New York City, you don't automatically think of *Chock full o'Nuts*.

Strangling your own baby, in order to grow, is far more common than you might think. If you have a successful monthly magazine, for instance, and then launch a weekly in the same category, you will inevitably weaken sales of your original title. This will follow as surely as night follows day. So should you launch the weekly magazine?

Yes! A thousand times yes! Why? Because if you do *not* launch the weekly edition, even though you know it is a good idea, then your *rivals* will do it for you. You will then be left with a damaged monthly and no weekly. This is called the 'Barbarians at the Gate' principle.

Let's imagine you have a herd of sacred cows inside a fortress. The barbarians are at the gate and you are under siege. Killing sacred cows is a horrible crime, even though your defenders are running short of food. If the barbarians overrun the fortress, the sacred cows will die anyway. If you kill *some* of the cows, you will be stronger and possibly able to turn back the barbarian attack. Ergo, you eat one or two sacred cows – even if those same cows were the meaning of life last week. Learning to evolve or die is a cardinal virtue.

This same argument has been used for centuries, both in commerce and in politics. Recently, the growth of the internet has begun to destroy the music industry. More and more people download songs without paying for them, despite it being illegal.

As a result, CD sales have been in tailspin and record companies have watched in horror as billions of dollars have been sucked out of the market, crippling their share price.

These record companies, who have grown fat for years by charging very high prices for little bits of cheap plastic, reacted foolishly, at first. They were far too slow to begin devouring the sacred cow of the CD. What they wanted was for the pirating and illegal downloading to stop. That's where they concentrated their efforts. Dumb move. The barbarians were not about to quit any time soon.

After all, what the record companies were faced with was nothing new. It was merely a kind of forced diversification. What they *should* have been busy doing, since the creation of the Napster website, let alone Apple's iPod, was weaving themselves new baskets – not defending the old, worn-out basket. Today, as a result of commercial pressure, that is exactly their strategy.

Let's not be too hard on them. As you will discover when you start your own business, it's difficult and scary facing up to swiftly changing realities on the ground. Most of us would prefer that things stayed the same so that we can carry on making money in ways we have grown comfortable with.

But things do *not* stay the same. Either you learn to go with the flow and change as rapidly as you are able, or you will be left stranded, like the last dinosaur, by the last warm lake, on the last continent the ice age has yet to reach.

Let's take another example of building more baskets just as quickly as you can. Richard Branson has done it. Some of his Virgin enterprises are not as strong as others (did you ever *try* Virgin Cola?), but that's not the point. Western capitalism will have to sink into an ocean of darkness before *all* of Richard's Virgin businesses go broke.

He has built scores of baskets, ranging from financial services to airlines, from music super-stores to railway passenger services. He's a canny man. I know from experience. I used to wake him up occasionally on his longboat, moored in central London. Before I even got a mouthful of coffee for breakfast, I was answering his damn telephones, ringing off the hook while he showered. In those days, he was probably showering in his trademark jumper.

Richard has perfected one cardinal rule: he owns or part-owns more baskets than almost anyone alive. It's certainly one way to become a billionaire.

How many baskets should you go for? As many as make sense. In the beginning, it would be best, if you can, to keep them related to your core business. Just like Richard did. He started off importing 'grey' record albums from the USA – they were the illegal downloads of their time, except they weren't free. Richard followed up with record stores and then a record company. Or was it the other way around? No matter. Different apples. But basically all from the same orchard.

You will not have to be as exceptional as Richard Branson to get rich. But his policy is a good one. No, a *great* one. I've failed the basket test a few times, and perhaps I should confess to one or two of them.

○ When I had the chance (i.e. when flush with cash), I should have bought more magazines. Even a newspaper, if I could have afforded it. Local newspapers, until recently, made a ton of money from their classified ads. I missed a trick there.

○ I should have considered going into radio or television production earlier than I did. Many popular television shows are based loosely on a 'magazine' format. There are a lot of similarities in the boys and girls who create television and create magazines. Not to mention the content.

○ I should have invested in one or two internet start-ups I knew were going to do well. That was a stupid error and came about because, by then, I was spending too much time each day writing poetry. No excuse, though.

There would be other tricks I missed, if I could bring myself to evaluate them. But nobody likes to dwell on past failures. They're just too painful.

Of course, not all baskets are worth investing in. Dennis Publishing did a great job as far as the internet was concerned. While most of the big magazine companies in the world were pouring cash into massive internet expansion seven or eight years ago, we decided to back off.

The sums being bandied about were insane. One British publishing company I know planned to invest $50 million over a couple of years on their internet business, housed in some massive building to give them room to expand. (It never did expand. It sank.) This strategy was executed solely to assuage institutional investors who knew nothing about the current state of play on the internet. Naturally.

Dennis Publishing built its websites carefully and well. We stuffed them with content and we advertised them in the pages of our magazines. But we didn't allow ourselves to be suckered into weaving a basket the size of the Super Bowl which would be obsolescent before it returned a penny. We couldn't afford to.

This sensible policy was mainly thanks to Guy Sneesby, who still works for me. Despite loving the internet and everything about it, he was dead against throwing money at it. 'Wait until it grows. Match investment with growth. Make it pay,' was his game plan. Turned out he was right. Probably saved me $10 million or so. Maybe more. Thanks, Guy. (You see, it pays to hire talent smarter than you are.)

Meanwhile, on the other side of the Atlantic, Guy's counterpart in my company there was a long-time Dennis staffer, a British ex-pat called Roger Munford. Roger has never been known to waste a buck. He's naturally thrifty. His second name is 'Frugal'. I have always suspected that when Roger's coffee from Starbucks goes cold, he warms it up in the microwave. *More than once!*

Roger was running Dennis's American internet division, and his instinct was similar to Guy's. But he spotted that things were different over there. Most magazines sell more copies via a paid subscription than on the newsstand in America – quite the opposite situation a publisher is faced with in Britain and Europe. Obtaining paid magazine subscriptions is a costly business. On average, it can cost between fifty and one hundred dollars to obtain a 'live' subscriber – one who will eventually renew their subscription and pay off the cost of having attempted to acquire scores of others.

Still with me? So Roger goes into overdrive when he finds he can sell subscriptions on the *Maxim* website. This strategy isn't working for Guy in the UK, but who cares? It's working in the USA. So Roger, that thrifty, frugal soul, begins pouring hundreds of thousands of dollars of my money into our American internet operation, weaving a massive new basket we never knew existed.

It must have been painful for him, but it paid off. We were selling subscriptions for pennies instead of fifty or sixty bucks a time. Hundreds of thousands of bloody subscriptions. It was exciting, it made great sense, and it allowed us to build the *Maxim* website into one of the most powerful internet portals for young men in North America.

And the beauty was, the newsstand purchasers of the ink-on-paper version of *Maxim* had paid for it. They had provided the cash to invest in our website. Thanks, Roger. (You see, it pays to hire talent smarter than you are.)

Just remember that this advice is not designed for your start-up phase. During the start-up, you concentrate on that one basket as if your life (and the life of your first-born) depends upon it. But once you have something that's working and making some money, start looking around quickly for another opportunity. The more baskets the better.

Diversifying not only ensured that I had more chances to lay more eggs and somewhere to incubate them, it also gave me the confidence to concentrate on any one egg at any one time. When one of my projects was in trouble and needed more work, or needed rethinking, the fact that I had other eggs in other baskets gave me the confidence to do what was right. Like re-engineering or folding it.

One of the problems with being a start-up entrepreneur is that you tend to think of what you have created as some kind of surrogate child. It becomes your 'baby', if you're not careful. This is dangerous and counter-productive. You are not in the egg-laying and basket-weaving or baby business. You are in the business of getting rich.

If you have only one set of eggs in one basket, then selling it (let alone folding it), can be surprisingly hard. The thought of letting go because it's just not working may be more than you can bear, however logical such a decision is. By having other eggs doing well in other baskets, you ensure that you can approach such problems at least semi-dispassionately. (It will only be 'semi'; trust me.)

It's for this reason that I am often, along with my group CFO, Ian Leggett, the only one voting to close down one project or another at my various companies. To the young people involved in that project, it is a matter, seemingly, of life or death. To a man with many other fish to fry, it is just another problem in need of a solution.

The reverse of that medal, of course, is that I do not bring to any project the passion and insight of those more closely involved. Even so, by diversifying and building other baskets in other countries, I believe I have become better able to make hard decisions more often. That's a definite plus.

The biggest basket I ever built wasn't my first or second. It was my twentieth. But if I hadn't built the second, I would never have reached the twentieth. And maybe, just maybe, I have a couple more baskets yet to build.

LISTEN AND LEARN

Then the Gods of the Market tumbled,
and their smooth-tongued wizards withdrew,
And the hearts of the meanest were humbled
and began to believe it was true
That All is not Gold that Glitters, and Two and Two make Four—
And the Gods of the Copybook Headings
limped up to explain it once more.
RUDYARD KIPLING, 'THE GODS OF THE COPYBOOK HEADINGS'

A lot of strangers ask to come and see me during the course of a year. And I mean a lot. I have three highly trained, full-time personal assistants at my private offices just handling the calls. In fact, they share another assistant who answers the phones – a kind of assistant to the assistants.

You might think that's excessive or just showing off. But if you were there in the middle of a busy day, you'd revise your opinion. The only description that comes close is organised chaos. Pretty often I find myself in two meetings at once. Which is why I have a connecting set of stairs to my flat upstairs from the offices. There just aren't enough meeting rooms, and a kitchen table always makes for a friendly substitute.

Not for me the quiet executive office floor with minions toiling their nuts off down below while I smoke huge cigars and ready myself for a soothing massage. I want to be where people can reach me on certain days of the week. Why? Because I want to hear what they have to say.

That's not because I'm a sociable chap. In fact, there's little I like better than my own company. But when you stop listening, you stop learning. And if you stop learning, it's time to get out of the kitchen and let someone else do the cooking.

Listening is the most powerful weapon after self-belief and persistence you can bring into play as an entrepreneur. And yet

I'm familiar with numerous senior executives running large companies who might spend two or three weeks in between listening to a 'stranger' – or a 'minion'.

Talking to your own executives and senior managers is necessary, of course. But talking to people you do not know, or who work in some obscure corner of your industry (or even in your own company), is just as necessary. More so, perhaps.

If you have experience, a little investment cash and will make the time, then the world will bring to your door an amazing collection of visionaries, con artists, madmen and budding entrepreneurs. They all have something to say. Most of your time will be wasted. But what is not wasted will make you richer. Much richer.

A digression. Allow me to slip in here a few words concerning courtesy. I cannot give it a chapter or even a subheading to itself, because being courteous and always failing merely makes you a courteous loser. Courtesy is not a cardinal virtue in getting rich, I admit. But it helps. It works. It greases wheels where force will not prevail. Out of the mouth of anyone on their way to becoming rich, it lends a certain gravitas and creates the impression of someone you might like to do business with. This is true in any country in the world, in my experience, but it is especially true in the USA. Americans worship courtesy almost as much as they worship money.

But the courtesy of listening is not an excuse for inaction. Unfortunately, this is often the very use to which it is put. How virtuous we all feel listening, taking notes, interjecting our own two-penny-worth and promising to consider the matter and get back to whoever has come to visit. Trouble is, business is not a talking shop. It relies on decisions, often hard decisions, being made in as short a time as makes sense.

My advice, based on thousands of such meetings over the years, is to keep them short – unless your gut tells you that you have stumbled upon a winner. Set the meeting for twenty minutes. Have somebody interrupt you after twenty-five minutes and usher the caller swiftly from your room.

It's usually better to leave no doubt in your visitor's mind if you're not interested in their project or idea. In a way, it's kinder, as well. While the temptation is to say, 'I'll confer with my colleagues and get back to you,' this will eventually come back to haunt you and waste more of your most valuable resource. Time.

I'm feeble at this balance between courtesy and efficiency and always have been, but I've got a little better over the years – especially with the help of my personal assistants, Wendy, Caroline and Ashleigh. They're trained to interrupt me if they sense either my visitor or I is flying on autopilot. And they can be ruthless about it!

Piling up meeting upon meeting in a brutal schedule actually helps. Your visitor sees others waiting to see you and will procrastinate less. If you *do* need time to mull over a suggestion, then make it clear that it will be *you* getting back to *them*. People with an idea are desperate, and will call and call and call unless you set clear ground rules.

Now let's talk about ideas and who owns what. If someone comes to see you with an idea you're already considering or are already working on (no matter how loose the connection), then stop them abruptly and tell them the situation. That's only fair. It is curiously common for new ideas to arrive independently from more than one source at a time. Science can't explain it, and neither can I, but it's a fact, all the same.

Ideas, by the way, cannot be 'owned' by anyone. You cannot trademark or patent or copyright any idea. You can only protect the *execution* of the idea and trademark the name. This is an important thing to know in any business and is often misunderstood by people who come to you with an idea. Such people often request you sign an NDA (a Non-Disclosure Agreement), and I am usually happy to do so.

Why? Because the force in law of most NDAs is limited and they do not work in the way most people think they do.

For example, the idea for 3M's Post-it Note could be described as follows: 'Paper of any size, one edge of which which will attach itself by way of gum to most surfaces, especially paper, and which can be detached, without leaving a residue or mark.' A lawyer would shorten that to 'paper with a repositionable adhesive'. No matter. If you had tried taking that description to the patent office after 3M's research scientist, Dr Spencer Silver, discovered the adhesive but before Art Fry, a 3M new-product researcher, hit upon a use for it – it would have availed you nothing. Why?

Because 3M *owned* the formula for the gum. The *formula* was a way of *executing* the idea. If you had come up with an even better gum and had created your own name for such notes and marketed them, then 3M would have had a devil of a job to stop you, because no one can copyright or patent an *idea*. You can only protect the *execution* of the idea, which must be unique. If your gum really was unique, you would be in business. And what a business!

Similarly, the Walt Disney Corporation does not own the rights to all imaginary talking mice. Talking animals existed in the minds of writers and artists long before Walt Disney himself was born. The Disney Corporation only owns the 'look and feel' (and a host of other attributes) of two *particular* talking mice, Mickey and Minnie Mouse. If you are in the business of executing ideas to make money, then this is something you are going to have to come to grips with and become a minor expert on. There are many books to help you out there.

To get back to our meetings where people are attempting to persuade you to consider their idea or project: what about ideas put forward by a member of your own staff? What if they come up with an idea which the company then develops and which proves to be a huge success. Who owns it?

The answer is that the company does. *You* do, if you are the owner of the company and your employee put forward the idea in the course of working for you. (*Now* do you see why you must always hire people more talented than you?) The only exception to this would be if an agreement had been entered into between you and your employee, or between the company and its employee, or if the idea had nothing to do with your industry and had been conceived (and developed) in the employee's own time, using no company materials.

Other than that, in the ordinary course of business, you do not owe your employee a single cent for bringing his or her idea forward. That's especially true if *your* money, or your *company's* money, was used to test and develop the idea.

This seems unfair. It was *her* idea. *She* pushed it forward and probably worked very hard on it. Shouldn't she enjoy *some* of the financial benefits of her idea? We'll get back to that, but first let's look at another scenario. The non-employee who comes in with a thumping great idea and wants you and your company to help execute it.

This is a different kettle of fish. You must proceed cautiously. Just because NDA agreements usually have little force, doesn't mean you can be cavalier and reckless. How far has this person gone towards *executing* the idea? If she came to see you and said, 'I have an idea for a coloured note that can be stuck onto paper, that you can write on, and that can be removed later without leaving a mark,' then she is a fool. She should not have come to you without protecting that idea very, very carefully indeed.

However, if she then brought out a sample that did not work very well, but which worked to *some* degree, the case is altered. She *has* executed her idea, however badly. If you wish to invest in the idea, you would almost certainly have to come to a legal agreement with the inventor.

This all sounds hypothetical and theoretical. But it's not, you know. In more situations than you might imagine, it becomes critical. Ownership is all. When *who owns what* is in dispute, the only people who are going to get rich are the lawyers. There have been many, many bitterly contested ownership disputes in business which not only wrecked the companies involved, but destroyed the sanity of the main participants. The invention of the television set in America was one such.

But what of the young lady who works for your company and brought you (or her manager), the great idea that worked so well? What of her?

That's up to you, buddy. You're the owner. If you're a sensible, decent, worthwhile human being, you will reward her handsomely and promote her. And you will thank her publicly.

If you're a rotten, ingrate scumbag, without any decent feelings whatever, you will not reward her. And you'll get rich. But perhaps not quite as rich as a more enlightened owner. Because if your clever employee has had one such great idea, she may well have another later. And she is unlikely to stay working for a company that stiffed her so badly, or to hand them another gem, is she?

I'm fully aware that this isn't a book about becoming a worthwhile human being. As I keep attempting to drum into you, riches aren't particularly worthwhile in themselves in any case. They don't make anyone a better person, at least as far as I have seen. But listening continuously, *listening* and *learning*, is one of the vital components for those of you who wish to be rich. What you choose to do with your loot is up to you.

But listen and learn if you want to be rich!

10

A FEW WORDS ABOUT LUCK

Born under a bad sign
I been down since I began to crawl
If it wasn't for bad luck,
I wouldn't have no luck at all.

BOOKER T. JONES AND WILLIAM BELL, 'BORN UNDER A BAD SIGN'

THE INVINCIBLE WORM OF DOUBT

Army chaplains who have seen bullets fly, sometimes boast that 'there are no atheists in the foxholes'. In the same way, as bullets fly around our head in life, most of us are believers in luck. Secret believers for the most part, it's true. But believers none the less.

The major religions of the world have worked tirelessly over the centuries to eradicate 'superstitions' among their flock; 'superstitions' which appear to mock, or at least to be at odds with, 'holy' writ. Which is another word for supernatural dogma. In this, they are at one (just for once) with philosophers and scientists, although for very different reasons. And it is true that a great many ancient superstitions no longer hold very much sway in large parts of the world. But with 'luck', and with omens of good or evil fortune, scientists, philosophers, religious leaders and wise men have, for the most part, laboured in vain.

You think not? How many times have you 'knocked on wood', perhaps rising from your chair to find a piece of wood to knock upon, or even tapped your head in a self-deprecating nod to the pagan gods of fortune? Many times, I would wager. I do it myself, and so do most people I know, however sheepishly.

We are all in thrall to Lady Luck, and therefore to superstition. Even those of us who rolled our eyes in disbelief when we heard that Nancy Reagan insisted on consulting an astrologer before allowing her husband, the most powerful man in the world at that time, to sign a disarmament agreement with the Russians. Even those of us who roared with laughter recently when yet more revelations emerged of odd and arcane behaviour involving the use of 'healing crystals' at No. 10 Downing Street. Not that the crystals were the half of it.

We may mock Mrs Blair and Mrs Reagan all we like, but this invincible worm of doubt, this nagging feeling that some are born to win and some are born to lose, that we can perhaps propitiate Fortune with ritual or prayer or sacrifice – this death-less wriggler infests most of us, to one degree or another. So what can we do about it on our quest to get rich?

The truthful answer, of course, is nothing. We can do nothing at all. And every word I now type opens me to well-deserved mockery and contempt from those very few souls (a Freudian slip, that last word, I'm afraid), who steadfastly deny the existence of any such thing as luck. Or destiny. Or the gods of good fortune.

And yet, and yet … Just like you, I have seen it at work. I have watched my own idiocy transformed by a piece of good fortune. I have stood, amazed, as catastrophe transformed itself into another chance – or, even more ridiculously, into a home run. And I have witnessed genuine achievement and hard work undone by a series of astonishingly unlikely events – mostly in others, I hasten to add. (I have just realised that those last seven words were a nod to the gods of good fortune. I shall leave them there as a penance.)

Then there is negative luck, or luck disguised. When I was thinking small and acting big in the late 1980s, I collapsed at my cottage in Connecticut. It later transpired that I had contracted legionnaire's disease in a hotel in Los Angeles.

Legionnaire's, caused by the bacterium *Legionella pneumophila*, which breeds in the air-conditioning units of hotels, hospitals and other large buildings, is a killer. It is especially lethal to coked-up, overweight, cigarette-smoking, malt-whisky-swilling idiots with too much money who believe they are built of titanium.

After the plane had touched down in New York, I insisted that my chauffeur drive me straight to the cottage, despite his appeals to take me to a hospital closer to the airport. My real reason was that I had a girlfriend waiting at the cottage and I knew she would be frightened to spend the night there alone. She was also a very beautiful girl – even when men are dying they think of sex! Little did I know that sex would be off the menu for the next few months.

That irrational decision, made in severe pain and through waves of nausea, saved my life. It was lucky, although I didn't feel too lucky at the time. It was luck disguised.

Hospitals in Connecticut have 24-hour diagnosticians on duty. Connecticut is one of the richest states, per capita, in the union and the emergency wards of their hospitals in no way resemble the scrum and chaos of many an inner-city hospital in large cities nearby. Within minutes of being rushed to Danbury Hospital by my cottage neighbour (more luck: he was a pharmacist and knew a potentially lethal fever when he saw one), the diagnostician there made a brave and, as it turned out, correct diagnosis.

If I had taken my chauffeur's advice, it might have been hours, even days, before a harassed and frantic A&E doctor in a New York City hospital finally diagnosed a set of bewildering and very rare symptoms. By then, of course, I would have slipped into a pulmonary coma from which there could have been no return.

That disease was also double luck disguised for me. It forced me to change my way of life. I came so very close to death that it jolted me back to reality. How close? Close enough for the doctors to ask what my religion was. Did I want to see a minister or a priest?

I am proud to report that, lying there on a bed of ice hooked up to more tubes than you'd find in a sack of spaghetti, I managed a weak joke through gritted teeth, which raised a laugh from a pretty nurse. She was thoughtfully pouring ice water on my genitals to keep me awake at the time. 'No minister or priest, thank you, doc. But do you have a venture capitalist handy?'

Let's return to the altogether happier world of making money and disguised luck. I once made several million pounds through a piece of luck that was also pretty heavily disguised at the time. Back in 1990, things were going well at my British company. Or so we all thought. I was busy with my partners in America building a brand new beast that needn't concern us here.

The UK company had expanded so fast we were operating out of five separate locations in an area of central London called Fitzrovia. This was obviously an inefficient state of affairs. The managing director of Dennis Publishing at that time was a fully qualified accountant who had once been our finance director.

Lesson No. 1: *Never* make your finance director or CFO the MD or president of anything!

Secure in the knowledge that our finances were in good order and we were making a decent profit, I asked my MD (we will call him Christopher, although that is not his real name) to scout around for a new headquarters building in Fitzrovia. He found one. An absolute beauty. We could not afford to buy it, of course, but we could certainly afford the rent because of all the savings we would make by working together under one roof.

Negotiations commenced and were concluded on Christmas Eve. I was already on vacation in the Caribbean with a gaggle of girlfriends, inhabiting several hotel suites and villas.

Lesson No. 2: Never go on vacation when a deal is going down.

I was so proud of our new headquarters building that I actually took a photograph of it with me on holiday. It was called Chadwickham House and still stands today in Bolsover Street, London. It's an odd but elegant structure, which might be described by a cockney lad as 'all mouth and no trousers'. That is, it's more show than substance. But what a show!

The frontage of Chadwickham House is immense, guarded by imposing wrought-iron railings. It features numerous stone gargoyles on pillars and literally scores of panelled windows. The entrance portico is handsome and austere. Unfortunately, the building had very little depth. But who cared? It absolutely *looked* the business and was more than big enough for us.

Then came a fateful telephone call. My vacation was wrecked. Christopher had been so busy as managing director he had not been watching our accounts closely enough. Far from making a big fat profit, Dennis Publishing UK had barely broken even that year. A black hole had appeared in our annual accounts and we had been living in a fool's paradise. There was absolutely no impropriety or shady dealings going on. It was just faulty accounting, exacerbated by a change in our computer accounts package.

Lesson No. 3: When you change accounting systems (or accountants, for that matter), have the numbers checked over and over again. I'll eat my hat if errors are not discovered in the next iteration.

Looking back, I suspect Christopher shouldered a great deal of the blame that belonged to others. But that is what MDs and presidents and CEOs are paid for. If it happens on *their* watch, then *they* must bear the responsibility. To his credit, Christopher did just that, although I suspect he aged a year during the crisis.

Desperately we attempted to back out of the Chadwickham House deal. No dice. There was no escape clause. I flew back to London and underwrote a loan at a very nasty rate of interest.

That was foolish. By this stage in my life I should not have been personally underwriting business loans.

Lesson No. 4: Never personally underwrite business loans for your company unless you absolutely, positively, are forced to. Even then, set limits in the agreement so that, as the loan figure is reduced over time, you are released from your undertakings commensurately.

Dennis Publishing moved into its fancy new headquarters. We were happy with them, but remained as poor as church mice for a few months. Christopher was offered a new job by a rival publisher based in America. He took it and still resides today on the west coast of America; very happily, I might add. I appointed a new MD and a new finance director. Life moved on.

A while later, my partners and I made a killing in America and I found myself awash with cash. Tens of millions of pounds of cash. Naturally I set about spending it just as fast as was humanly possible, which, in my case, must have set some kind of world record.

New cars, new houses, new women and new wine cellars. But I'm not a complete fool and my new finance director, Ian Leggett, proved to be a gem. He forced me to invest in a few sensible things apart from the company itself. One of them was Chadwickham House. I bought the property from the landlords for a song and sold it six or seven years later, when we moved to an even larger office block. The profit was handsome. Very handsome indeed.

Lesson No. 5: Listen to people who are good with money and always invest in property with a good address – providing you can pay cash for it and will not need to sell it for a few years.

So where did the negative, disguised luck come in? It came in the shape of the black hole in the 1990 company figures. Think about it.

If we had known the truth, I would never have entered into a lease for a fancy new building. I would then not have been in a position, as a tenant, to purchase it from the landlords. After all, I'm not in the property business. Furthermore, we would not have been in a position to squeeze a sensational price from the property developer who subsequently bought it from me. (He was forced to pay above the odds because Ian discovered that Chadwickham House was slap bang in the middle of a city block the developer had been acquiring site by site.)

It wasn't a clever business brain that made me all that money. It was dumb luck. But I was ready to seize the opportunity that disguised luck had delivered.

One of my favourite philosophers, the first-century Roman Seneca, coined the following: 'Luck is what happens when preparation meets opportunity.' I have never come across a better definition – that's why I'm repeating it. Preparation multiplied by opportunity. Say it again. Learn it off by heart. Let it become a daily mantra. Luck is preparation multiplied by opportunity.

Over the centuries this has morphed into cracker-barrel soundbites, as in the golfer Gary Player's: 'It's a funny thing, luck. The harder I practised, the luckier I got.' But Seneca's original quote is far more profound and is worth a moment of our time. Preparation is the key. Be prepared. Do the heavy lifting and the homework in advance. Get on with the job, but remain alert enough to spot an opportunity when it arrives. Then hammer it.

If you haven't prepared yourself, the opportunity will go begging. It will be yet another regret in your life, another 'if only ... ' And even if you *have* prepared, but are too busy, probably buried in the minutiae of management, or a messy divorce, or moving house, or a hundred and one other things, then luck will again evade you. Months or years later you will be saying, 'If only I had spotted that opportunity. I was ready for it, but I wasn't paying attention.'

'If only ... ' are the two saddest words in the English language.

Then there is the case of a man I have known for thirty years. He is a better publisher than I am and has been a better publisher since we both set out on our own back in the early 1970s. He is a better businessman, too. He networks more and is always one of the first to understand which way the wind is blowing. His writing skills are way above my own – not that that's saying much, I know. But even so, good writing skills can be important in our business.

He listens to others more often and more closely. He is a fierce but fair negotiator and has more patience than I. And, by God, he has needed more patience, more patience than Job.

Like a modern-day version of that tormented biblical figure, misfortune dogs him. No sooner has he struck gold than it crumbles into dross. No sooner has he dug another mine than it fills with water nobody guessed was there. Nothing will work. Nothing has ever really worked for him. It must be absolutely galling.

His personality has changed for the worse in recent years. He now exhibits, perhaps not unnaturally, a degree of resentment towards those who have done so much better with so much less talent and less determination. I notice I have begun to avoid his company. And so have others.

Is it because I feel guilty? Is it because I wish to avoid his flashes of bitterness and dark humour? Is it because I am leery of vile, involuntary gloating? Or is it because in some pagan corner of my heart, I believe that *bad luck might be contagious*?

I don't know the answer to that. But I do know that he *ought* to be rich. At least as rich as I am, and perhaps a great deal richer. So what is it that separates us? Perhaps a dispassionate analysis will help to us to peer dimly into the murky world of what we humans call 'luck' and 'misfortune'.

THE NATURE OF ALBERT'S MISFORTUNE

You will find a great deal of poetry in this book. Both by me and by much better poets. There's a good reason for that. Poetry forces a writer to condense and crystallise his thoughts and often represents a short cut to truths unsuspected by the author himself. Here's a short poem I wrote a while ago concerning the laws of unintended circumstance and 'luck'.

Two Left Feet

The laws of unintended consequence
Have nimble limbs; they mesmerise the dance.
With two left feet, our dancing makes no sense:
Are not all ballerinas born by chance?

Perhaps. But I shall tell what I have learned—
The gods of fortune recognise no debt;
Bouquets strewn on a stage are mostly earned,
And luck is one more dividend of sweat.

But is luck just 'a dividend of sweat'? How many times can one person 'dust themselves down, pick themselves up and start all over again' before they lose heart? I have already mentioned Winston Churchill's 'If you're going through hell, keep going'. All very well if you are a cigar-smoking, ageing hero at the nadir of his career, who is nevertheless certain he is destined for greatness. But what about the rest of us?

The only truth about luck, good or bad, is that it will change. The law of averages virtually guarantees it. And here, I think, is one difference that separates me from my 'unlucky' friend, whom I shall call Albert.

Albert is so close to the cross currents of the market that his antennae lead him astray. When he hits yet another bump on the road, or has a head-on collision, he attempts to change his luck by changing direction. It's not that he lacks stamina. Albert has tons of energy and stamina. But he doesn't, as Churchill put it, 'keep going'. Instead, he keeps looking for pastures new – the golden sunlit uplands, the philosopher Leibniz's 'best of all possible worlds'. Perhaps there, in a new place, he will find his fortune and change his luck?

Instead, he immediately encounters the evils of an unfamiliar and perilous country, without the benefit of the road maps he so painstakingly put together in his last adventure. He does not 'keep on truckin'' as the cartoonist, Robert Crumb, would have it.

This 'flight not fight' behavioural trait is the sign of a prey animal, not a predator. Despite what you will read in many self-improvement tomes, 'partnering' and 'symbiotic evolution' are no way to get rich. They may be a way to a better world. They may make you a happier person and a better manager. But they will not make you rich – except, perhaps, in spirit.

To become rich you must behave as a predator. I will go further, you must *become* a predator. Albert is not a predator.

By moving so adroitly and so swiftly from one thing to the next, Albert does not place himself in the way of luck. He does not draw luck to him. He does not make his own luck. He is much too much in love with the green, green grass just over the next hill.

Then again, Albert is more intelligent than I am. He had a grand education and read all the right books at university. He is not a self-taught scholar, as I am. But there is a downside to all this intelligence and imagination. He thinks a little too much before he acts. He weighs the options *too* carefully. *He is capable of imagining defeat.*

So while he is clever enough to want to minimise his risk by switching to yet another new and uncontested marketplace, he leads himself into uncertainty. And into error.

Uncontested markets are usually uncontested for a reason. Nature abhors a vacuum and if no one else is contesting a market, it may well be that no such market exists. Albert is always slightly ahead of the media game. He is a visionary, I guess. Very few visionaries get rich, begging the lads at Google's pardon.

New software often faces this problem. Brilliant software designers come up with fancy software that solves no known problem. They are forced to discover or invent a problem their software might solve. Should they fail, there will be no users and no investors. And no money.

Take electronic spreadsheets, for example, today one of the most ubiquitous tools of any finance department anywhere in the world. Prior to the invention of spreadsheets, nobody spent much time playing 'what if' games and mapping possible alternative financial business models. Today, everybody does it as a matter of course.

But few visions or new technologies result in such a serendipitous outcome. Yet Albert wastes too much of his time seeking them out, coming to understand them and making all the rest of us feel inferior as he wearily explains this exciting new concept for the umpteenth time to Luddite chumps like me.

There are other differences between Albert and me. He is a great believer in partnering and share options and employee profit participation. I shall be devoting an entire chapter to this subject (See Chapter 14: **A Piece of the Pie**), but I will mention, here, that in Albert's case, this division of the spoils is undertaken in the minutest detail, long before there are any profits whatever to share. Albert believes they encourage his co-workers. But such arrangements are immensely time-consuming and a distraction from the tunnel vision necessary to become rich in the first place.

Albert is a ferocious negotiator, as I've mentioned, and a whizz at assimilating and mastering detail. But he is a perfectionist and his powers of delegation are stunted. He's so good at what he does that he is unwilling to accept even slightly second-best. This means, for him, that he must do it himself. And if by chance he doesn't get it exactly right the first time, then he will do it over and over again until it *is* right. Until it is perfect.

We shall come to the importance of delegation later in this book (See Chapter 13: **The Joys of Delegation**), but Albert's reluctance to permit young managers to make their own mistakes has cost him dearly over the years. Not just in the time wasted, but in management turnover.

While he is fair, and sometimes more than fair, with his staff, they don't love him. They don't love him because they do not get the chance to grow, and if there is one good thing about a well-managed company in a capitalist society, it is the opportunity to groom talent and encourage it to grow. Apart from the money, it's the best thing about getting rich.

As a result of trying to do everything himself, Albert also sometimes misses out on good fortune and luck when it's staring him in the face. He reminds me of a groom-to-be who is so keen to redecorate the church, the reception rooms and his new house to ensure a perfect wedding day that he fails to notice his bride-to-be has grown tired of waiting and has married another man.

Also, Albert cares too much (because he is growing desperate in his mid-fifties), and takes himself and his destiny too seriously. I know this because I have got drunk with him a few times – always a good way to really get to know somebody. In vain I have pointed out to him that we are nothing but merchant princes. Who will give a hoot whether we made $10 million or $500 million in a hundred years from now? Nobody will.

Having too much money isn't important. Breaking your neck is important. Getting cancer is important. Having nothing to eat is important. Losing someone you love is important. But too much money is absolutely *not* important, it's just a part of the game. As H. L. Mencken put it: 'The chief value of money lies in the fact that one lives in a world in which it is overestimated.'

That's a fair summary. If we lived in a world where seaweed

was overestimated, I would collect tons and tons of it. And I would enjoy doing it. But I wouldn't kid myself it was all that important. It's just seaweed.

But Albert doesn't get it. He won't laugh at himself enough; he won't dance in the moonlight stark naked at a party for the hell of it; he won't sing the words to 'Duke of Earl' or 'Doo-Doo-Ron-Ron' out loud when we've imbibed too much malt whisky he doesn't even *know* the words to those songs, for chrissake. He cares what people think about him. He cares about his gravitas. He can't empty his mind during negotiations, stare straight through an adversary and walk away from a table with millions of dollars piled on it.

How can I put this another way? Lady Luck doesn't love star-struck suitors like Albert. She wants crazy bastards who will tell her to take a hike or get lost if they feel like it. She won't come calling to anyone who needs her or needs to worship her.

If Albert stopped *trying* to be lucky and just got on with the business of making loads-a-money; if he ignored the rotten cow even when she came calling; if he cursed her out loud for every little favour she bestowed … then who knows? She's a fickle bitch at best and making nicey-nicey is one certain way never to get a piece of her.

Lastly, Albert has a penchant, and always did, for calling himself unlucky. He's subtle in the way he does it, but he does it none the less. And he does it too often for my taste. You do not have to read Norman Vincent Peale's *The Power of Positive Thinking* to know that if you repeat something negative often enough, then you are training yourself in the ways of negativity. The mask of misfortune Albert so ironically dons for the amusement of those around him fits rather too well these days. He is becoming the mask. It's a dangerous, stupid game and he ought to know better.

Maybe he does know better. But unless he gets lucky, he will never be rich.

No one can pretend that luck – or chance, at least – does not exist: in life, in love, in business and in the getting of money. If you reject any notion of the supernatural whatever, if you are a true atheist or a humanist with a capital 'H', then you must also accept that life itself on this planet arrived by luck. You can't have it both ways.

'Fortune favours the brave,' says the old proverb. And that's right enough. But it seems to especially scorn anyone who wants money too badly. And it positively appears to despise men or women who fear to lose what fortune they already have. As William Shakespeare put it in Othello:

> Poor and content is rich, and rich enough,
> But riches fineless* is as poor as winter
> To him that ever fears he shall be poor.

My advice concerning luck is to laugh in the face of the Lady when she presents herself. Take what you will of her bounty and act swiftly to take advantage of good fortune. But never thank her for it. And forget her the moment she leaves to seek another victim.

In modern, sexist parlance: 'Treat her mean to keep her keen.' Pimp her, don't court her. And don't go looking for her or make enquiries about her. It isn't exactly the act of a gentleman, but then you didn't ask me to teach you to be a gentleman.

You asked me to show you how to get rich.

So here are my last thoughts on this vexing and baffling phenomenon.

○ Prepare yourself for luck, but don't seek her out. Let her come to you.

○ Make your own luck.

* boundless, infinite

○ Don't whine or ever describe yourself as 'unlucky'. (You're alive, aren't you?)

○ Be bold. Be brave. Don't thank your lucky stars. The stars can't hear you.

○ Stay the course. Stop looking for the green grass over the hill.

○ Don't try to do it all yourself. Delegate and teach others to delegate.

○ Remember that most predators are lucky most of their lives, unlike their prey.

○ Whiners and cowards die a hundred times a day. Be a hero to yourself.

○ If being a hero isn't your style, then fake it. Reality will catch up eventually.

○ Just do it. It is much easier to apologise than to obtain permission.

○ Never take the quest for wealth seriously. It's just a game, chum.

○ Next time you bump into Lady Luck, giver her a whack on the rump from me.

○ Be lucky. Get rich. Then give it all away. (We'll get to that bit later.)

○ Don't call your son 'Albert'. (Just joking!)

11

THE ART OF NEGOTIATING

The fortress that parleys is already half taken.
RUSSIAN PROVERB

THE BALANCE OF WEAKNESS

Reams of highfalutin nonsense have been spoken and published on the subject of negotiating, especially by politicians. During John F. Kennedy's portentous inaugural speech, the new president exhorted his fellow countrymen: 'Let us never negotiate out of fear. But let us never fear to negotiate.'

This is typically muddled thinking from one of the most overrated presidents in US history. A good looker, but a bad egg.

If you 'negotiate out of fear' you are not 'negotiating'. You are surrendering in all but name. As to the second half of his pronouncement, he is saying that it's always worth listening to the other side in the search for mutually beneficial agreements. Did we need the world's most powerful man to tell us that? It's just common sense.

Negotiating is a popular subject, too, in big fat books from US corporate management pundits with titles like *The Art of the Steal* or *The Sun Tzu Split Second Manager*. It's amusing stuff, but has little to do with getting rich, except in the mind of authors hoping to join the comfortably poor by writing catch-word tripe.

Serious negotiations, however, have everything to do with getting rich. This is both because a great negotiator *can* make a real difference in some situations and because many people, astonishingly, believe themselves to be great negotiators. In my experience, the reality is somewhat more prosaic:

○ Most of us are rather poor negotiators.

○ Most negotiations are unnecessary.

○ 'The other side' is often just as smart (or stupid) as you are.

○ In the end, 'the balance of weakness' almost always decides the issue.

○ In Greed vs. Need, the former usually 'wins'.

All negotiations arise from weakness, unless you are one of that strange tribe who finds themselves intoxicated with the process of bargaining and negotiating itself. Sure, haggling can be fun, but it's only a means to an end as far as this book is concerned.

If you are overly fond of haggling, my advice is that you quit thinking about making money the old-fashioned way and consider becoming a politician instead. That way you can rob and plunder your fellow citizens year after year without risking your own financial security or capital – you bastard. (By the way, please get used to people thinking of you as a bastard. After all, it's what nearly everyone thinks of politicians, except themselves.)

As for us working stiffs, serious negotiating (just like turning to the law to dig you out of trouble), should be reserved for seri-ous occasions. Most 'negotiations' are not negotiations at all; they are merely part of the fabric of everyday living. The manner in which they are conducted will depend on the parties involved, the subject under discussion, your day-to-day management style and what side of the bed you got out of that morning.

Take a small example. You have an employee who wishes to deposit and collect their child from school each day. This will supposedly interfere with his or her 'normal' working hours. Big deal.

If the employee is important to you, you will probably bend over backwards to 'negotiate' a solution. If they are not, you will probably enforce the letter of the law applicable in the country or state in which you work, or muddle through with your company's 'in-house rules'. (Personally, I'd allow them to do it. But that's because I'm both an idle manager and a big old softy – in personnel matters, at least.)

Whatever you decide to do, you are *not* involved in 'negotiating' – you are problem solving. The same applies to mid-level salary negotiations, most human-resource issues, job-title dickering, job-performance reviews and the price of wet fish. Serious negotiations are like falling in love. You may have fooled around a few times and been strongly attracted to one or two lovers. But when you fall in love, brothers and sisters, you will know all about it. Right off the bat. Boom! That's what serious negotiations are like. It's probably happened once or twice, right?

MANAGEMENT BARGAINING
vs SERIOUS NEGOTIATIONS

Do not mistake serious negotiations with management bargaining. They require very different skills.

All great companies, all well-run organisations, need great managers and great staff. That much, at least, is pretty obvious. You forget it at your peril.

But the acquisition of managers who can bring a sense of mission to even mundane tasks, who can identify potential candidates, nurture late bloomers, fire dullards and whiners and adapt to changing circumstances – that searching, identifying and nurturing is not about negotiating. It's about setting an example of true meritocracy in a company where nepotism hasn't a chance and where those who wish to succeed are given every opportunity and encouragement to do so. So far, so straightforward.

Similarly, all organisations are a reflection of the people who start them. This sounds crazy, but history has shown it to be true. The effects of even long-dead founders often linger for decades. I'm told by Hollywood film buffs, for example, that MGM movies in the old days were normally slightly less 'dark' than Warner Bros movies. It was the 'house style', a style that had filtered down from the original founders over the years and somehow pervaded individual directors, producers and even actors at each studio.

The only 'style' I assume you're interested in developing is an efficient money-making machine which is also a great place to work. That's a wise and laudable aim, but however necessary, however laudable, such aims are, they belong in the realm of senior- and middle-management problem-solving.

Please remember: *you are not reading this book to become a successful manager*. Managers rarely become rich. Most managers are lieutenants. *You*, on the other hand, have to keep your eye on another ball – several other balls, in fact.

You may well have to *masquerade* as a manager (for a short while) on the way to becoming rich, and you should strive to be a good manager while the role is forced upon you. But even if you discover that you truly *have* a talent for the minutiae that management demands, it's best to abandon the role just as soon as you can afford to hire appropriate personnel.

You just will not have the time to choose who gets to work in which office, where the Christmas party should be held or what company policy should be regarding the provision of in-house tea and coffee facilities. If, as the owner, you *do* find you have the time to involve yourself in such decisions, then I have news for you. Your organisation is in deep trouble.

Personally, I don't think I was a very good managing director or CEO of any of my companies, so my advice concerning your choice of middle management is limited to the following: *the world is full of aspiring lieutenants.* Most people seek job security, job satisfaction and power over others far more than they seek wealth. And thank goodness for that. If all the great managers in the world were dead set on becoming rich, and willing to take the necessary risks to do so, there would be little hope for the likes of you and me.

Management efficiency really does count, of course: loyalty counts, fairness counts, a steady disposition counts, a sense of appropriate compromise counts. An organisation will fail without managers who apply such virtues consistently. But they are not necessarily attributes you should invite into the room during a series of tough *negotiations* when the big money is on the table and your future is on the line. They are the attributes of first-class managers. Not negotiators.

Serious negotiations are very different from day-to-day bargaining and should be approached differently. They imply a weakness in the position of at least one of the parties involved in the negotiations, unlike day-to-day bargaining, where no such weakness need exist. The first thing to be done, perhaps the most vital thing, is to establish exactly where those weaknesses lie.

Weaknesses in serious negotiations usually exist in both camps, of course, at least to some degree or another, and it becomes important to swiftly determine which weakness is most pressing and most potentially catastrophic to which party. An *immediate* balance of weaknesses may well prove more decisive than any long-term balance of strengths.

It is for this reason that small companies and individuals have sometimes managed to out-negotiate larger rivals, especially in emerging markets and technologies. If a big, powerful organisation convinces itself it absolutely *has* to have some whizzo new technology, or whatever, it will sometimes permit itself to pay way over the odds for it. We've seen it a zillion times reported in the financial press.

The balance of weakness is also the reason why farmers in Britain, for example, are utterly in thrall to the power of the supermarket chains and why British people pay more for much of their food than almost anywhere else in Europe. British food isn't better (in fact, it is somewhat worse than, for example, French food), but British supermarkets are undisputed champions when it comes to exploiting the balance of weakness.

Farmers are poor negotiators. Supermarket chains are great negotiators. Supermarkets have a lot of cash and many possible sources of supply. Farmers need to fix that broken tractor and pay their veterinary bills right *now*. The balance of weakness is overwhelmingly in the farmers' camp and the result is therefore preordained unless central government interferes.

Supermarkets have a slight weakness – very slight. They need to buy food regularly and in wholesale quantities. And they need quality and consistency. If food became scarce, the balance would tilt and farmers would begin to clobber the supermarkets. But, right now, farmers haven't a prayer. There is too much food of reasonable quality too consistently available from too many sources and our government has chosen not to interfere.

(The rights and wrongs of all this are immaterial. If I could arrange the magazine publishing and internet website business the way British supermarkets have arranged their business, I would do it in a heartbeat. Providing I was a supermarket and not a farmer.)

Or take the attitude of banks towards start-up or small companies. If you need a loan because you cannot meet payroll, you almost certainly won't get one. (Er, make that 'you *absolutely*, *definitely* won't get one'.) The balance of weakness is so obvious and utterly immediate, nobody will want to waste time listening to your entreaties.

But if you need a loan, say, because you wish to take a private company public with a reasonable chance of success in the not-too-distant future (in other words, you don't really *need* a loan, it would merely be convenient to be offered one), then loans will shower upon you like confetti. After all, banks need to make money by selling professional services as well as charging interest, and you are now a potentially important customer, a customer who may well require those professional services – not a suppli-cant grovelling on his knees with a dog eared business plan.

THE ELEPHANT AND THE FLEA

If all this sounds to you as if the controllers of capital are the 10 ton elephants in the jungle, then you're right. But there is another side to it. Your little outfit may be nothing but a flea in a corporate elephant's patch of jungle, indeed one he has barely noticed until recently, but just how much might the elephant be willing to pay to be rid of you, or to buy you out? Especially if your business, however small, is growing and the elephant's busi-ness is not?

Because the elephant has a master, a *mahout*. And his master is an unforgiving son-of-a-bitch with a nasty barbed iron stick and an elephant gun. He is otherwise known as an institutional investor. All start-up entrepreneurs should say their prayers for institutional investors, those fabulous beasts, every night. 'Dear Lord, thank you, thank you for institutional investors in big companies.'

An institutional investor, often a pension or savings company, is just jargon for an entity that owns a big chunk of stock in a publicly traded company.

So why? Why should you say your prayers for them? What do institutional investors in huge corporations have to do with developing serious negotiating skills as an entrepreneur and getting rich? Everything, my friend. Everything.

For the elephant must show his master that he is an *up-to-*

date elephant. A *savvy* elephant. An elephant that knows what's just *round the corner* and what the next big thing is going to be in his patch of jungle. Otherwise he risks his *share price dropping* and being hurt by the nasty iron stick, or even shot by the fierce institutional investor, who will then acquire a new elephant, leaving the bones of the old one to rot on the jungle floor.

Now *you* have had an idea. You have nurtured it with your little company and it is now a reality, however tiny. Better still, it looks like it's already working, or might work soon. The elephant is concerned that his master may hear of this little flea's idea and that he might well be punished for not having thought of it himself. (Most elephants are a trifle lazy, you know.) The elephant knows what he must do then. He lumbers over to meet you. He has done it many times before, with many other fleas.

Thus it is that the elephant comes to the flea – not because he wants to (in his monstrous, corporate heart he would really like everything to stay the same), but usually because he fears his *mahout* more than he despises the flea. And sometimes, too, to be fair, because elephants are as curious as the rest of us.

But never forget why he came calling in the first place. He does not love you. He is not your friend, although he may pretend to be. He might not hate you, he may even admire you a little. He will certainly flatter you. But remember he *had* to come. His fear drove him. His fear of his master, the institutional investor.

And the day when he does come – hurrah! – the day when he makes that hateful call – hateful to *him*, that is – that is the day when the fun begins and when serious negotiating skills and a dispassionate understanding of the balance of weaknesses in *your* particular patch of jungle, at *that* particular time, can change your life overnight. And can change it for ever. Just as it changed mine.

Let's look at a couple of examples of the elephant coming to the flea. (Of course, sometimes the flea must approach the elephant. Not so good. We'll come to that later.)

THE ELEPHANT MISJUDGES HIS NEED

Are you sitting comfortably, children? Then I'll begin.

It is 1981. Personal computers are a new thing in the world. They are not the everyday objects we now take for granted. They have little presence inside the offices of any sensible company, large or small, except in those companies helping to create them, or the software for them – and those very few companies publishing specialist magazines about them.

Dennis Publishing Ltd is just such a small specialist magazine publishing company, with a turnover of a few million pounds in Britain and a slippery toehold in the USA. Its finances are precarious. Its owner is a greedy little flea, determined never to be sent back to prison and never to report to another human being in his life.

The flea has managed to acquire a controlling interest in Europe's first personal computer magazine from the man who launched it, Angelo Zgorelec. The magazine is called *Personal Computer World*, or *PCW* for short. It is not exactly a big magazine. Angelo and the flea have also helped to build up a series of exhibitions allowing hardware and software manufacturers to show off their latest products. All this helps to boost sales and credibility for *PCW*.

The flea's company has done its best to staff *PCW* with good editors and writers. This is an easier task than usual, because there are so few rival magazines. The magazine also has a first-class designer and one or two very hungry advertising sales people. While it's not exactly living off the fat of the land, *PCW* is an exciting place to work. The industry it reports on is a new, exciting industry. There is a whiff of revolution in the air, a technological revolution. *PCW* is right at the heart of it and the staff and owners know that perfectly well.

Other magazine fleas have begun to take notice. They launch their own personal computer magazines. But they do not invest in them sufficiently and they are not quite as good as *PCW*. In time, the majority of them shut down or wither on the vine. The flea redoubles his efforts to obtain cash by publishing rubbish one-shot magazines about pop music and panda bears. He pours this cash into *PCW*. Without question, this decision to invest is the second or third most important business decision the flea will ever make in his life.

Above all, the flea and his magazine are swimming with the tide, not against it. *PCW* is growing with the market. More readers come on board every issue. And more advertising begins to arrive. A lot more advertising. Angelo Zgorelec and the flea are both immensely proud of themselves.

Then disaster strikes. The flea has foolishly launched a pop-music weekly. He has begun to believe he walks on water. This weekly is an initial success and then a dreadful, cash-devouring failure. The flea is in panic and even entertains the idea of selling half of his little company to friendly partners – 'white knights' they are called in business jargon. Fortunately, this deal falls through, because his partners want him to close the pop-music weekly immediately and the flea hasn't the courage or the wit to do so. When the 'white knights' walk away, catastrophe stares the flea's company in the face. There is simply not enough cash being generated to feed the growing monster called *PCW*.

The flea closes the pop-music weekly. He is forced to. By sheer, dumb luck, his intransigence has kept him from selling half of his company's shares. But the cash deficiency is looming still. And you must remember that the flea is still a greedy little mite and wishes to become a millionaire at the earliest opportunity.

He is approached by a tall, affable man who, together with his sidekick, has helped to build EMAP (East Midlands Allied Press), one of the biggest magazine elephants in Britain. His name is David. David and the flea have many meetings. Later, David and his sidekick, Robin, will become good friends with the flea. But this is not a time for friendship. This is a time for serious negotiations.

David and Robin are a legend in the magazine jungle. They are polar opposites in character and appearance. David is sophisticated, slim, very tall, friendly and non-threatening. You can tell he went to university without even asking. He would have made a first-class diplomat. He is wise in the ways of prising properties from fleas. I think the first time I ever drank a decent bottle of wine was with David.

Robin is cranky, hugely talented, sometimes bad-tempered; he does not suffer fools gladly but he knows the magazine business backwards and is immensely respected by the EMAP elephant employees. He has no time for meals in restaurants and buttering up clients – or fleas for that matter. I don't like him when I meet him. (I will get to like him very much in the years to come.) David senses this and keeps Robin out of the picture.

David and the flea arm-wrestle over the possible sale of *PCW* to EMAP. The flea speaks to tax advisors, to Angelo and to lawyers. He speaks to his white-knight partners in America. The negotiations intensify and the flea realises that David, while as calm as ever on the outside, is becoming anxious to close the deal swiftly. There is a particular meeting in the flea's flat in central London. Very, very nearly David persuades the flea that he *must* sell *PCW* now; that he *must* shake hands on a price of £700,000 or thereabouts. This is an astonishing price for a new magazine. And remember, the flea is very, very greedy.

But just as dumb luck saved the flea before, instinct saves him now. Instinct and the advice of the white knights and others. Besides, there is a slightly glittery cast to the elephant manager's eyes the flea doesn't much care for at this meeting. He asks for more, much to David's annoyance, and this time, understandably, that annoyance is openly expressed.

For a few weeks, the flea wonders if he hasn't allowed his greed and naivety to wreck his salvation. Perhaps he has pushed the elephant too far? Certainly there are those around him who hold precisely that view. But what has actually happened is that the EMAP elephant's managers have been talking to other fleas. They think they can obtain something rather similar to *PCW* for less than the £1 million the flea is asking for.

Just for once, the EMAP elephant has misjudged the balance of weakness and has underestimated his need. It is an error for which he will pay dearly in the years to come. For within a short time, the flea *will* sell *PCW*, but not for £700,000, not by a long chalk. What follows is the story of how he came to sell it and how much for.

ANOTHER ELEPHANT COMES TO CALL

There is more than one elephant in any jungle. Which is just as well. Fleas stand little chance when there is only one elephant – monopolies and entrepreneurs don't get along.

Soon after the fateful meeting in the flea's flat with David, another elephant comes to call. This is a Dutch elephant called VNU, with homes all over Europe. It is a massive beast with a lot of experience in all kinds of magazine publishing. In the UK, it has a large business-to-business operation, including magazines serving large, traditional, mini-computer and mainframe computer departments.

The usual preamble and mating rites take place. The flea is coming to enjoy lunches in fancy restaurants and bottles of good wine – especially when he is not paying for them. But the flea has also learned to shrug off flattery and keep his eye on the balance of weakness. This particular elephant has a huge need, almost a unique need, and the flea is determined to exploit it.

The flea suspects that big computer installations will always be around. But *personal* computers, desktop PCs as they will come to be known, are the coming thing. They are a different kettle of fish entirely from mainframes and systems that require men in white coats and machines the size of a small room. The Dutch elephant's *mahout* will be especially angry if the old beast misses out on the coming thing, the desktop PC. That is his unique weakness. And he is such a big elephant. And his *mahout* is such a terribly fierce master.

Naturally, the flea also has a weakness, one we already know about. He is very short on cash and is greedy. Can the flea survive his cash shortfall and curb his youthful greediness for long enough? Long enough for what, you ask, children?

Long enough to make the Dutch elephant become truly, truly desperate. Can he do it?

This is the flea's plan. His professional advisors hate the plan. It is stupid. A flea cannot outwait an elephant! But it can, you know; for a little while it can. And all the time the flea's magazine is swimming with the tide, growing bigger each issue and increasing its advertising revenues. The flea even licenses an Australian edition of *PCW* to a young man who strolls into his office while on vacation. (A young man who will subsequently become a millionaire as a result.) All the while the market is growing. And the Dutch elephant's *mahout* is not getting any happier.

The Dutch elephant's first offer is perfectly reasonable. It is made over lunch by a very nice Dutchman called Francis. 'We can offer you a million pounds,' he says, peering over his spectacles. The flea stares him in the eye and says nothing. 'And a little more. Say £200,000, which we will hold in reserve and pay to you depending upon the performance of *PCW* over the next year or so.'

This is a handsome offer. Almost *twice* the EMAP elephant's offer. But the flea judges that the Dutch elephant is not desperate enough. Very politely he declines and pours himself another glass of delicious wine. Francis, wisely, let's the matter drop. He is an older man, and a skilled, courteous negotiator.

Some weeks later, the Dutch elephant brings along another of his managers. This one is British and his name is Graeme. The flea likes him immediately. But he is careful to mask his likes and dislikes. These managers are not here to be liked or not to be liked. They are here to negotiate and to rob the flea if they can. That is what they are paid for, after all. That is what their *mahouts* expect.

A big meeting is held in the Dutch elephant's palatial offices. The flea has with him only his lawyer, called Michael. Prior to this meeting, the Dutch elephant has tried to send an emissary to talk to Angelo Zgorelec, the minority shareholder in *PCW*. The flea is angry about that. There can only be one negotiator. Any house divided is a house that will fall.

The flea has asked Angelo not to listen to the Dutch elephant's minions, and Angelo has willingly agreed. The flea masks his anger at the meeting. This is a big day. He knows it will not be *the* day, for the Dutch elephant is still not desperate enough. But it's a big day, all the same.

The flea has warned his lawyer, Michael, to keep all their business papers close to hand. To be ready for an abrupt and immediate departure. Michael is unhappy about this. He is a canny, considerate man, and he is the flea's friend. But he is not a negotiator and the flea is his client. He will do what is asked of him. That's why he is a professional.

Around the table there are several managers from the Dutch elephant. And maybe a lawyer or an accountant or two, it's difficult to tell. The meeting begins and a new offer is made. The offer is almost exactly what the flea has guessed it would be: nearly two million pounds, with a big chunk held 'in reserve'. It is a magnificent offer. Absolutely magnificent. Three times what was offered by the EMAP elephant.

For a while the flea does not respond. Instead, he talks about how well the magazine is doing, about the Australian edition, about the growth of the exhibitions. He also mentions that he will be launching at least one more personal computer magazine quite soon – one aimed at the personal computer trade itself this time. At companies who sell personal computers and personal computer software. It will be a business-to-business magazine, precisely the type of magazine the Dutch elephant specialises in.

Eventually, the discussion comes back to the offer. The flea looks Graeme and Francis in the eye. He totally ignores everyone else present. He *empties himself mentally* and stares straight through them. He convinces himself that he does not care what the outcome of these negotiations will be. He clings to this illusion of emptiness while he negotiates. He doesn't care if he becomes a millionaire or not.

'The price is *three* million pounds,' he says, 'and only one *twelfth* can be held in reserve. That is the price and it will not be changed.'

There is consternation around the table, whether real or feigned it is difficult to say. The flea nods to his lawyer, who collects his papers and puts them in his briefcase. They both rise to leave. Just as they are leaving the flea stares once again at the two Dutch elephant managers, his mind and eyes as blank as a zombie.

'Thank you for your offer, gentlemen,' he says. 'As I said, the price is three million pounds with only a quarter of a million pounds held in escrow. In addition, the buyer of *Personal Computer World* must permit me to launch my new computer magazine to the trade. If I do not hear from you shortly, then my next price will be four million pounds. Good afternoon.'

We walked out into the Soho sunshine and stopped at local café. My hands were shaking as I spooned in the sugar. So were Michael's.

'You're mad, my friend,' he murmured, shaking his head. 'Utterly mad. Worse than that, you have been stupid. They will not pay that kind of money. Also, you have *walked out* on them, you have *threatened* them and you have made a sudden, *unreasonable* demand. Are you really planning to launch a PC trade magazine?'

'No,' I admitted. 'I only just thought of it while I was sitting there. I haven't got the money to launch anything. You know that.'

We both sat sipping our coffee, Michael smoking one of his small cigars from a tin. Ironically, they were Dutch cigars. I paid the bill, and while the waitress was bringing my change, Michael tried one last time to persuade me to do the sensible thing. 'Felix, I am your lawyer and your friend. Let me go back and apologise. Two million pounds is an unbelievable sum of money. I don't know of any new magazine that has ever sold for two million pounds in Britain. Listen to me and let me go back. You don't have to go yourself.'

And I very nearly allowed Michael to do just that. But something held me back. Something I had sensed but could not explain or articulate. Finally, I smiled a little ruefully and patted Michael's arm: 'Michael, their need will outweigh my greed. I am sure of it. Let's wait and see.'

So we waited.

Before we bring the story to its conclusion, let us pause and reflect on what has happened here.

○ The flea has established to his own satisfaction the elephant's urgent need.

○ The flea has learned to ignore flattery.

○ The flea has learned that an elephant cannot be your friend in negotiations.

○ The flea has learned he is not a good negotiator.

○ The flea has learned to 'empty' himself and make himself believe he does not care.

○ The flea has overcome his lack of skill by setting a price he will not deviate from.

○ The flea has hardened his heart and has walked away when the price was not met.

○ The flea has introduced a rogue element (the trade magazine) into the negotiations.

○ The flea has weighed Greed vs. Need. He believes Need will
outweigh Greed.

Of course, you know the end of the story. We all met again round
the big table, this time with a lot more accountants and a lot
more lawyers. The price agreed was three million pounds. The
escrow was a quarter of a million pounds. Angelo got his million
pounds. My company got the rest. I got to launch my trade
magazine, called *MicroScope*, which kept me in the loop of a new
and growing market but out of VNU's way – for a while.

And what did the Dutch elephant get? It got a wonderful
magazine which is still being published and which still makes
money today, twenty-four years later. They also persuaded me to
help launch two more personal computer magazines for them,
one in the UK, which was a flop, and one in Holland, which was
a success.

Lastly, and very cleverly, VNU kept me out of the personal
computer market (except for my trade magazine) for three years.
Three vital years. They did that with a non-compete clause in
the sale agreement. (Non-compete clauses can be a bugger for
those selling an asset. Keep the period of non-compete as short
as you can.)

And what of EMAP, the first elephant who had come calling?
EMAP never really succeeded in the personal computer magazine
business. Not in *PCW*'s patch of the jungle. In virtually every
other sector they reigned (and continue to reign) supreme. They
have whipped my butt time and time again in other sectors. But
they missed their chance with *PCW*. They underestimated their
need and were, probably rightly, appalled by this little flea's greed.

Not that I blame them. I've been on the receiving end as a
buyer, rather than a seller, too often now to blame them even

remotely. But it was still an error. Had David upped the ante to one million pounds or more in my Soho flat, my greed would probably have overwhelmed me, and Angelo and I would have missed out on an additional two million pounds.

In today's figures, by the way, that two million pounds would be worth about six million pounds, give or take. That's a huge chunk of change to waste through making a mistake in negotiations.

A FEW TIPS ON NEGOTIATING

○ Remember that few of us are any good at detailed negotiations. That includes your opponent, by the way.

○ If you are a poor negotiator, like me, then set a limit on what you will pay or accept and on any conditions attached. Do not deviate. Your first thought is your best thought.

○ Most negotiations are unnecessary. Don't enter into them. Remember that 'the fortress that parleys is already half taken'. Save serious negotiations for serious occasions.

○ Do your homework. And do it rigorously. What you don't know or haven't bothered to find out can kill you in any type of serious negotiation.

○ Despite my jungle book examples above, the devil really is in the detail in serious negotiations. Get all the professional help you can trust. But do not surrender control of the negotiations or the agenda to such professionals. They are not the ones who will have to live with the consequences – you are. Professional advisors are there to explain and advise, not to decide.

○ If your advisors are leading you down a path you don't approve of during your negotiations, call a 'time out' and tell them privately that if they continue along that route you will get yourself some new advisors. The world is full of them.

O Never fall in love with the deal. A deal is just a deal. There will always be other deals and other opportunities.

O Avoid auctions in business like the plague – unless you are selling something, that is. You will nearly always pay more than is wise if you are the 'winner' of an auction process.

O The negotiator opposite you is not your new best friend. He is not your partner. He is not your confidant. You have no obligation, outside of ordinary courtesy, to please him or satisfy his demands. He is the enemy. If you do not understand that real winners and real losers emerge from serious negotiations then you will be robbed, whatever the circumstances.

O Take no notice of management manuals that tell you to leave passion and emotion out of the negotiating room. If you are emotional or passionate about something, then let it show. But leaven emotion with courtesy, and, if possible, with wit. If you're not the witty type, then flattery and self-deprecation are good substitutes.

O Listen when engaged in serious negotiations. Then listen some more. You are in no hurry. Nobody ever got poor listening. Also, use silence as a weapon. Silences are disconcerting. People tend to fill silences with jabber, often weakening their bargaining position as they do so.

O Choose a rogue element to your advantage and bring it into the negotiation at a late stage. You'll be amazed at how often this tactic produces results.

O The British created the largest geophysical empire in the world with one tactic: divide and rule. It always works. It never fails if you can get to exploit it. Get to know the other side. There may be slight differences in the individual approaches of their senior managers and, possibly, in their goals. Drive a wedge and keep hammering.

○ Permit no such weaknesses in your own camp. I have often banned senior executives from taking part in negotiations simply to avoid this trap. Better you are in there on your own, outgunned, outflanked and outmanoeuvred, than to have two or three of you silently squabbling.

○ Everyone thinks they are a great negotiator, but most of us simply are not. If it's *your* company, then, for better or worse, *you* are the final arbiter. That remains true whether you are a good negotiator or a bad one.

○ If you suspect you perform badly on such occasions, do not attend, even if you are the 100 per cent owner. Get someone else to do it after setting out your response to every conceivable option that might arise. This tactic can be devastating to the other side, and Peter, Bob and I have used it on many occasions in the past. You have to trust your nominee completely, though.

○ Above all, establish where the balance of weakness lies in any serious negotiation. Most strengths are self-evident, especially strengths like cash and infrastructure. Weaknesses are usually hidden. Ferret them out, hold them up to the light and make a battle plan.

○ Whatever you agree to during a negotiation, fulfil the bargain. Nobody wants to do business with a weasel or a chisler. Written in the Zoroastrian Scriptures two-and-a-half thousand years ago was this: 'Never break a covenant, whether you make it with a false man or a just man of good conscience. The covenant holds for both, the false and the just alike.'

Aye, that it does.

I will leave you on this subject with the words of Britain's closest rival to Machiavelli: Francis Bacon. Bacon 'negotiated' his way from relative poverty to the very pinnacle of wealth and power in England under King James I. Then lost it all, and spent his last years writing and studying. His *Essays* are among the wisest, most thought-provoking (and meanest) set of instructions ever published in English. I sleep with them by my bedside.

This is from a short essay (short even by Bacon's standards) entitled 'Of Negotiating', published in 1625, nearly four hundred years ago. Every word of it is true today:

> *If you would work [negotiate with] any man, you must either know his nature and fashions, and so lead him; or his ends, and so persuade him; or his weakness or disadvantages, and so awe him, or those that have an interest in him, and so govern him. In dealing with cunning persons, we must ever consider their ends to interpret their speeches; and it is good to say little to them, and that which they least look for. In all negotiations of difficulty, a man may not look to sow and reap at once; but must prepare business, and so ripen it by degrees.*

Thank goodness Francis Bacon did not live in my time and go into the British magazine business. I would *never* have got rich with such a rival in the same city!

12

OWNERSHIP!
OWNERSHIP!
OWNERSHIP!

How can you buy or sell the sky, the warmth of the land?
The idea is strange to us. If we do not own the freshness
of the air and the sparkle of the water,
how can you buy them?
CHIEF SEATTLE, NINETEENTH-CENTURY
AMERICAN INDIAN CHIEF OF THE SUQUAMISH

Private property began the instant
somebody had a mind of his own.
EDWARD E. CUMMINGS, AMERICAN POET

THE PARADOX OF OWNERSHIP

How can anyone truly 'own' anything? Surely the answer is that
we can claim no such thing.

No animal but man lays claim to owning things or places.
They merely defend them – their lives, their mate, their cubs,
their pack, their territory, their food. If you introduce a new dog
or cat into a household which already contains one or two of
these excellent creatures, there will be a short, trying period of

testing the waters and perhaps a scuffle or two, and the thing is done.

A new animal soon finds its place in the collective hierarchy easily enough. And it requires no parliament, written laws, police force, bailiff or army to do so.

Human beings are different. We purport to believe that individuals can 'own' the most astonishing things; that they can own islands, mines, mountains, forests and areas of the sea. Even more astonishingly we pretend that mere names can own such things, for what is a partnership, a corporation or a country but a name?

And to top it all, we believe that a name can own an executed idea – for that is the basis of corporate intellectual ownership. The very type of ownership that has been the foundation of my own wealth.

Perhaps even more preposterous is the universally accepted proposition that an individual or entity can 'own' land, rivers, hills and deserts where dinosaurs freely roamed for uncounted millennia. Roamed, mark you, long before *Homo sapiens sapiens* was a twinkle in a small, shrew-like mammal's eye. Not to mention that those lands, hills, rivers and deserts will be there when not even a whisper of evidence survives to show that humans existed on the blue planet.

This is not a book about philosophy, sociology or the history of human law, but I believe it is worth remembering that ownership of any kind is nonsensical. It is absurd and defies reason because we are all mortal and we cannot (as yet) take it with us.

So what's this got to do with getting rich? I could say, 'Nothing, but thank you for letting me get it off my chest'; but I won't say that, because my amateurish musings illustrate very nicely just how idiotic the getting of wealth, as a goal in and of itself, really is.

'Ah,' but you could argue, 'that's all very well for *you*. *You* have already made *your* pile. It's easy to be philosophical when you've already amassed a fortune.' And my reply would be that there is truth in that, but there is also truth in the assertion that I may well have been *only able* to put a few hundred million dollars in the bank because I recognised that this getting rich malarkey is *just a game*. A delusion, if you will.

Being rich is fine, and at the very least is better than being poor. But it shouldn't be the be-all and end-all of your life, or anyone's life. If you can laugh in the midst of early poverty and in the face of real adversity, and if you can still laugh when you're coining it in, then you will almost certainly continue to coin it in.

But if you chase money desperately in the earnest belief that you can never be happy without it and seriously think that the chase is a meaningful occupation, I doubt very much you will succeed. You have to be fiercely determined, true. But an appreciation of the absurdity of the chase helps enormously.

As the author G. K. Chesterton puts it in one of his Father Brown stories: 'To be clever enough to get all that money, one must be stupid enough to want it.' Mind you, Chesterton wasn't exactly averse to fine food and wine himself.

OK, OK, enough musing. Now we'll get on with the job of stimulating your accumulation of money as quickly as possible. But don't say your Uncle Felix didn't warn you.

WHY OWNERSHIP ISN'T THE IMPORTANT THING – IT'S THE *ONLY* THING

A poor virgin, sir, an ill-favoured thing, sir, but mine own.
WILLIAM SHAKESPEARE, *AS YOU LIKE IT*

So if ownership is a delusion, and we are all nothing more than consenting thieves, how can we become successful thieves as early as possible? The answer is simple. Very simple, and if you want to be rich then I ask you to stop skipping paragraphs and pay close attention.

To become rich you must be an *owner*. And you must try to

own it all. You must strive with every fibre of your being, while recognising the idiocy of your behaviour, to own and retain control of as near to 100 per cent of any company as you can. If that is not possible, in a public company, for example, then you must be prepared to make yourself hated by those around you who are also trying to be rich. That is the dirty, rotten little secret of it all, my friend. Just like Gollum, it is *your* Precious and *they* are all 'filthy little thieves'.

You won't read *that* in any of those *Become An Instant Millionaire In Your Sleep* manuals I mentioned earlier. Such works, nearly all written by men and women who have never made a million anything in their lives, usually witter on about becoming a better manager (who bloody *cares* about becoming a better manager?) or creating 'partnerships', thinking 'outside the box' and exploiting 'insanely great' ideas in totally innovative ways.

To put it bluntly, this is all bollocks. It has nothing to do with becoming rich.

To become rich, every single percentage point of anything you own is crucial. It is worth fighting for, tooth and claw. It is worth suing for. It is worth shouting and banging on the table for. It is worth begging for and grovelling for. It is worth lying and cheating for. In extremis, it is even worth negotiating for.

Never, never, never, never hand over a single share of anything you have acquired or created if you can help it. Nothing. Not one share. To no one. No matter what the reason – unless you genuinely have to.

Do you remember my old 'rivals' Robin and David from the EMAP elephant? They were both far better publishers than I will ever be. On my best day they would have wiped the floor with me. But after a quarter of a century of jointly creating one of the biggest media companies in Britain for EMAP shareholders, what did they get for their pains?

I don't know exactly, of course, and I wouldn't tell you if I did. But I'll guess, using current market norms. £3 million? £5 million? £10 million? (I doubt the last, but it could have been.) You mean that's *it*? That's all there is after busting your balls for the best part of your working life and making hundreds of shareholders and lawyers and banks immensely rich? A few measly million pounds less tax? That's shocking.

I've made more than that in deals I can barely remember now. I once made half a million by selling a magazine I had not even published yet to a rival. Half a million pounds for a day's work. And why? Why? *Why?*

Because I *owned* it. I owned it all. And my dear friends David and Robin never owned anything during their time there except for a pile of EMAP share options, a good salary and a lovely pension. Please think about this if you want to be rich. Ownership is not the most important thing. IT IS THE ONLY THING THAT COUNTS.

Nothing else counts in the getting of money. Shareholder thanks do not count. A good salary and a company car and health plan and pension don't count. Most share options (usually nothing more than the promise of chickenfeed to salaried employees, and a promise broken half the time, too), don't count. The gratitude of colleagues doesn't count.

Nothing counts but what you own in the race to get rich. If you haven't much skill, or much wit, or much talent, or much luck, and yet you insist on owning more than your fair share of any start-up or acquisition, then you can become rich. If you take what you're given, you will probably not get rich.

Years ago, in the early days of my company, four of my colleagues got together and had a long talk, I assume in a pub, although I cannot be sure of that. One was a senior manager, one was a publisher, one was a designer and the other an editor. Together, they hatched a small conspiracy. Knowing how important they were to my little company, they confronted me and demanded a share. They bearded the lion in his lair.

They were polite and civilised about it. They pointed out that

I owned 100 per cent of the company and could easily afford to share out, say, 20 per cent between them. It wouldn't cost me anything and it was only fair. Those were the words they used. They were working just as many hours (10–12 hours on a good day) as I was and they were committed to making the company a huge success. They were even willing to discuss a slight reduction in their salaries in return.

In addition, they went on, I should remember that such a 'dispersal' (I remember they actually used that word, too) would incentivise them mightily. Such a gesture would never be forgotten. And my remaining 80 per cent of the company would ensure that I was still the boss.

However, should I not 'disperse' these shares among them, they intended to leave. And leave immediately, virtually without notice. They would have no option but to do so, although they didn't want to.

The company would suffer dreadfully – and might even fail altogether. They had already agreed the name of their new company, in case I wouldn't play ball, and had even registered it. They would set up as rivals. They were serious and they meant business. All of this unpleasantness could be avoided if I would just hand over a pitiful 20 per cent to them, perhaps based on future performance?

Both as friends and colleagues, they earnestly advised me to consider their demands dispassionately and honestly. In my heart, they argued, I knew they were right. It was only fair.

I fired them on the spot. Or they walked away. I can't remember which – it didn't matter then and it doesn't matter now. What mattered is that I held on to every single share in my company. I would run the entire bloody company myself, write the articles, design the pages, answer the phone and sell the ads if I had to. But I would not part with a single, solitary share. Not for love. Nor for fairness. Not for loyalty. Not for anything. And certainly not for moral blackmail.

They set up their new company. They launched their magazine. Either it folded or they gave it away, I don't remember now. Two of them came back to work for me. There were no recriminations. I am on friendly terms with all four of them to this day. Not one of them ever got rich. Nor ever will, I guess.

I didn't blame them, by the way. I would have tried the same stunt myself if the positions had been reversed. But if I *had* tried it, I would have made a damn sight more certain of its success.

'Why doth treason never prosper? For shouldst thou fail, thou must hang. And if it doth succeed, why, 'twas never treason!'

Over the next thirty years, I estimate that their suggested 20 per cent, had I handed it over, would have earned those four gentlemen around $80,000,000 – say it again – eighty *million* dollars, in current asset value and past dividends. This is the problem with sharing ownership. The laws of simple mathematics are relentless and obdurate.

And if I *had* given 20 per cent to those four employees, should I not have had to do so with many others as they joined the company and worked hard to make it a success? Where would it all end? I'm not a bloody charity. I'm an entrepreneur trying to make a small fortune, not the Salvation Army. I pay people to get a job done. And I pay them well. I try to make it as much fun as I can along the way. I reward senior managers with bloody huge bonuses based on performance and results. Millions of dollars have been paid out in such bonuses over the years.

But I will *not* give them a share. Not one. Not for love. Nor for loyalty. Not to be fair. Because capitalism isn't fair. Life isn't fair. The lottery of what genes we are born with isn't fair. The moon and the stars and the gas clouds of Alpha Centauri aren't fair.

Except for your loved ones or closest friends, it's every man for himself in this world, in case you haven't noticed: 'No prisoners! The Lord will know his own!' Or, in the rapier advice of Benjamin Jowett, a nineteenth-century master of Balliol College, Oxford: 'Never retreat. Never explain. Get it done and let them howl.'

The best kind of fairness is the kind that makes money. Lots of money. Then you can decide to do with it whatever you wish. There's a whole chapter at the end of this book about it. (See Chapter 18: **How to *Stay* Rich**). But we can't be wasting time thinking about and debating fairness while we are in money-making mode. Money making and fairness having nothing to do with each other.

Just how nasty can this all get? Say you have a brother and you want to start a business together. You should begin with the proposition that *you* will own the business and *he* will work for it. Fight for this tenaciously. Begin by assuming it.

If that won't fly, then absolutely insist that you own 75 per cent of the shares. The reasons are immaterial. Make a spurious list of them and wave it about. Say you won't go into business unless you own the majority share. Have a temper tantrum. Shout. Scream. Wave the bloody bit of paper about again. Say you'll work longer hours. Say you will find more capital than he will. Say anything. But GET A BIGGER SHARE OF THE COMPANY FOR YOURSELF.

Then, and only then, should you return to being a reasonable human being. You can now afford to be reasonable. You are going to be richer than your brother. Perhaps a lot richer. It is as simple and as vile and as nasty as that. Would I do it to *my* brother, Julian, whom I love very much? Yes. In a heartbeat, if I had to. Would I *give* my brother all the money I ever made if he needed it? Yes, I would. But I WILL NOT GIVE HIM A SHARE IN MY COMPANY!

Because ownership isn't the important thing. If you want to be rich, it's the only thing.

THE JOYS AND PERILS OF PARTNERSHIP

'He ain't heavy ... he's my brother.'
SONG TITLE, BOB RUSSELL AND BOBBY SCOTT

Come to think of it, I never have. Given a share to my brother, that is. And he never asked me for one. He's a sensible man with a loyal wife and two lovely children. He doesn't want my bloody shares.

Nor have I ever *given* a single share to anybody. And yet, unlike most entrepreneurs I know, I have enjoyed a wonderful thirty-year-plus relationship with my 'white knight' American partners, Peter Godfrey and Robert Bartner.

In the UK, I clung to my 100 per cent ownership like a limpet. In the USA and elsewhere, I happily hitched up with Peter and Bob. And we are still hitched, decades later. We have together created many companies, which have operated in many countries. We have split the ownership of those companies in a dozen different ways. Once, I owned 80 per cent and they owned 10 per cent each. On another occasion, we owned 33.3 per cent each. On more than one occasion I have been a minority shareholder.

It never mattered. The partnership has held like a rock through all the stormy weather and the trials and tribulations that are the lot of any long business life. We have shouted at each other a few times and we have cried on each other's shoulders more than once. We have enjoyed the thrill of the chase immensely. We have helped to make each other millionaires times without number.

Once, and only once, I even acted as an honest broker when Bob was thinking of suing Peter (or was it the other way round?) – I honestly cannot remember over what. But the point is, the partnership held, and has always reflected just two principles as far as sharing the pie was concerned. These are:

1. Who is putting what capital into a venture?
2. Who is doing what work on that venture?

I believe I have been a good partner and an honest one for Peter and Bob. And I *know* they have been good and honest partners for me. We make a good team.

I am the creative maverick and usually the risk-taker. Peter is the cautious, stubborn and worldy-wise one. He's hard to convince. But he is a great negotiator in a clinch. Bob is the nuts and bolts wild card. He does not suffer fools or errors gladly. He goes through 'the numbers' with a voracious appetite for them.

Bob is willing to voice misgivings that Peter and I (especially me, it has to be said) might quietly sweep under the carpet. It was Bob who refused, years ago, to invest one more personal cent in one of our companies. He had realised, long before Peter and me, that we simply were not rich enough to feed this particular monster. We would have to do what we had never considered before. We would have to go public. That was Bob's doing.

While Peter was working the longest hours of his life to keep this beast afloat, and I was stripping my own UK company of senior managers and hurling them into the American monster's maw, Bob simply went to some people he knew and told them we needed to go public. Without Bob, Peter and I might well have worked and worried ourselves to death. We were rich men by then, but not rich enough to fund what became a $2 billion corporation.

That's the best part of a true partnership. You always have a brother to help carry the load. And if things go wrong, you have a built-in drinking buddy with whom to drown your sorrows! And you have a built-in conscience, too. No bad thing.

So if this is the case, why am I so insistent upon outright ownership, or, at the very least, as much as you can wangle? It's simple. I could always *walk away* from the partnership with Peter and Bob if we fell out. I had my *own* company doing my *own* thing under my *own* control three thousand miles away.

And I believe the same has been true for them. Despite our close friendship and real affection for each other, this knowledge, that any one of us *could* walk away from the others if he wished, that illusion of freedom – if illusion it was – made it possible to compromise with each other when things got tough in our partnership business.

If Peter and Bob had represented every iron I had in the fire, if our partnership had been the only hope I had of making real money, then I believe it might well have disintegrated almost before it began – never mind lasting for three decades. A partnership is *not* a marriage. In a marriage, you should be willing to die for your partner. To share everything. To kill for them, if you have to.

But in a partnership, the making of money comes first. Friendship and affection comes later – if you're lucky, as I have been.

I hope that you too, dear reader, will one day be lucky enough to find such partners and enjoy similar success. But my earnest advice is that you establish *yourself* first, retaining as much control of any start-up or acquisition as you can, and then, and only then, seek pastures new with partners in the picture. That's a great way to spread risk. Partners are a wonderful thing. But they are not a marriage – except of convenience. Ideally, you should keep something of your own to fall back on.

Why else is ownership so vital to anyone who wants to get rich? Ownership buys you the luxury of time. Not only the luxury of occasionally considering a partnership or an investment elsewhere. Ownership means never having to waste time saying sorry that a business didn't work out. It means not having to spend weeks and weeks trying to persuade your partners that a certain course of action is necessary. It means that, for better or worse, you can concentrate on building the business and making money. Or losing it without the added burden of guilt.

Which brings us to minority shareholders and investors. I have owned companies with minority shareholders. And I have always gone out of my way to be fair to them and their interests. But I cannot pretend that they were not a burden. Let me explain by way of example. Should I wish the company we co-own to invest all its profits for three years to build itself, a minority shareholder might (understandably) complain: 'It's all right for you. But I depend on the dividends the company would pay me if we did not invest so much. I want to protest at your investment strategy.'

Then begins a long, tortuous affair of meetings and spreadsheets and jockeying for position. Not because I could not force the issue. But because to force the issue will waste a lot of precious time and energy. Even more time and energy than those endless meetings will take. Time is the only thing we cannot replace, apart from our health and our lives. I resent wasting a moment of it.

But if you want to be rich and you are forced to take minority shareholders on board, then I guarantee that, sooner or later, you will waste weeks or even months in the attempt to obtain mutual agreement. It is unavoidable.

One of the more amusing, and deadly, clauses that can be inserted into any shareholder agreement is worth bearing in mind here. This clause is the 'Mexican Shootout'. I have only seen it used once, and it all got pretty hairy before it was done, but there's no question it resolves disputes between shareholders quickly. Here's how it works.

In the Articles of Association of a company, both sides agree to insert a clause that governs serious disputes. If the dispute cannot be resolved, then the following takes place. Each side in the dispute, each shareholder who wishes to participate, considers carefully what they would be willing to pay for the *whole* company. It doesn't matter how many shares they own, but they must have access to the sum they have indicated, less the worth of their own shares valued on an equal basis.

The parties then go to a neutral lawyer or professional on a certain day and bring with them a sealed envelope with nothing inside it but their estimate of the company's entire worth. Or, at the least, what they are willing to pay in total for the company. The lawyer then opens the envelopes. Whoever has bid the highest amount is now the owner of the company and must pay the losing side for their shares, based on the winner's valuation.

The Mexican Shootout is a brilliant, hair-raising solution, and there are many variations on it. But there are drawbacks. It rather depends which side of the fence you are on. In general, it favours the minority investor.

From the *minority* sharcholder's point of view, it offers the only chance he or she will ever have to own the company for *certain*. It's true that the majority shareholder *might* consider selling to the minority. But he or she doesn't have to if the clause is omitted from the Articles. Only the shootout can force the issue, providing the minority bids high enough.

From the *majority* shareholder's point of view, providing they have sufficient cash, of course, it offers the only certain chance to be rid of a troublesome pest. But the majority shareholder has more to lose. The balance of weakness is in his or her court.

If you start off as equal partners with 50 per cent each (and I *told you not to do that*!) then the 'Mexican Shootout' can save months, even years of weary argument, lost sleep and soul-numbing, teeth-grinding negotiation. If I was the majority shareholder, I would never permit the shootout to appear in the Articles of Association. If I was a minority shareholder, I might not invest without it being there.

Naturally this book is going to be read by millions. I can therefore expect thousands of emails and letters from successful minority shareholders or minority partners who have never owned the whole of their business and yet have prospered mightily. They will claim that I am exaggerating the problems of shared ownership.

And perhaps they are right and I am nothing but a greedy little sod who, all unknowing, has been cowering in his solitary shell since the day he was thrown into prison. Quite possibly. But at least I am a fairly *rich* little sod cowering in his shell. What I have written here about ownership has worked for me, that is all.

I believe you should be cautious, very, very cautious indeed, before you take up with a partner or invest as a minority shareholder. At the very least you should spend hours with a patient, sensible lawyer (if you can find such a creature), going through the Memorandum and Articles of the new company. Every minute you spend on that task may well be repaid a thousandfold, a millionfold at some point in the future.

Unlike a marriage, you must contemplate the end game before taking the plunge. Just how will it end? How can it be ended with least damage to the business and the hearts and minds of the partners? These are questions you must consider seriously before you sign the partnership documents.

In summary, unless you already own a successful business outright, then I do not recommend you enter into a partnership of any kind if you can avoid it. It's time-consuming and distracting. If you have any choice whatever in the matter, walk your narrow, lonely road to riches all on your little ownsome.

As I mentioned before, it's a nasty, lonely business getting rich.

WHY GOING PUBLIC IS DIFFERENT

The public be damned! I work for my stockholders.
WILLIAM H. VANDERBILT, US RAILWAY MAGNATE

There is absolutely no comparison between running and owning a private company and running a public company. (Note: by definition you cannot 'own' a public company, although you can certainly control one, providing you are willing to put up with a great deal of scrutiny.)

We may be getting a little ahead of ourselves here, as you have yet to get rich in any environment, presumably. But should you manage to achieve that objective successfully, you can be certain that the subject of 'going public' will creep its way onto the agenda in due course. And as going public is one way to become very rich indeed, we need to take a cursory look at it.

I once helped to found what became a fair-sized public company, MicroWarehouse, and I was a part of the process of taking it public. A small part. That is, I owned a lot of the shares and I was asked to sign a lot of papers. My American partners, Peter and Bob, did most of the heavy lifting to get us public. Peter in particular.

This was because they knew damn well that if they foolishly permitted me to play a major role in the *process* of going public, the whole shebang might come crashing down about our ears. That would *not* have been a good idea. There was a lot of money at stake. Hundreds and hundreds of millions of dollars, in fact.

Let's face it, I've worked hard over the years so as to be able to tell anyone I want in business to take a hike. But just prior to, and during, the complicated process of taking a private company into the public domain (the NASDAQ in our case), creative mavericks and members of the Awkward Squad are not welcome at the table.

Which table? Why, the table where endless meetings with investment bankers and their ferret-faced lieutenants take place. Where lawyers drone incomprehensibly to each other about gobbledegook with faces that look like they're sucking a lemon. Where the sight of a woolly-haired Brit taking a cigarette out of his pocket would probably have caused the building to be evacuated and the fire brigade and building security to be called.

No, Peter and Bob were wise. It wasn't my scene. Nevertheless, I was forced to listen to enough lectures and to sit round enough tables and listen to sufficient corporate legal eagles to gather that my partners and I were entering a different world. We were about to be entrusted with massive quantities of the public's cash. And if we screwed up in any one of a hundred ways, then it was chokey for us, go straight to prison, do not pass go, game over.

I learned, for example, that after we were a public company and I was a director of that company, then should I be foolish enough to accept a call from anyone, or meet them over lunch, and casually mention that business was particularly brilliant right now and that we would be announcing that fact formally in the near future, then I placed myself in peril. Worse still, I would place Peter and Bob and my other fellow directors in similar peril.

Should the person I had so casually spoken to then rush out and buy my company's shares, I might well find myself in prison. Should he then send me a case of the finest Pomerol wine on the planet merely to thank me for what I'd told him, then I would *definitely* go to jail. And so might Peter and Bob.

This is kind of an odd thing for an entrepreneur to take on board. Entrepreneurs are always bullshitting each other about how great business is; it's virtually an epidemic disease with us. But what I would have done within a public corporate environment by telling this mythical buddy what I told him and drinking the wine he sent, even with the best of intentions, would have been *insider trading*. A big no-no in the world of publically traded stocks and shares.

(Insider trading is an easy one to understand. If you help to run a public company, nobody gets to know how you are doing before *everybody* gets to know. Got that? It doesn't matter if the news is good or bad. It must not be alluded to outside of your professional advisors and company colleagues. *Especially* the upcoming quarterly earnings and revenues. Just don't mention it. Not even to yourself in the bath.)

And this was just *one* of hundreds and hundreds of such rules and regulations we had to remember. Peter would sit with me over a drink and lecture me endlessly on keeping my mouth shut about our business. I became so paranoid that I almost turned into a voluntary mute. It was crazy and depressing. Of course, I got the hang of it in time, and everything went well in the end. But, boy, was I glad to sell those shares a few years later and get the hell out of there.

Now don't get the wrong idea. Going public made me a fortune. And unlike a private business, it seemed that the more we divested (sold off) our shares, the richer we became, because more people bought them and the more those shares we still had left were worth. That sounds weird, but it's exactly what happened. In a private company I would virtually have to be pried away from my shareholding with a crowbar – until I was ready to sell the whole shooting match, anyway. But with a public company, everything seemed to be topsy-turvy.

And that included selling shares. Just as directors of a public company cannot use their inside knowledge to enrich their lunch buddies, even inadvertently, so they must not use that knowledge to enrich themselves. By selling shares when things are going badly, for instance. Not unless *everyone* knows things are going badly. Got it?

There were other weird rules and mantras we had not faced as a private corporation. Growth was apparently all that counted. Growth in share price. Growth in corporate revenues. And being in the 'right' markets (like the internet, at that time). Profits were not the issue. Nobody seemed to care that not a cent had ever been made by any company *trading* on the internet back then. All that mattered was that we achieved compound growth in flavour-of-the-month markets.

When I say '*we* achieved ... ' what I really mean is that '*Peter* achieved'. Peter Godfrey was the lead partner on MicroWarehouse, both before and after it went public. He took to it like a duck to water. Here, the power of trust in a true partnership revealed itself in letters of fire.

Day after day, month after month, year after year, Peter drove himself and his Connecticut management team to the brink of mental and physical exhaustion. He had elected himself chairman, CEO and president – and I thank my lucky stars to this day that he did. Both his steely temperament and attention to detail were uniquely suited to this ball-breaking task – and suited, too, to marathon board meetings (which sometimes lasted ten hours or more) and to smoothing the ruffled feathers of institutional investors.

The paperwork alone was beyond my comprehension. I remember staggering into one board meeting carrying two huge bags stuffed with reports, agendas and memoranda. Then Bob arrived with *three* bags full. Then Peter marched in with an associate buckled under the weight of a filing-cabinet-sized pile. We all burst out laughing, perhaps a little sheepishly. But the strain was beginning to tell. Public company management was testing to the limit what had once been an easy-going partnership.

As MicroWarehouse grew from a half billion, to a billion, then to nearly two billion dollars of revenues from operations in half a dozen countries, Bob and I knew we were virtually tagging along for the ride. We did our best and we kept our heads down, but we never really got the hang of it the way Peter did. We kept thinking like entrepreneurs, making unhelpful entrepreneurial suggestions. Personally, I was way out of my depth – and was all too aware of it.

A private company could never have operated in the way Peter was required to run MicroWarehouse. A private company lives on profits and reserves. There has to be a balance between investment and profit-taking. Between growth and the bottom line. In a private company, growth is not a goal in itself; you only grow if it makes sense to grow.

But a public company exists only to boost its share price, and its share price is determined, incredibly enough, by 'analysts' – spotty-faced youths who live on another planet where growth-at-any-price is the only deity one is encouraged to worship. Medium- or long-term strategies were for wimps and amateurs, in their estimation. *This* quarter's results, *this* quarter's growth, were the only things that mattered to them. It almost seemed, at times, as if profit was a dirty word. If we were making 'profits', asked the 'analysts', weren't we in danger of 'wasting' money that could have been invested to produce more 'growth'?

Huh?

Madness! But it made me very rich. It made all three of us very rich. I cannot deny that. Sales of our MicroWarehouse shares put hundreds of millions of dollars in our collective pocket. Peter's *tour de force* had paid off. All was well that ended well.

And how did it end? It ended when we engineered the sale of MicroWarehouse back into the private sector via a huge investment consortium. Suddenly, our services were no longer required. The so-called 'professionals' had taken over. As far as I was concerned, they were welcome to it. I think even Peter was glad it was finally over. I categorically *know* that his wife Barbara was!

I remember the evening Peter came to join Bob and me at a quiet celebration in a small Manhattan restaurant following the sale. I barely recognised him as he approached our table, casually dressed in a leather jacket and baseball cap – I hadn't seen him without a suit and tie for nearly five years. Nor was he carrying the ever-present bags full of paper. But the strain of the past few years' toil was etched all over his beaming face as he threw his hands in the air, to the astonishment of other diners, and recited a joyous imitation of Martin Luther King: 'Free at last! Free at last! God Almighty, I'm free at last!'

Bob and I had our partner back from the salt mines, and all was well with the world. Even today, I wonder how the three of us ever found our way out of that nightmare labyrinth.

That's all I know, and all I want to know, about public companies. From my perspective, they are not sane places and their share prices are not decided by sane people. Perhaps it's different when a company has been public for many years. But the first few years of any such enterprise are ones of gut-wrenching adjustment, soul-destroying workloads and barely concealed terror. It's a high price to pay for those at the sharp end.

But hey! If you want to be rich, sometimes you have to sup with the devil. And nobody cares, least of all 'analysts', how long or how short your spoon is.

13

THE JOYS OF DELEGATION

*Work is of two kinds: first, altering the position of matter
at or near the earth's surface relatively to other such matter;
second, telling other people to do so. The first is unpleasant
and ill paid; the second is pleasant and highly paid.*

BERTRAND RUSSELL, 'IN PRAISE OF IDLENESS'

This will be one of the shortest chapters in my book. The quote above from the philosopher and mathematician Bertrand Russell says it all. Well, nearly all. Not that Russell was ever a rich man. He was too wise for that.

Try reading his quote again and reflecting for a moment. Under what circumstances is his statement not quite true? Quite a few, when you begin to think about it.

For example, I understand that the foul-mouthed and amusing US 'shock jock' Howard Stern is now about to earn *hundreds* of millions of dollars by switching his shows to a new satellite radio network. Good for him. He has the right to have as much fun at the expense of others as he wishes and to get as rich as he pleases. But how much would Mr Stern earn if he *delegated* his show to others?

The answer is that, after a short while, he would get nothing. His listeners and viewers want Howard Stern. He must 'alter the position of matter at or near the earth's surface relatively to other such matter' himself. He cannot tell others to do it. His audience would not put up with a substitute. Actors, celebrities, kings, politicians, artists and a host of others, either do the job in person, or they lose the job – and the income that comes with the job.

Sure they can delegate certain things to others. But Queen Elizabeth II, for example, ensures her role by appearing, in person, in a punishing round of personal audiences and appearances that would tax the stamina of someone a third of Her Majesty's age. For the Queen, as with Mr Stern, personal attendance is mandatory.

Back in 1861, the young Queen Victoria was shattered by the death of her husband, Prince Albert and went into self-imposed seclusion from public life. This did not go down well with her ministers or with her subjects. 'The Widow of Windsor' was informed after some years, pretty brutally, that either she must get back in the spotlight or she must abdicate. Not surprisingly (and probably deeply unamused), she tottered back on stage.

Delegation for many, then, will only stretch so far. But for most of us with a desire to get rich, it will take us further than the inexperienced could believe. And, as Bertrand Russell noted, it is by far the most pleasant part of the whole business.

I say this not because I am idle – I'm anything but – but because the exercise of delegation, used responsibly, allows you to bring out the best in others and *to make yourself rich* in the process. It is the nearest thing to a 'virtuous circle' imaginable. Just imagine getting rich while you're helping others to help you get richer and prove their worth in the process. Magic!

It used to be surprising to me why so many people appeared to have a problem with delegating. But I finally figured it out, and the answer isn't a pretty one. It concerns our old bugaboo, ownership.

If you own a company and that company's purpose is to make you wealthy, you will be content, delighted even, for any amount of glory to go to anyone who works there, *providing you get the money*. It is in your best interests to delegate whenever it makes sense in such circumstances.

If you do *not* own the company, or a part of it, then it is possible you are only a senior manager because you like power. It is not true of everyone, of course. But often enough. You like bossing people about. You enjoy telling them what to do. If that is the case, then you might be understandably reluctant to delegate real power or opportunity, in case the person you delegate to proceeds to excel. This, in turn, may well demonstrate to the rest of the company what a ho-hum manager you really are.

This is a warped way of thinking. But I am convinced it lies behind much of the reluctance to delegate I have encountered in my business life. I used to be surprised at this reluctance of others, both in and out of my own companies. Now I'm not surprised at all.

Bossy people and glory hounds are mostly interested in building a power base so they can have yet more people to boss about. It's pitiful and a little sad, but we have all seen it. We saw it in school. We saw it in the playground. We saw it in college. And we saw it in our first job. If you are observant, you have been seeing it nearly all your life.

Such bullies and toads appear to cover the earth. They often gravitate towards jobs that give the appearance of power but which require low(ish) skill levels – security companies, the prison service, immigration and customs, minor civil service roles, non-commissioned officers in the armed forces, and so on. I am not suggesting that these organisations are made up solely of such creatures; but who would disagree that they have more than their fair share of them?

This is fine, because they are easy to spot in such roles, and they have to work somewhere. They are mostly an obnoxious nuisance. But cleverer specimens are also probably working right next door to you today. The truly evil ones, through a combination of fawning, flattery, smoke, mirrors and luck (and occasionally, even talent), have risen to the middle ranks and have people reporting directly to them.

This type of managerial toad will often talk about training and delegation in sepulchral tones, but then, as the old proverb tells us, 'the Devil can quote scripture for his own purpose'. Such toads know they are unlikely to rise further, but take pleasure in ensuring that you won't, either.

When they *do* delegate, they enjoy delegating tasks they believe are either impossible or beyond the recipient's ability to complete satisfactorily. How do you counter this idiocy? You don't – unless you own the company, in which case you fire them. I have fired a few. It was the only time I enjoyed firing anyone.

You can't deal with bossy, puffed-up sods who won't train you and won't delegate. You can only move departments or change your place of work. It isn't worth the time to do anything else.

The whole point about getting rich is not to have to deal with this nonsense. Office politics can be fun, as can all forms of politics, but to many people they are upsetting. They reduce productivity and dent morale. They can take up astonishing amounts of time. They increase the number of 'sick days' in a department – which is often a good indication that a toad is in charge and needs to be winkled out of its hole.

True delegation is an entirely different matter and can often be a joy to be involved in. On both sides. As an owner, or an owner in training, you must always be alert for the telltale signs that here is a candidate for promotion and delegation. They are smart. Perhaps smarter than you are. They work hard and they appear to love the work they do. They ask intelligent questions and don't waste time gossiping and mucking about. They listen and correct their errors, and don't repeat them. They want your job.

Especially in the early days of your company, delegation and promotion are among your most powerful weapons in getting rich. Men and women with spirit will be prepared to leave safe, comfortable jobs and work for you, providing the atmosphere of the new operation is loaded with optimism, adventure, the sweet scent of delegation and the promise of promotion.

Not everyone works to get rich. In fact, most people do not. But almost everyone wishes to be respected. With promotion comes respect. And with delegation comes promotion. If your company is young and a bit rickety, meritocracy, delegation and promotion are the bricks and mortar that will make it stronger.

Do not seek a replica of yourself to delegate to, or to promote. Watch out for this, it is a common error with people setting out to build a company. You have strengths and you have weaknesses in your own character. It makes no sense to increase those strengths your organisation already possesses and not address the weaknesses.

If you are bad at keeping records and filing and tend sometimes to shoot from the hip, for example (that sounds a familiar description!) then bring in people who have the organisational skills that you lack and who tend to be of a more even disposition. It's so easy to delegate important work to people who are similar in temperament and skill-sets to you, or to promote them. So easy and so wrong. You may be the founder or the owner, but you cannot do everything yourself – even if you *could* make time stand still. By setting an example early on with a programme of carefully tailored delegation and well-deserved promotion, you will create an atmosphere of loyalty, efficiency and camaraderie that feeds upon itself. An atmosphere poisonous to toads.

Any leader will tell you of the importance of morale. And it *is* important. It cannot compensate for sloppy work, or for lack of persistence or belief in yourself. It cannot compensate for a lack of determination to succeed or for ill fortune. Nonetheless, good morale, a pervasive feeling of 'us against the world', combined with the promise of responsible delegation and promotion based on achievement, can move mountains. And under those mountains is gold. Your gold.

But what exactly *is* delegation?

Let me put it this way. The work undertaken by your colleagues and employees is more important than your work. Your job is merely to lead, perhaps just to point in the right direction. This is advice I suspect will fall on stony ground for the uninitiated. Let me be crystal clear.

I am not suggesting you will have an easy time of it or that you will not work long and unsociable hours. You will. All of us who made our own money did and it will be little different for you. But I have the benefit now of hindsight. I look back along the years and see myself working like a proverbial Trojan. A stupid Trojan. You can avoid this trap.

I see a young man who would think nothing of working a sixteen-hour day – going out into the London night for a drink and a swift curry, coming back into the office for a few hours' kip on the office sofa and beginning the process all over again. And I see the same young man, dragging himself in on Saturdays and Sundays, pale with self-inflicted exhaustion. Snappy. Quick to criticise and too slow to delegate and praise others. I see a young man *trying* too hard, but not *delegating* enough.

Month after month, in those early days, I battered myself and my staff into setting world records for stamina and effort. Did it make me rich? No. It made me tired, bad-tempered and arrogant. It led me to make errors of judgement which I would have avoided had I gone about it a smarter way.

In essence, all I did was show my 'troops' that I possessed awesome stamina. I was the toughest digger in the mine and I could shovel more coal than any two of the rest of them put together. Big deal.

I had forgotten that I wasn't *in* a bloody mine. I wasn't being paid for the hours I kept. Miners rarely get rich. They merely build a legend if they are strong enough or unlucky enough to waste their life in an unhealthy and poisonous environment. Fortunately, this fit of madness (it lasted about three years) eventually passed.

I only started to get rich when I began to delegate and to ease up on my work schedule. How exactly this occurred I'm not certain. Selecting good people has never been a problem for me – yes, I know everyone thinks that, but I have a pretty good track record to back it up. Perhaps those talented people began to edge up on me without my knowing. Perhaps they 'stole' work inch by inch. And perhaps I had just enough wit to let them.

I'm sure my 'vanishings' on a boat in the Norfolk Broads helped. I would just take off (no notice, no plan), summer or winter, and allow the boat to wander among the reeds and herons and riverside villages for a week or two. Alone mostly. Or with a friend from my school days called Bruce Sawford, who had the companionable knack of not talking too much.

During those unscheduled absences, life in our tiny company had to go on. There were some smart young boys and girls there, and they grew used to my peripatetic absences. In the interim, they would 'delegate' the work to themselves and often keep those responsibilities when I returned. Yes, I think that was how it happened.

It wasn't a good way to go about growing a company. Nor a very smart one. But I had no role model, nor even the vaguest grasp of management techniques. I just assumed the world revolved around *me* and everything would turn out OK if I worked an insane number of hours every day. Rather like setting a billion monkeys typing incessantly in the hope that one of Shakespeare's plays would emerge.

My company was lucky to survive those early days and I owe a real debt to the colleagues who worked with me back then. It probably helped that my company was a fun place to work, otherwise it might *not* have survived. Added to which, hard work never bothers the young. They think they are built of steel.

But *you* don't have to go about starting up a business like that. *You* have the benefit of reading this book and examining all the ridiculous errors I made as I stumbled from one catastrophe to another. Then again, there are a lot more entrepreneurial role models, like Richard Branson, to learn from these days. There weren't so many back in the early 1970s, or at least it didn't seem as if there were.

How do you learn how to delegate wisely? Trial and error, I would say. I have been constantly surprised all my business life at who faces up to challenges best. It is very often not those who talk the best talk.

For example, I used to fancy myself as a great negotiator in big deals, but I have learned that I am not. The reason is that I never do negotiate. I only dictate. That's fine if the other side's need is greater than yours in the balance of weakness. But what if there is a potential win–win situation to be reached through patient and reasoned negotiating?

That's when I delegate. Automatically and without thinking. I have people who work for me who are patient, who listen better than I do, and who are quietly determined to get the best deal they can with a potential partner while not scaring them off. They are willing to compromise, but not to surrender. Long after I would have lost interest and wandered away to find something more interesting to do, they will still be patiently negotiating until an agreement is reached. These are not people I would ask into the room to negotiate the sale of a large asset. They have too much empathy with the other side. But for the majority of symbiotic deals and arrangements a company needs to make, their skills far surpass mine.

What else do I delegate? Almost everything now. I do not run my companies and have not done so for many, many years. Rivals do not believe this. They smile knowingly when I tell them that. Perhaps because many of them are not good delegators. But they are wrong. I don't run my companies. And I have no desire to.

Instead of attempting to stay in day-to-day control, I have devised a system where I keep overall control, but do not involve myself in running a business unless I wish to get involved for a particular reason. I use the power of veto instead.

By making myself the chairman of all my companies, I can choose to attend or not attend senior management or board meetings as it suits me. On average, I will attend four to six such meetings a year for each company.

The chair is usually taken in my absence by the MD, the president or the CEO. Verbatim minutes are taken. (I *do* read all the minutes of these meetings very carefully, and I can get a mite cross if they are not produced promptly and accurately. For me, they are not a memorandum of past events. They are a tool to understanding current positions.) I also have Ian Leggett, my personal financial manager as well as my group CFO, placed on all these boards. If I am not present, you can be sure he is.

My vetoes are carefully explained and very well known to all of my executives, who agree to abide by them before they join the board. It's a short list, but has worked well for many years.

Without my express permission:

1. They may not vote anyone on or off the board.
2. They may not physically move the headquarters of the company.
3. They may not dispose of, or shut down, any substantial asset.
4. They may not purchase, or launch, any substantial new product or business.
5. They may not award themselves bonuses or salary increases.

That's it. No more vetoes. Within those guidelines, the managers of my companies are free to get on with their jobs, grow the business and reach the margin return agreed upon at the beginning of the year. A margin that they will have arrived at among themselves by consensus. With Ian's beady eye on them while they do it!

If things go wrong in a particular part of the business, then I *will* get involved. When we are about to launch, sell or close something, I am always involved.

To run a group of companies like this you have to trust your managers and directors. You can only do it if you have learned, by long experience, the art of delegation. It is important to distinguish between delegation and abandonment. Absentee landlords never prosper. I am not absent. But I am not exactly toiling with the troops side by side, every minute of every day. My days of toiling in those particular mines are well and truly over.

To be honest, I suspect my managers prefer it that way. They certainly get to take more scary decisions more often. And that's half the thrill of their job, I hope. As our senior management turnover rate is one of the lowest in the industry, and has been for years, my system must have something going for it.

In fact, I must somewhat shamefacedly admit that in 2007 Dennis Publishing was ranked by the *Sunday Times* newspaper as 'One of the Top 100 British Companies to Work For' and was the only magazine publisher included in their list. Dear me, it is obvious that I am losing my grip and must fire a few people on a mere whim if I am to salvage what is left of my fading reputation as an entrepreneurial tyrant.

One thing I do to compensate for this style of ownership is to look hard for signs of excellent work. When I spot it on one of our websites, or in a magazine, or from management minutes or financial results, I drop a handwritten note to whoever is responsible. And I do it often.

I also invite folk who work for me to visit me in my private office, which is about half a mile from our company headquarters, usually after work. And when I visit any particular company in the flesh, it's usually without warning, on the spur of the moment.

Why do I do things this way? Because I want to write poetry and plant a forest in the heart of England, and that takes a lot of time. Because I have a life and intend to lead it. Because I have discovered that many, many people are better managers than I am. Because I have learned that obsessive micro-management scares away talent.

And most of all, because I learned to delegate a long time ago and to accept that you must allow young managers the opportunity to make mistakes without crushing them or blaming them when things go wrong. (You can always fire them if they make the same error over and over.) Because I love to see talent grow in the stable and watch it come hurtling out of the box at full gallop. Because it makes me a little proud to be a part of such a process. Because I get easily bored. For all of those reasons.

I'm not saying mine is the greatest system ever devised, and I am sure you will devise your own. You need great senior managers to keep my particular way sweet. In any case, you may be one of those who feels guilty when you are out of the office while others toil to keep your company humming and growing. I can relate to that. That's just how I used to feel.

On a related note, let me make a plea concerning the pernicious role of electronic communication in delegation. I'll start by confessing that I am something of a Luddite when it comes to emails and texting and Blackberries and downloads and mobile phones. Quite frankly, I hate the things and all their works.

It enrages me to see senior managers wasting their time (often hours each day) wading through emails, which are often informing them that the receptionist's sister has just had a baby or some such nonsense. I have been known to wreak physical violence on a cell phone that begins to squawk in the middle of meetings, or on a Blackberry which is being used surreptitiously under the table by its owner. Not only is it bad manners, such interruptions break the flow and concentration necessary for real decision-making.

All this is bad enough. But have you ever considered how the growth of such devices has conspired to damage and corrupt delegation in the workplace? If you go on holiday or a business trip and keep obsessively in touch via a mobile phone or Blackberry with the office, what does that say about your management style? About the trust you have in your colleagues 'minding the ranch'?

It says you don't trust them. It says you cannot delegate meaningfully. It says you are a meddler and a micro-manager. So don't do it!

If you want to get rich, then learn to delegate. Don't learn to *pretend* to delegate. Delegation is not only a powerful tool, it is the *only* way to maximise and truly incentivise your most precious asset – the people who work for you.

Real delegation can help make you rich. But only if you work at it.

14

A PIECE OF THE PIE

What is robbing a bank compared with founding a bank?
BERTOLT BRECHT, *DIE DREIGROSCHENOPER*

SHARING AND GROWING THE PIE

*In most of mankind, gratitude is merely
a secret hope for greater favours.*
DUC DE LA ROCHEFOUCAULD, *MAXIMES*

Despite all my hard words about establishing ownership and caution where partners are concerned, I am a great believer in sharing the *annual* pie around. That is, I believe in incentives that help concentrate the mind and bring a sense of competition and purpose to management.

What I do *not* believe in, are incentives handed over as a kind of sop (you will find these everywhere) or in an owner sharing the proceeds of an asset sale unless contractually bound to do so.

Use the annual profits of a company to grow the business by all means. One of the ways of making it grow is to carefully craft bonuses for those who work for you to achieve margin, cost and revenue targets. This is a great idea even if you are going short at the time yourself and your sales manager is earning more than you are that year. Sounds crazy? Well, it worked for me!

But when it comes to a sale, when you cash in your asset for big bucks, then I dispute the necessity (or even the fairness, not that life *is* fair) of handing over substantial chunks of the big bucks to people who did not risk their cash or livelihoods to create the business.

Handing over a substantial portion of the proceeds from the sale of an asset to employees makes no logical sense. Almost certainly the people now working for an asset sold by you will continue in their employment under a new owner. If not, they will be compensated – the law, not to mention common decency, ensures it. Why then would you want to hand them a windfall? You're not responsible for motivating them any more. The new owner is.

Gratitude? Don't make me laugh. I have had many, many employees whom my company encouraged and groomed over several years suddenly leave my company for a wonderful position elsewhere. Often without a second thought. Nor did I blame them one iota.

To the contrary, I am proud, as proud as Lucifer, that we have been able to offer them the opportunity to grow and excel and build their skills to the point that they have been poached by a rival. Why would I not be?

Dennis Publishing alumni litter the senior management offices of my rivals. I love them all. I'm proud of them. And many of them are rather fond of the 'Bearded Dwarf', my nickname among them. But neither they, nor their ex-colleagues still at my company, deserve a piece of the *asset* pie.

So am I just an ingrate? Is this 'the unacceptable face of capitalism'? I don't believe so. Employees work for a salary. That salary is guaranteed. They are also awarded pension contributions from their company and, in some instances, health care and other perks. They risked nothing but a small potential embarrassment when they applied for the job in the first place. They are not owners. The financier John Paul Getty put it best half a century ago:

The meek shall inherit the earth, but not the mineral rights.

Exactly. Risk equals reward. 'An honest day's work for an honest day's pay' is not risk-taking.

If you work in my mine, I'll pay you fairly, try to make it a great mine to work in, incentivise you if it makes sense for the company to do so, contribute to your pension, perhaps contribute to your health care and the health care of your family, teach you to grow your skills and thereby improve your personal net worth, ensure you have paid vacations, ensure you are not bullied or in any way discriminated against, and concern myself with your personal safety at work.

I will do all these wonderful things in a thoughtful and consistent manner. BUT I WILL NOT SHARE OUT THE PIE WITH YOU WHEN I SELL THE MINE AND ITS MINERAL RIGHTS. Fair enough? If you don't think it's fair, please take a job somewhere else. I accept that that is why I am rich and you are not. But that is how the system under which we labour is constructed. If you want to change it, go into politics. (You won't change it there, either, but that's another story.)

There are exceptions, of course. Important exceptions.

Very senior managers who turned down attractive offers from elsewhere to stay with the company and grow it, perhaps. Very long-term employees. Key employees who made a crucial difference to the viability and growth of the particular asset about to be sold. They should certainly be considered for a piece of the asset-sale pie, but generosity should be tempered with the facts set out above concerning risks and rewards. And they *are* facts, you know.

What about incentives from annual profits offered to senior employees? They are absolutely necessary, but they represent a problem which has vexed me all my business life. I do not think I have ever got it right. Your aim, as an owner, is simple: it is to improve management efficiency, productivity and frugality, and thereby improve future profits while still encouraging growth.

But the balance is crucial, and many managers attempt to reach their targets simply by cutting costs. This can be fatal.

Any fool can cut costs anywhere at any time. For one shining moment it will look as if he or she is a genius at increasing the bottom line. Then the moment will pass (unless the cuts were from an excessively fat cow) and quality will collapse. Keeping costs down is vital in almost any business except government (how I *wish* I owned a government) but it should not be the main focus of senior managers.

Instead, the balance between annual profit and investment for future growth is the key. Revenues versus costs is important, but the latter should not be cut merely to meet management bonus targets.

There is also a truth that is antithetical to the tenor of this book. For whatever reason, a surprising number of first-class employees (managers or otherwise) are not overly motivated by money. They want security, or respect, or the chance to learn or the opportunity to shine. Often they require little more than a decent salary in a company where they feel motivated and valued.

You and I, on the other hand, for the purposes of this book, are greedy little sods solely bent on the pursuit of wealth. We must be very careful not to load our own sins on the shoulders of the innocents described in the last paragraph. They are what the English call 'the salt of the earth'.

You won't get far if you attempt to financially 'incentivise' the salt of the earth. Praise, the ability to discern when a good job has been done and the courtesy to say so, fairness, integrity and camaraderie should be employed instead. It takes more trouble than mere bribery, but it produces wonderful results.

There are arguments to the contrary, too, about *any* thought or consideration of the financial reward that ownership and keeping most of the pie brings in its wake. Most of them come from the central tenets of world religions – organisations whose assets and resources rival that of many multinational corporations, it might be added. Even so, these religions have been credited in the past, rightly or wrongly, with carrying the flame of eternal truths, truths that men are apt to forget from generation to generation. Let's take a brief look at their attitude towards gathering wealth.

Take the Bible first. In Matthew 19, v. 26 we learn, in words taken directly from the Son of the God of Christians, that: 'It is easier for a camel to go through the eye of a needle, than for a rich man to enter into the kingdom of God.' Pretty strong stuff when you consider the alternative on offer in the Old Testament.

Or again, from Matthew: 'Lay not up to yourself treasures upon earth, where moth and rust doth corrupt, and where thieves break through and steal. But lay up for yourself treasures in heaven.'

Stirring words, but for many hundreds of years it was taught that one way for a man to lay up 'treasures in heaven' for himself was to give *money* to the Catholic church. The more you gave, the more you were likely to be saved – and to hell with the widow's mite, was the cry of Christian bishops then. (Bishops, in those days, lived like kings. Archbishops lived like emperors. I do not think it would be wise for me to comment about those higher up the chain, although the evidence is there for those who wish to read it.)

And again, in the Bhagavad Gita, a Hindu holy poem from a religion which was old before the coming of any Jewish prophet, we read: 'Set thy heart upon thy work but never upon its reward. Work is not for a reward: but never cease to do thy work.' Just as the Devil can quote scripture for his own purposes, this might cynically be viewed as a more beautiful rendering of the old canard: 'I never meant to get rich. I just did what I love doing and I got rich by accident.' But I will not say so. It is difficult to comprehend meaning down the long centuries.

If I were writing a book about how to be happy, then I would recommend much to you along the same lines. Love of any work, diligently undertaken, no matter what it is, brings contentment and, eventually, respect. But it will rarely bring you riches. And that is what you are reading this book for, is it not?

In the Koran, too, and in Taoism and scores of other religions or philosophies there are warnings about the very attitudes extolled in this book. Even today, the morality tales at the heart of Hollywood films like *Wall Street*, and many others, warn against greed. They warn with a wink, it is true; but they warn just the same.

So is it worth it? Should we pursue the Pie at all?

This is not a question for me to consider here at any length. I have become a poet, a serious one, too, and I wrestle with such questions every day in the three hours I put aside to write verse. But you are not to consider this. You are to consider that I might well be a hypocrite, because I took to writing poetry *after* I had 'laid up my treasure' on earth.

I have wasted vast amounts of my life 'laying up treasure'. I have exiled myself for months at a time to plunder the riches of the USA and to bring them back to Europe. Many are the nights I lay awake in my New York apartment, listening to the eerie sirens and street sounds which define that great city, while I dreamed of spring in an English country garden thousands of miles away.

Let's pause, just for moment, to consider how I came to regard that trek in hindsight and in sonnet form:

Prodigal Son

Often I ventured in Babylon's towers,
Never a friend I met – never a one,
Playing the part of the prodigal son.
Many the weeks and many the hours,
Barely a moment to think of the flowers
Patiently budding in Warwickshire's air.

Never a thought of a snapdragon there,
Or May on the hedge. All of my powers
Spent upon gilding the lilies of gain
While blue-eyed forget-me-nots lowered their gaze,
Their beauty unmourned in an English lane.
Yet now, as I lie amidst Babylon's maze,
Decked in the trappings of fabulous dross,
By the sirens of night, I weep for their loss.

Well, I can weep all I want. Not a moment of those long, long years worshipping Mammon can be brought back. Just as I cannot bring back the dead forget-me-nots from past spring days I never saw.

Does it matter if I now *own* the lane, or half of the county for that matter? Or that it was purchased with treasure brought back from across the Atlantic after years of sweat? You might want to think about that.

But don't think too long if you want to get rich.

PROTECTING THE PIE

The Queen of Hearts, she made some tarts,
All on a summer day:
The Knave of Hearts, he stole those tarts,
And took them quite away!

LEWIS CARROLL, *ALICE'S ADVENTURES IN WONDERLAND*

Sooner or later someone is going to try to steal your pie. This will not be unfair. You almost certainly set out to steal someone else's in the first place and may well, to some degree, have succeeded. There is very little that is new under the sun and the supply of pie is not infinite.

But enough of philosophy, already. Here comes another wannabe or a great big corporation. They like the look of what you've been baking in the kitchen, and decide to bake something very similar. They want to put you out of business.

What to do? First let's take a look at the nature of rivalry and competition in a capitalist society.

'Competition is all that makes capitalism bearable.' Without rigorous competition, all forms of Western-based societies would soon be ruled, not by parliaments or their equivalent, but by fat, bloated and impregnable monopolies. (Some would argue they already are.) You wouldn't like it much. People of my age and older have personal experience of it.

You think I'm joking? Obviously you're not old enough to remember the days before rationing ended. Or the days before Freddie Laker introduced the concept of cheap air travel. British Airways and their American cousins ruled the roost at the time, and charged whatever the hell they wanted to charge for you to fly. They had virtually no competition. You paid up, or you stayed grounded.

Or perhaps you cannot recall when the GPO (the General Post Office) was in charge of *telephone* communications – which were then hived off to British Telecom in a bogus 'public flotation'. They, too, had no competitors. 'You'd like a new phone in your flat? Certainly, madam. That will be loads-a-money up front and we'll come to install it at our convenience – shall we say in four months?' Four months if you were lucky, that was. And if you didn't complain.

Britain in the 1950s, 1960s, 1970s and much of the 1980s was ruled by a combination of monopolistic, undemocratic unions who spent all day arm-wrestling with a bunch of monopolistic, undemocratic nationalised industries. British citizens never got a look in. The word 'customer' was alien to almost everyone involved, except what was left of 'private industry'.

Around the world, by friend and foe alike, the UK was called the 'Sick Man of Europe', and that's exactly what we were. All because so much competition had been sucked out of the country by the creation of monopolies, which, if they were not owned by the government, were regulated by them to the point of virtual control.

I have little time for many of Margaret Thatcher's policies. By my lights she was a warmonger and a damn sight too full of herself. But she smashed the union's grip on Britain's economy and helped create a climate in which denationalisation of major industries became the cry for Socialist, Liberal and Conservative alike. And if you don't like my reading of history, ask Tony Blair. He'll tell you much the same, although his words will be softer and altogether more prudent.

She did not reduce taxes fast enough. And she did not listen to anyone except her 'inner voices' concerning Europe, pensions, red tape, bureaucracy, the health service and a hundred and one other things. But I, and many thousands like me, will always be grateful to the old handbag for bringing the sweet aroma of competition back to what, after all, is a nation of shopkeepers.

I am a Labour man born and bred. I will die voting Labour. It's a tribal thing. It's plain stupid. But I still believe (well, just) that 'the inch of difference', as my friend Richard Neville put it, 'between the Conservative and Labour party, is the inch in which my friends and I live'.

Even so, that lack of competition nearly ruined Britain. It wasn't entirely Labour's doing – much of it had to do with the loss of markets and lack of capital following the devastation of World War II. But it brought us to the edge of an abyss from which I doubt we would have crawled out in my lifetime. Thatcher dragged us back from that brink, and nobody knows that better than the current Labour administration. After all, they stole many of her and John Major's policies, and made them their own. Very successfully, too.

Now *that's* how to handle competition!

Competition isn't some misty-eyed concept that should be confined to students of the 'dismal science', Economics.

Competition is the heart, soul, liver, lungs and kidney of the beast we call Western capitalism. How you react to it, how you face up to it, defines whether you can stay rich, and probably whether you can get rich at all.

I'm a fighter. My natural reaction to provocation in business, as in life, is to attack. But this basic instinct has led me astray many times, and I have learned to think a little more carefully before tearing into the enemy with fangs bared. Let's take an example.

At the beginning of the 1990s, my company owned more than half of the personal computer magazine titles in the UK. We were making a small fortune. Most importantly we owned a brute called *Computer Shopper* (we still do), one of the only magazines in Europe which clocked in one *thousand* pages of advertising in a good issue. This was a magazine worth defending. My biggest rival in Britain was the Dutch company VNU, headed up by Graeme Andrews, the chap who had masterminded VNU's purchase of *PCW* magazine from Dennis Publishing in 1982.

I was contacted by Ziff Davis, a powerful magazine-publishing company based in Park Avenue, New York City. Ziff Davis was owned by one of the finest magazine publishers who ever lived, Bill Ziff, and he wanted to talk to me on the telephone. I had met Bill a few times, and had sold him the American edition of *MacUser* in 1986, a magazine I'd launched in the USA with my partners, Peter and Bob.

Everyone had done well out of the deal, not least because Bill had persuaded me to spend a year babysitting *MacUser* in New York after selling it. He had achieved that feat by offering to increase the sale price substantially if we hit ambitious targets. I had hit them, all right – there was a lot of money involved. Close to $20 million.

But that had been a few years back. Our conversation went something like this:

'Hello, Felix.'

'Hi Bill.'

'How are you?'

'Very well, thanks. What's up?'

So far so breezy. Being breezy with Bill was like whistling in the dark when you know there's a ravenous Doberman somewhere in the vicinity. It doesn't do any good, but it makes you feel slightly better. His answer was chillingly courteous.

'We're coming to Europe, Felix. Soon.'

'Oh.'

'I thought that at least I should let you know.'

'Great, Bill. We'll do lunch. Japanese for you, isn't it?'

'No, that's not what I meant.'

'Oh.'

'I meant that we are going to launch PC magazines in Europe.'

'Which magazines, Bill?'

'Two of them to start.'

'Where, Bill?'

'I think you can guess, Felix.'

'Oh.'

The conversation was downhill all the way from there. This was a catastrophe of terrifying proportions. I knew that. And Bill knew that I knew. It ended roughly as follows:

'I think we should talk, Felix.'

'Sure.'

'We would like to buy your company. Or at least 51 per cent of it.'

'Oh.'

'You could be involved with us launching in France, Germany and Britain.'

'Uh-huh.'

'You could even head it up.'

'Uh-huh.'

'I'll have Phil call you, Felix.'

'Sure.'

'Do think carefully about our proposal, Felix.'

'Sure.'

'Together, we could conquer Europe in the PC magazine business.'

'I'll think it about it, Bill.'

It was about all I *did* think about for the next year or two.

So that's how lives are altered. One phone call. A conversation that would have meant nothing except to those in the personal computer publishing business. To me, it meant the world crashing down about my ears.

It was flattering, but it meant ruin, of a kind, if I sold 51 per cent to Ziff Davis. It meant loss of independence. It meant that if I agreed, and Bill or his CEO called me up on a Monday morning and asked me to pee in the blue urinal that week, then I would have to pee in the blue urinal. I would be transformed into a hired gunslinger, trampling over Europe, swamping rival computer magazine publishers with launches of high-quality product backed by huge investment.

I would become something like a travelling salesman. A very *rich* travelling salesman, true. But still a salesman. A hired gun.

But what choice did I have? Bill Ziff was not a bluffer. If he said he was coming, then he was coming. Soon. If I spurned Phil's advances (Phil was one of Bill's senior legal advisors) then I was toast.

Because Ziff Davis in those days were the best. Simply the best publishers of PC periodicals in the world. If I was a fox, they were a tiger. And a tiger with huge amounts of money to call upon from their American investment-banker buddies. If they launched competing magazines against me in Britain, it would be like Russia invading the Isle of Wight. All over before it began.

Or would it?

Britain is not America. Britain has only sixty million souls compared to North America's three hundred million. British advertising agencies were insular, awkward, cantankerous and nothing like the suavely dressed pond-life I lunched with on the east and west coasts of America.

Costs were higher in Britain for printing and paper. Salaries were cheaper. As we have seen, newsstand sales were more important than subscriptions, unlike in America. Margins were smaller. The balance of revenues between advertising and sales of copies was reversed. Advertisers tended to pay less per thousand readers per page; much less. Budgets were tighter. We drank warm beer. And we didn't do power breakfast meetings.

Europe was a different environment. Ziff Davis would probably think that Britain (and Germany and France) were just mini-versions of the USA. They would be utterly wrong. And it would take them time to find that out. Time would cost them money. How much money were they willing to lose? –

Maybe there was a chance. To fight. To prove I was better than them, better than anyone, in my own backyard. Maybe it wasn't totally hopeless. But I needed allies. And I needed money. So I did what I never did, I got down on my belly and squirmed over to see my rival, VNU, who had a fancy office building several blocks away in Soho.

Here was money – VNU were a public company. *Here* was international clout. And VNU didn't like Ziff Davis. In fact, one got the impression they positively disliked them. And the enemy of my enemy is my friend. Especially when my enemy is on the attack with his dagger at my throat.

Now VNU are a decent bunch. Most Dutch people are decent. That's stereotypical, maybe, but it's always been my experience of them. Good negotiators, good traders and nearly all straight arrows. But if I was a fox and Ziff Davis was a tiger, then what was VNU? VNU was a woolly mammoth. It was so big it didn't bother with animals that kept away from it. In a snowstorm, the fox could probably snuggle in downwind of the mammoth, providing it behaved itself.

Dennis Publishing and VNU got on in Britain. We poached each other's staff (mostly, I poached theirs) and made orang-utang breast-beating noises to advertisers. But, quite honestly, the two companies liked and respected each other. And I especially liked their CEO, Graeme Andrews.

I filled Graeme in on the news. (I suspect he had already heard.) He was concerned. Very concerned. VNU was a huge company in Holland and had a growing worldwide business. They were bigger than Ziff Davis. Ziff could never buy them, and would probably never want to buy them. But the tiger could damage them in Britain and elsewhere. It would be a bloody fight and no quarter asked. So we talked, Graeme and I.

A public company has to be careful. It cannot make alliances like private companies can. There are a million ways it can fall foul of the laws governing the governance of public companies. Graeme could not exactly *promise* me that VNU would join with Dennis to see the invading tiger off, but he could suggest various hypothetical scenarios and leave the rest to silence and a raised eyebrow.

I got busy. VNU got busy. I turned down Bill's offer, and I believe that Bill was a little mystified by that decision. Together, but without colluding (honest!) we fought Ziff Davis on the beaches, on the landing grounds, in the fields and in the streets, in the hills, in the offices of advertising agencies and on the news-stands of Britain.

Ziff Davis were game. They kept coming. They threw millions of dollars, then more millions at their British beach head. It was awe-inspiring. They poached our columnists and our editors in droves. They paid a fortune to their staff and rented fabulous office space down by the river. Sales incentives were juicy. Their staff car park looked like an automobile show, the models were so new. All that was missing were the girls in bikinis.

They wined and dined even tiny advertisers. They flew a half-page *Computer Shopper* advertiser down from Scotland, with his wife, and took them both to the opera! British publishers had never seen anything like it. It was the American Way writ large in a country one quarter the size of Texas.

I worked as I hadn't worked in years. Together with Alistair Ramsay, my managing director, and the entire Dennis computer publishing team, I used every dirty trick and stratagem I could think of to attack the Ziff juggernaut. We nearly had nervous breakdowns. And we spent money like water to take the fight to them. We would not give in.

And we won. Eventually, they folded their tents and drifted away into the night. The combined forces of VNU and Dennis, with a teensy bit of help from EMAP and my friend Chris Anderson at Future, saw the buggers off. But at what cost?

At the cost of two years' entire profits, my friends. *Two years'* profits is what it cost us to defeat Bill Ziff. Not just the profits from *Computer Shopper*. But from the whole company. And today, knowing what I know today, would I still have done it?

No. Absolutely not. It was stupid. Glorious, but stupid.

I would have *listened* more closely to Phil and Bill. I would have *negotiated* my balls off. I would have *become* 'the enemy', and I would have led the charge to rip the limbs from any bastard who stood in the way of Ziff Davis Dennis in Europe. That was going to be the name of the company: Ziff Davis Dennis, ZDD.

That's what I *should* have done. It doesn't pay to be a hero. But am I glad we did it. Yes, I'm glad. Because I proved that my own people, with their backs against the wall, facing an enemy with superior firepower and massive confidence, could slow, stop and, finally, beat that enemy. It was exhilarating. But it was ultimately a pyrrhic victory. If my memory serves me right, either VNU or EMAP ended up with the remnants of Ziff Davis's two magazine launches. So what?

I'm in this business to get *rich*, aren't I. So what did I *do* it for? Was it because Bill had *assumed* I would be his junior partner? Was it because I secretly desired to prove that, in the UK anyway, I was as good as everyone said his organisation was? Because the approaches from his people that followed our conversation *assumed* I would take their wonderful offer (and it *was* a wonderful offer). Did that rankle a little? Subconsciously?

I don't know now. Too much water under the bridge and wine through the arteries. But I do know I would have been a *richer* man if I had joined with Bill and run with the tiger as his jackal. I'm certain of it.

And what of the competition *you* will be facing? What do I think I know that might be of use? I know that you must dodge more bullets than you try to catch. I know that competitors can be a source of inspiration as well as irritation. And I know that it is a foolish fox that attacks a woolly mammoth, except by stealth, in the dead of night, when calves are born. I know keeping your head down doesn't always work. And I know your competitors will keep you honest.

My advice on competition is always to ensure that you *want* to fight, and *ought* to fight on a larger competitor's ground. If he is anxious to buy you, determined to park his tanks on your lawn, maybe you should let him. *For the right price.*

If your competitor is smaller, try to hire him or buy him or join with him. If he won't budge, take drastic action and smash him. If that won't work, then learn to be friends and collude against the woolly mammoths together.

But don't fight tigers, my friend. Not if you want to get rich.

TWENTY-ONE WAYS TO MAKE MORE PIE

*It is not that pearls fetch a high price because men have
dived for them. On the contrary, men dive for
them because they fetch a high price.*

RICHARD WHATELY, ENGLISH PHILOSOPHER AND THEOLOGIAN,
INTRODUCTORY LETTERS ON POLITICAL ECONOMY

Here is what I have learned as far as owning, sharing and growing your annual pie is concerned. None of this should be written in stone. The way I got rich and shared (and continue to share) my annual pie may not suit you or your own circumstances. That said, I suspect some of the points that follow are universal truths:

1. **Make annual bonuses generous.** If you want your managers to concentrate on improving margin and profitability while growing the business, then they have to feel the light is worth the candle. Pay them well for performing well. (They will have many excuses to make to their lovers or spouses for working late to achieve the goals you set them.)

2. **'Ring fence' investment costs from 'ongoing' business.** You want the business to grow but you also want to make profits. Balance is the key. By 'ring fencing' all investment money for new projects and growth in your annual accounts, you can encourage managers to work on margin and profit from their 'ongoing' parts of the business while offering them the chance to grow and take some risk. This equation requires patience and goodwill on all sides. But it can be done, and it works.

3. **Keep costs down.** Always. 'Overhead walks on two legs' and will eat you out of house and home. No company, new or old, can avoid 'stealth' growth in overhead. It occurs, as it were, by osmosis. Prune overhead regularly. Stop only when the pips squeak.

4. **Never delegate bonus arrangements.** I once did so, like a fool, and twelve months later my company was forced to pay ludicrously high bonuses for a very small improvement in profit to six senior managers. Four of them voluntarily returned half of their bonuses. They knew they were not equitable. The other two insisted on keeping their bonuses. Neither of those two managers works for me today, or will ever work for me again. But it was *my* fault. *I* had delegated a task to them I should not have delegated.

5. **At senior level, insist on collective responsibility for bonuses.** Part of the annual incentive bonus for senior managers should result from their *combined* efforts to bring home the bacon. One cannot make a senior manager's *whole* bonus rest on this edifice. But peer pressure is a powerful force. If senior managers sense one of their number is slacking and fear they may all suffer for his or her transgressions, they are likely to let their feelings be known. Forcefully.

6. **Praise excellent work.** But do not waste your praise on ho-hum performances as a sop. Employees respect a boss who knows the difference between the mundane and the exceptional. Remember that not all employees respond well to incentive bonuses or a dangled carrot of any kind. They seek recognition, not bribery.

7. **Fire malingerers, incompetents, toads and glory hounds mercilessly.** Not only does firing them make *you* feel better and contribute to a more pleasant working atmosphere, it cheers up the whole staff.

8. **Turn a cold eye on company 'perks'.** These can add up to huge sums. While I am considered terribly old-fashioned on this subject, I am still uneasy about company-issued credit cards;

company-issued mobile telephones; travel and entertainment of any stripe at the company's expense; company air travel in any class but economy.

9. **Avoid all 'jollies'**, the generic British term for flying the sales team to Florida in winter to 'boost morale' and issue tub-thumping speeches, all of which are forgotten the second the crew hit the beach. You can't afford 'jollies'. Ignore protestations from sales managers to the contrary. A day set aside in a quiet environment, prepared for carefully, to assist sales teams improve their presentations to clients, is sensible. As is sales training from reputable training agencies.

10. **Offer legal perks that you have paid for yourself to employees.** This sounds crazy, but it works. I allow my employees, for example, the use of my Rolls-Royces or Bentleys for their weddings. I permit them to stay at my homes around the world if they have performed well. I send every child born to an employee (well, I used to in the early days – there are too many of them now) a massive soft toy. Such perks are legal because I paid for them myself from after-tax dollars or pounds.

11. **Set an example.** If, as an owner, you want fancy furniture in your office or works of art or Persian rugs, then bloody well pay for them yourself. How can you expect frugality when a junior manager, who works in a cubicle, comes to visit you, knowing that the *company* paid for those accessories? There is nothing wrong with them being there. It's who *paid* for them that counts.

12. **Encourage senior managers to go over annual results with you one-on-one.** You will learn more from off-the-cuff remarks and opinions expressed at *one-on-one* meetings while looking over financial results than you will in a dozen board

meetings. This tactic never fails to produce food for thought, often on both sides.

13. **Back up your managers.** With delegation comes responsibility. Back up your managers, in public, whenever and wherever you have to. If they do not perform, speak seriously in private to them. If they still do not perform, fire them. But do *not* undercut them or engage in meetings that appear to undercut them. Reprimand other managers who bad-mouth their peers. Nearly everyone's ego and self-confidence is more fragile than the outside world believes.

14. **Search out and promote talent.** Talent comes in all shapes and sizes and is often inarticulate and shy. Talent isn't necessarily the woman in the Calvin Klein suit who talks the talk and bamboozles meetings with stunning graphics on her PowerPoint presentation. Talent is often to be found dressed in T-shirts down in the lower reaches of your organisation. Set a bounty on talent among managers. When you find it, test it. Groom it. Work it until it's ready to drop. Load it with more work and responsibilities. Praise it. Reward it. It will make you loads-a-money.

15. **Interview your rivals' talent.** I have never known a single person in a rival organisation, however well paid or cosseted, who has refused to meet me for a quiet drink after work. I have discovered more about what my rivals are up to in this manner than any other. In addition, I have often been so impressed with the people I met in this way that I poached them later. No intelligence-gathering exercise is ever entirely wasted in business. There is only so much pie. Talent bakes that pie.

16. **Discourage secrecy.** The more you take middle and senior managers into your confidence, the more they will respect you

and the harder they will work for you. Many managers disagree with this policy. They love the feeling of power that comes from knowing what others do not know. I don't care about power. I care about getting rich.

17. **Save a little bit of pie for suppliers.** Save a little of the annual pie to wine and dine key suppliers. Or let them wine and dine you. If you like them enough, invite them to your home. We all remember to call often upon our major customers. But it is worth remembering suppliers. And they often have important market information.

18. **Never bad-mouth rivals.** It's a sign of stupidity and weakness. I try to go out of my way to praise my rivals when I can. Often enough they deserve praise and they're sure to learn about my comments sooner or later. Why go out of your way to antagonise them? (Secretly feeling sorry for them, because they do not own as much of their own company as you do, is definitely permitted.)

19. **Sell early.** Real money rarely comes from horsing around running an asset-laden business *if you are an entrepreneur*. You are not a manager, remember? You are trying to get rich. Whenever the chance comes to sell an asset at the top of its value, do so. Things do not keep increasing in value for ever. Get out while the going is good and move on to the next venture. More money is usually lost holding onto an asset than is made waiting for the zenith of its value. I should know – it's my own biggest defect.

20. **Enjoy the business of making money.** The loot is only a marker. Time cannot be recaptured. There is no amount of pie in the world worth being miserable for, day after day. If you find you dislike what you are doing, then sell up and change your life. Self-imposed misery is a kind of madness. The cure is to get out.

21. Never miss an opportunity to promote your asset. Try purchasing one (or both) of my books of poetry: *A Glass Half Full* or *Lone Wolf* for instance. If they are not in your local bookstore, then go to www.felixdennis.com and check them out. Each contains a spoken-word CD and may well transform your entire life. (Sorry, I just couldn't resist that.)

15

THE POWER
OF FOCUS

The vulgar thus through imitation err;
As oft the learned, by being singular;
So much they scorn the crowd, that if the throng
By chance go right, they purposely go wrong.
ALEXANDER POPE, 'AN ESSAY ON CRITICISM'

FOCUS ON KEEPING YOUR EYE ON THE BALL

I have been very poor the greater part of my life,
and have borne it as well, I believe, as most people,
but I can safely say that I have been happier
every guinea I have gained.
SYDNEY SMITH

It was Alexander Pope who wrote the immortal lines concerning learning, and how a little of it 'is a dangerous thing'. Much the same could be said about certain people's behaviour following even the most modest success. It blinds them.

What is it you are attempting to achieve here? You are trying to become rich. This must be the main focus of your business life. Becoming rich. Not becoming one of the world's most famous athletes, or taking on Rupert Murdoch in the newspaper publishing and television business, or having your name appear a thousand times when you type it into a Google search.

You want to get rich. And you want to do it legally and as quickly as you can.

That is what we are supposed to be about. Unfortunately, as John Lennon pointed out, our lives are 'what happen while we're busy making other plans'. And that is precisely what happened to me and a great many other people I know. We forgot we were supposed to concentrate on getting rich and concentrated, instead, upon excelling in the first sphere we succeeded in.

Why am I a magazine publisher? Is it because I love magazines? No. It's because I had a tiny success back in 1967 selling a hippy magazine on London's fashionable King's Road. That's right. I discovered that at two shillings and sixpence a time (half for me, half for the owner, Richard Neville), I could earn more money than I could as an R&B drummer or a high-street-store window dresser.

I even learned that by dressing up one or two girlfriends in the shortest skirts they owned and instructing them to approach every guy under thirty with a big smile and the following words: 'Hi! Have you got your copy of *OZ* this month yet?' I could triple my earnings. (Some wits might say that having created the world's biggest men's lifestyle magazine, *Maxim*, I'm still at the same old game. Well, let 'em say it.)

It was nothing unusual for me to return to Richard Neville's basement flat in the King's Road days to divvy up the loot and discover a hundred pounds in my satchel. A hundred pounds! In those days, nobody I knew had ever earned a hundred pounds in a fortnight. I could earn it in a day or so.

And so I became a magazine publisher. That was OK, but I forgot to keep my eye on the ball. The ball was to get rich. Instead, I decided to become one of the world's *best* magazine publishers. Not smart.

Why wasn't it smart? It took me way too long, for one thing, and it cut me off from more lucrative endeavours for another. I became a multi-millionaire in 1982. By then I was thirty-five years old. Barmy! By thirty-five I was already half dead.

With my talents I could have been a multi-millionaire by the time I was twenty-five or twenty-eight. All that was stopping me was my conviction that I was a born magazine publisher. How stupid. I wasted eight or nine years when I could have been drinking Petrus, swilling down Retsina and lager instead.

The truth is I led myself to believe I had fallen in love with publishing. That wasn't a tragedy in itself, but I allowed my liking for the magazine publishing business to blinker me from so many other avenues where I could have coined cash.

If you have entrepreneurial flair, then you can go into just about any business and make money. But instead of rushing to where the money was, I kept on digging in the relatively poor pit of ink-on-paper until the money, reluctantly, came to me.

This is so important, gentle reader. It pains me to think about it. If you wish to become rich, look carefully about you at the prevailing industries where wealth appears to be gravitating. THEN GO TO WHERE THE MONEY IS! *That* is where you should focus your efforts. On the ball marked 'The Money is Here.'

Let us say I had done something worthwhile with my life, which I have good reason to doubt, and had raised a son or daughter. Would I allow either of them to go into the magazine business today? You must be joking.

What is the magazine business? It is a business where our main activity is chopping down millions and millions of trees, flattening the pulp and printing hieroglyphics and images on both sides of it. Then we send the end product out in diesel-guzzling trucks to shops where perhaps 60 per cent of them sell to customers. We then pile the remaining, unsold magazines into more diesel-guzzling trucks and take them to a plant where they are either consumed as fuel, buried or shredded, or used to make cardboard boxes for refrigerators. That's the magazine business.

Does this sound to you like a great business? Of course it isn't. Do you imagine I would allow any grown child of mine to go into such a business? Of course I wouldn't. The magazine business will have faded to a shadow of its former glory within a decade or three. It is a *mature* business, and few fortunes are made in mature industries, unless you are lucky enough to create a monopoly in one. I was luckier than I knew.

So what businesses *should* I have gravitated towards? Computer software, technology and dot com start-ups, cable and satellite television, property, environmental waste clean-up, alternative energy services … any one of these might have created a much larger fortune for me in less time than I took with magazines. Do I know anything about these industries? No. But, then, I didn't know anything about magazines in 1967 either.

So this is the first lesson in the power of focus. Keep your eye on the ball if you wish to get rich. And do not forget which ball.

It's the one marked 'The Money is Here.'

TIMING

The time you won your town the race
We chaired you through the market-place;
Man and boy stood cheering by,
And home we brought you shoulder-high.
A. E. HOUSMAN, 'TO AN ATHLETE DYING YOUNG'

There is no substitute for good timing. There is always luck involved, but it's often the kind of luck you help make yourself.

With my friend Don Atyeo, I wrote two biographies many years ago. The first one was about the martial artist and film star, Bruce Lee. We received a pitiful advance from a very small firm in London called Wildwood House run by a publisher of the old school, Oliver Caldecott. Oliver was a kindly soul, and he thought he might just be able to sell a few thousand copies of what would be the first biography written about Bruce Lee. Lee was a cult figure in Hong Kong and the UK at the time.

Don Atyeo and I were broke. We knew nothing whatever about kung-fu and nothing about Bruce Lee. Neither of us were film buffs. Neither of us had ever written a book before. Our only qualifications for this task were as follows: 1) It was our idea. 2) We owned a typewriter each. 3) We had visited Asia. 4) We were broke.

Our contract with Wildwood House gave Oliver rights to publish our biography in Hong Kong, Britain, Canada, New Zealand and Australia. No other territories were mentioned in his contract because it was inconceivable that the book would ever be published or wanted in them.

Don and I buried ourselves in research. We visited Hong Kong (on a shoestring budget) and got a lot of interview material (including, incredibly, an interview with Bruce Lee himself), and then we sat down in my Soho flat in London and began typing. Typing, rather than writing, would be the operative description.

This was hack work of the most demeaning kind. But it was fun and we needed the money. Then good timing arrived. Good timing for *us*, that is. Bruce Lee died suddenly and unexpectedly in Hong Kong in July 1973. Overnight, he became a global superstar. And we had almost finished his biography – the *only* biography then written about him.

The world erupted in Bruce Lee mania. His films began playing to packed audiences in scores of countries. For a brief moment, he was the most famous man on the planet. Most movies appeal only to movie-goers in one or two continents, but Bruce Lee became a star not only in Europe and North America, but in Africa, South America, India, Central America, the Middle East and Asia.

At my request, Don leaped on a flight to Hong Kong. A flight we could not afford. Oliver loaned us the money. There,

Don got the lowdown from the hospital where Lee had died, interviewed surgeons and nurses there and went on to obtain interviews with Bruce Lee's mistress and minders and pieced together what had happened on the night Lee died.

It was an explosive story, and all the more compelling because his death was considered suspicious by many of his fans. Meanwhile, Lee's movie company Golden Harvest, run by Raymond Chow, together with Lee's wife, Linda, were concocting a smokescreen designed to protect the filmstar's reputation. This was understandable (he had collapsed in his mistress's apartment) but rumours of criminal and even supernatural involvement in his death swirled around Hong Kong.

Eventually, these rumours reached the outside world. The result was an international media firestorm.

When famous people die, there are always rumours which coalesce into conspiracy theories. It's just human nature. In Bruce Lee's case, this speculation reached absurd levels and only served to heighten worldwide interest in his movies. In the Western world, Don Atyeo and Felix Dennis, two hard-up hippies living in a slum in central London, now became Bruce Lee 'experts'.

Hey! Compared to the hundreds of other journalists assigned to the story from around the world, we *were* experts. No sooner had Don flown out of Hong Kong, interview tapes and photographs bulging in his luggage, than a well-oiled machine rolled into place. Golden Harvest's machine. And Mr Chow was one of the most powerful men in Hong Kong. The worldwide media circus arrived too late.

Journalists from newspapers in every capital city in the Western world could find no one to interview. Lee's wife, his mistress, Betty Ting Pei, his producers, his housekeepers, his drivers, his studio colleagues, the hospital staff and anyone connected with Bruce Lee and his movie company clammed up. Our timing had been perfect. We had slipped in and out 'under the radar'.

We finished the book in record time and Wildwood House published *Bruce Lee: King of Kung-Fu* in the UK to the delight of legions of ecstatic Bruce Lee fans. It went straight into the British non-fiction bestsellers list. For the first time, Wildwood House had a bestseller on their hands. And Don and I had money in our pocket.

But there was far more money to come from this splendid piece of good timing – unless you happened to be Bruce Lee. I realised I owned the rights to our biography in many countries around the world – all of Europe, Africa, Central and South America, the Middle East, most of Asia and, most crucially of all, the USA. In addition, because my little company had designed the book, we had the negatives and typesetting on hand. Together with an old friend and lawyer, Andrew Fisher, as well as book agents Abner Stein and Nat Sobel, I got busy.

The result was a river of coin flowing into Don's pockets, my pockets, Andrew's pockets, the agents' pockets and my company's pockets from foreign edition after foreign edition of our book. There were translations into German, French, Italian, Portuguese, Dutch, Greek, Arabic, Spanish and a host of others. It also meant I got to meet up with a hero of mine again, Jann Wenner, who had founded *Rolling Stone*, the American music magazine.

Jann's book publishing division, Straight Arrow, bought the US rights. The book there was re-designed by Jon Goodchild, the very man who had taught me to design magazines in the early days of *OZ* in London, who was now living in San Francisco. *Bruce Lee: King of Kung-Fu* flew off the shelves in North America. I'm told it was one of Straight Arrow's best-selling books ever.

It was perched on Bruce Lee's metaphorical shoulders that I first tasted real money and built my first successful business, including a raft of kung-fu magazines and Bruce Lee commemorative mail-order items, masterminded by my old school friend, Bruce Sawford. Bruce had a lot of experience in mail order.

In the latter part of 1973 and through 1974, the post office delivered more than one thousand *sacks* of mail to our ramshackle office. The postmen (there were no women delivering mail in those days) got so pissed off with the number of sacks, they refused to carry them upstairs to our garret office and dumped them in the hall. On a good day there would be six sacks. Each sack would contain envelopes with postal orders, cheques or money worth $10,000 or more. Every *day*.

Then more good timing. A television presenter ranted and raved on her show on national UK television about one particular Bruce Lee commemorative item sold by my company. It was called the Bruce Lee Treasure Kit, and she thought it poor value for money. In tones resembling the announcement of the death of a family member (she was a sanctimonious phony if you ask me) this showbiz hack removed each of the items from the bag containing the Treasure Kit and showed them to the camera. There were maybe eight items, including a membership card to the British Bruce Lee Society, photographs, a couple of badges and stickers, and a bunch of other stuff.

The next day, thousands *more* orders for the Treasure Kit came pouring in our garret door. We actually went round to the post office ourselves and helped the postmen lug them up the street on hand carts. In those sacks was a small fortune, and I didn't want them lying around the post office sorting rooms too long.

Here is the power of timing. Don and I were not great writers, although we improved as time went by. We were not investigative journalists. My company was a hole-in-the-wall operation barely capable of publishing a series of pamphlets, let alone a stable of magazines. Wildwood House was not a home of bestsellers. We were broke. We were inexperienced. And yet, we made a ton of money.

Not everyone who wants to get rich is going to get lucky with their timing. But what made the timing so good in our case? Three things, I think.

One was the blind luck of one of the fittest men in the world keeling over and dying. (If you want to know what he died of, then buy a second-hand copy of our book. And don't believe anyone else. We really did those interviews with the hospital surgeons and staff and so we didn't have to make up conspiracy nonsense concerning 'bad feng shui' and Triad plots.)

Secondly, we followed our instincts and we persisted with this mad idea, despite our lack of experience or any credentials. But then, who *did* have the credentials?

Thirdly, we acted with extraordinary speed. We put ourselves in the right places at the right time, and we never slowed down from the moment Bruce Lee died. Within weeks, we had finished a book, sold lots of foreign language editions, sold the US publishing rights, published a ton of magazines, invented a lot of mail-order items and then manufactured and sold them to tens of thousands of fans.

And what did it all add up to? It added up to focus, following a stroke of luck in the shape of perfect timing.

What errors did I make? Plenty. I did not invent enough magazines and I did not invent enough commemorative items early on. Within a year or two, my company was organising 'Bruce Lee Memorial Conferences' and even sending fans on 'Pilgrimage Tours' to Hong Kong with Cathay Pacific airline. It was profitable business. But if I had managed to do those things within six months, I would have made far more money.

What other errors? I did not write and publish another book. I had enough material to have done so. I could easily have asked a couple of journalist friends to ghost it for Don and me for a pittance. It would have been another bestseller for sure. But, by then, I had fallen into a trap. I believed I *was* a biographer. I believed that our biography was a *great* biography. What nonsense.

What I *should* have done was published a book, with Wildwood House or any other book publisher, called *Who Killed*

Bruce Lee? And *this* time, I should have insisted on having my company named as joint publisher. Such a book, produced swiftly enough, would have sold millions of copies around the world.

My errors came partly from inexperience and partly from falling into the trap that I mentioned earlier. They also came from lack of focus. I was allowing my thoughts to wander towards expanding in new directions, mostly magazines, while there was still a cow in the shape of a new book bursting with milk and waiting to be milked. That was a serious error. A loss of focus.

Who knows? Perhaps I *will* milk it one day, but it will never yield the small fortune that would have resulted from a ghosted piece of exploitation published in 1974.

FOCUS ON CREATING THE RIGHT ENVIRONMENT

I was the better at getting and keeping,
You were the better at spend and spend;
I was the better at grubbing and heaping,
But who was the better man in the end?
Yes, who was the better man, my friend?
Who was the better man?
'THE BETTER MAN'

You cannot get rich all on your own. No one can. You have to create, or work within, the right environment.

Humans are a cooperative, if argumentative, race. If you were to be boycotted by your immediate neighbours, if nobody would meet with you or take your instructions or sell you anything or buy anything from you, you could never make money. You cannot do it on your own. Getting rich is mostly sleight of hand, but if you acquire no audience but a mirror, then there is no illusion with which to get rich.

Paper money itself is an illusion. It is a promise from a man you will never meet, who works for a bank you will probably never enter, who reports to a government you do not control. A £50 note or $100 bill is just a piece of paper with some fancy printing on both sides of it. And what is a credit card but a small rectangle of plastic with which you *promise* to buy a watch, car, a yacht or even a house?

When you bank or spend paper money or use a credit card, you do so as a part of a collective illusion. You already subscribe to what Charles Mackay once rightly called 'a popular delusion' or 'the madness of crowds'. You cannot use such devices alone. Others must believe in them equally for the magic to function.

When enough people share a short-lived delusion, vast sums of money can be acquired overnight. The 'tulip mania' in Holland in the mid-seventeenth century was such a time. Tulips had been imported into Holland for forty years before the madness hit. By 1635, a single tulip bulb was swapped for a collection of valuable articles, which included the following:

- four tons of wheat
- eight tons of rye
- a bed
- four oxen
- eight pigs
- a suit of clothes
- two caskets of wine
- four tonnes of beer
- two tons of butter
- one thousand pounds of cheese
- a silver drinking cup

The current value of the above would be $50,000 or more. And this was for a *single* tulip bulb! Fortunes were made or lost, especially the latter, when the music stopped. Within a few years, a tulip bulb was worth less than a dollar in today's money. Here is the wonder of collective short-term delusion writ large.

In the same way, it is almost impossible to build an individual fortune without colleagues, confederates and one or two professionals on board. You will need a lawyer, sooner or later. You will be a fool to set up in business without a qualified accountant somewhere in the picture. You will need others who believe in your idea or your talent to work with you and for you.

I suppose there is a 'James Bond' type scenario where an evil genius can work with a computer hitched up to the internet and steal all the world's money alone. But I doubt this is a part of your own game plan. In any case, even the evil genius will need someone to guard the gold bars while he works his evil on the computer, to make him the computer in the first place so that he can *be* evil, invent the internet to *allow* his evil to spread, force millions of others to *use* the internet as victims of his evil and hire minions to *pump out* the evil lavatory when the evil sewage pipe blocks.

You see? You just can't do it on your own. You need to create an environment.

This does not mean you require fancy offices and all the accoutrements. Human capital is by far the most important element of your environment, whether you are just starting up or deep into the game. By focusing hard on obtaining that human capital you will vastly increase your chances of becoming rich.

Stupid people are easy to hire. The world is full of stupid people. Many of them are extremely pleasant and will give you a lovely smile every morning. But such people will not add to your wealth. In the early days, you should avoid them like the bubonic plague. What you need are clever, cunning and adept people.

But why would clever, cunning and adept people work for a mug like you? Simple. There are many clever, cunning and adept people who are risk averse. You are *not* risk averse because you are dedicated to becoming rich. Believe it or not, much, much cleverer people than you will come and work for you if you ask them.

You don't believe me? Then I have obviously failed in this book. Do I strike you as a particularly clever person? Right! I'm *not* a clever person and I have just enough wit to know it. I never attended university and was tossed out of my school before I had 'graduated', to use the American expression.

You do not need to be clever. You do not even need to be that adept. You need only a little cunning and massive determination to become rich. Providing you can pay much cleverer but risk-averse people properly, and promote them and lead them in such a way that they are all rowing in the same direction, they will sign on to your little ship. I can guarantee that this is true because I did exactly that myself.

Persuading them to join is not the problem, but separating the wheat from the chaff is harder. They look so much alike. This is where you have to focus your energy and concentration.

Your employees, your colleagues, your suppliers and your customers are all human capital. Choosing among them is an art form. Yet creating the right environment in which money can be made is essential. I repeat, you can't do it on your own.

It takes effort, experience, focus and skill. If you get it right, you will become rich with an ease that will astonish you and everyone who knows you. If you get it wrong, you will be running around like a headless chicken for a year or so and then you will be bankrupt.

And you will deserve to be.

FOCUS TIPS WHEN CHOOSING 'HUMAN CAPITAL'

Here are a few discoveries I have made over the years about staying focused when choosing employees or suppliers.

○ **Never choose an important employee or a key supplier alone.** Get others to interview them or talk to them as well, either with you or separately. We are all far too fond of choosing those we instinctively like, those we respect or believe are similar to ourselves. This is not a good thing. You need the input of others to choose the right candidate, although the final choice, in the early days, must be yours and yours alone.

○ **Go further than reading a person's references.** It's such a fag, such a bloody nuisance, such a pain in the neck, to go well beyond the references and CV you've received, isn't it? And yet it pays. Make an appointment with a potential employee's last company or with a supplier's other customers. Go and see someone there. Make nicey-nicey. Listen hard. You will discover more about your potential employee or supplier in a few minutes in this way than in hours of conversation with them.

You can even tell the prospective employee or supplier you have done so if you wish. It cuts bullshit down to a minimum and shows, at the same time, that you cared enough to go beyond a CV and the usual references.

○ **Make notes. Speak little.** I'm terrible at this. Absolutely terrible. But I've learned to try harder as the years have gone by. Your notes need not refer in any way to what the potential employee or supplier is saying. It can be gibberish. Or it can, more usefully, be your impressions of the person and their responses. Have a series of questions handy to shoot out when they grind to a halt. Then focus like mad on what your instinct and your intuition is telling you – as well as your ears.

As to speaking little yourself, remember you are being interviewed, too. It is impossible for the other side to tell that you are not as clever as they are if you keep your mouth shut. 'Better to have the world suspect you a fool than to open your mouth and put the matter beyond doubt,' as the old saying has it.

It may appear rude to have initiated a conversation, as you have, and not to make small-talk to fill in embarrassing silences. But you are not conducting the conversation to be polite. You are conducting the conversation to get rich.

○ **Good suppliers respect attention to detail.** Don't hesitate to challenge quotes or invoices – after you have done your homework. At the beginning of a relationship, everything will usually be hunky-dory. Later, hidden or unacceptable costs may creep in. Challenge them. Constantly request quotes from your supplier's rivals. Demand refunds if a supplier screws up, based not on the cost of the goods or services, but the financial consequences of the screw-up.

(I've read acres of New Age rubbish about 'partnerships' between suppliers and customers. That's what it is: rubbish. If I could only get rich by bankrupting every supplier I ever dealt with, then I would do it in a heartbeat. I wouldn't feel good about doing it, but I'd do it. Getting rich isn't about vendor–customer 'partnerships'. And anyway, I have found that good suppliers respect a hard-nosed attitude providing it's logical and providing you pay on time.)

○ **Pay employees well. Bonus better.** Even young children know what you get when you pay peanuts. Monkeys! Your company's salaries must be competitive.

Bonuses should be more than competitive, they should be tempting, generous and based ruthlessly on meritocracy and delivery. That's the way to get employees to really focus. You don't want people to apply to work for you because of the salaries on offer – they should be driven by other desires. But if a salary isn't commensurate with the market, potential winners will not be able to afford to work for you. I made that error for some years before changing my ways.

○ **Be alert for 'cross overs'.** Many times I have been interviewing someone for a job and realised that they are not suitable for the job in question. However, the candidate would be perfect in another position in my company. Never mind that that position is currently filled. (All positions in your company, except your own, are temporary.)

These 'cross overs' occur often. Be alert for them. Nothing pleases a candidate who has failed to get a particular job more than being contacted some time later and offered a job out of the blue. It is like a vindication and they will almost certainly say 'yes' if the job title and money matches or exceeds their current position.

○ **Only hire winners.** There may or may not be such a thing as bad luck. But whether it exists or not, it is certainly contagious! Hire winners or people you believe will become winners. Fire whiners and moaners swiftly. That's contagious, too. You are trying to create an environment where making money is on everyone's mind most of the time. Losers and whiners usually have other priorities.

○ **Ignore your prejudices, likes and dislikes.** Easy to say and hard to do. Legally, you may not permit certain prejudices to colour your choice regarding any candidate. This is not only good law, it's good sense. Some of the most successful colleagues and employees who have worked with me and for me over the years were not my personal cup of tea at the beginning.

Likes and dislikes should not come into it. Loyalty, effectiveness, honesty, integrity and stamina are crucial. Cleverness and cunning can be useful. Professionalism is vital. A desire to shine in the world is worth more than a university degree. All of this is important. Who you like and don't like is irrelevant. If an employee makes money for you, you'll get to like them later, I promise.

○ **Promote from within when you can.** I recently had to hire a new CEO for one of my companies. An old friend, an ex-CEO and chairman of one of my rivals, Robin Miller, gave me a great piece of advice. He suggested that an external candidate, a candidate from outside the company looking for a senior position, had better be at least 30 per cent better than any internal candidates to get the job.

Why? Because, he reminded me, you know all the faults of an internal candidate – they may have worked for you for years. But external candidates come to you free from errors made in the past. All you are faced with is an impression at the meeting and a list of their achievements. Failures are not a part of anyone's CV. It was good advice from Robin, and just tipped the balance in my mind when I made my own final decision.

○ **Don't leave senior employees in any job too long.** If this happens, as it has in my companies occasionally, it means you are not focusing on that business. You will get the most out of any senior employee in their first year or two in a new position. After that, they enter a 'comfort zone'.

Do you really want them to be comfortable? If a man or woman heads up one of your companies and has been there too long, consider asking them to create a new division or company for you. But do not leave them to quietly go to seed – they will get bored and resign anyway, if they're any good.

FOCUS ON DOING AN OUTSTANDING JOB

Indeed the Idols I have loved so long
Have done my credit in this World much wrong:
Have drowned my Glory in a shallow Cup,
And sold my Reputation for a Song.

EDWARD FITZGERALD, *THE RUBÁIYÁT OF OMAR KHAYYÁM OF NAISHÁPÚR*

If on my deathbed I had only a very short time to pass on what wisdom I have accumulated about getting rich to a son or daughter, then it would be this:

> *Ownership Shall Be Half of the Law;*
> *Doing an Outstanding Job Shall Be The Other Half.*

There is no point in owning 100 per cent of a rubbish company. Whatever it is you intend to do to get rich, get good at it. Hire people who are better than you at it. Listen and learn and get better still at it.

Even if you produce garbage for morons to watch on television, make it the most entertaining garbage out there. Even if you are nothing but a scum-sucking, ambulance-chasing tort lawyer – the lowest form of pond-life that walks on its hind legs – be the best scum-sucking ambulance-chaser in town.

The American gangster Al Capone is said to have shot a man who kept brewing rotten beer for Capone's illegal beer-distribution racket during Prohibition. His gang lieutenants didn't get it. The business was illegal anyway. If a new supplier tried to muscle in with better beer, they would murder him. What did it matter if the beer was crap? But Capone, who would have become one of America's greatest businessmen if he had stayed on the straight and narrow, knew better.

He knew that rotten beer makes rotten business. He refused

to have his name associated with rubbish. He expected Prohibition to be lifted eventually, and hoped to be the legal beer king of America. Of course, he never *did* because he didn't pay his taxes and because he was a murderer and a vicious, brutal killer.

Even so, I am ashamed to say that if the above story is true, then I admire Capone for the sentiment, if not for his business methods. He was right about the beer. Having read his autobiography, I found myself wishing he had stayed out of the rackets and built his fortune legally. He had many of the attributes of a world-class entrepreneur and I suspect he could have become very rich indeed without having had to resort to crime.

Why does it count? Why is it important to focus on doing an outstanding job?

Firstly, talent will flock to your company. Talented employees mean you have more opportunities to make more money. Secondly, you will make fewer errors. The quality of your management will see to that. Thirdly, it places a premium on your assets and the worth of your business. That means you get richer faster. Fourthly, it's simply more enjoyable – which means you will enjoy coming to work and will spend more time focusing on doing an even better job.

So focus on your business, whatever it is. It represents what you are. It should be a source of pride as well as a source of money. Being the best, or at least striving to be, will speed up the process of getting rich. Trust me. I'm the best damn magazine publisher in England. (Well, at least I strive to be!)

Focusing on doing an outstanding job is an important part of getting rich.

PART FOUR

TROUBLE-SHOOTING & ENDGAME

16
WHOOPS!

Being young is greatly overrated.
Any failure seems so total. Later on,
you realise you can have another go.
MARY QUANT, FASHION DESIGNER

AN OWNER'S GUIDE TO KNOWING
WHEN TO CUT AND RUN

And this is the law, I will maintain,
Unto my dying day, sir,
That whatsoever king shall reign,
I will be the Vicar of Bray, sir!
TRADITIONAL ENGLISH FOLK-SONG

I do not believe the words 'a patient man' would necessarily spring to the lips of those who know me superficially. 'Irascible' would be more likely. But I can be as patient as the next man, and a great deal more so, when it comes to projects I believe will make me money.

Still, not all things work out. Nor do most of us have the time or the inclination to conduct a full autopsy on what went wrong. Past failures are not pleasant to contemplate. But if you intend becoming wealthy by owning a company or some similar entity, then, sooner or later, you will encounter failure. It would be wise, at that time, to figure out just what went wrong.

A failure in the offing represents one of the only times that minority shareholders or minority investors become a potential boon. If you can offload your share of a failing company on them and shimmy out the door, then you should certainly do so. They may be prepared to take over and attempt themselves to make a success from your failure.

Most people close very few companies or projects in their life and they are often unaware of closure costs. They nearly always underestimate them. The magazine business will provide a classic example which may surprise you.

Believe it or not, there are magazines that have been propped up on life-support by large publishing companies for years. The executives will be fully aware that their magazine is not viable and will never be viable. Let us say it is losing $3 million a year. Why not close it without further ado?

The answer is closing costs. The hidden cost of failure.

In our example, the cost of shutting down the magazine will far exceed the three million it costs to keep the wretched rag just breathing. Why so? Because magazines sell large numbers of subscriptions to readers. In America, these 'subs' are often sold at a knockdown price to encourage the appearance to advertisers and others of growth. It is a foolish practice, but it is ubiquitous.

Even if the magazine's 'subs' price is a reasonable one, there have been numerous cases of a form of petty 'bribery' where potential subscribers are wooed by publishers to subscribe with the offer of a free clock-radio or reduced memberships to health clubs, etc. These cheap prices and 'free gifts' create a massive liability in the publisher's balance sheet – which is fine as long as advertising continues to pour in. But when the magazine is no longer flavour-of-the-month and advertising is falling off, the misery begins.

Let us say a dying magazine has a million subscribers. Most of them are not 'real' subscribers, but, even so, they have paid their dollar per copy and are owed, on average, six more issues.

This means the cost of reimbursing the subscribers alone will exceed $6 million in refunds. (It will exceed it, by the way, because of the huge cost of collating and mailing the refunds to a million people.)

Of course, the publisher will also face other closure costs, including redundancy payments to magazine staff, rebates to advertisers and possibly to printers and paper merchants and a host of other creepy-crawlies that will come slithering out of the woodwork when news that the ship is sinking spreads abroad. In all, sudden-death closure costs might be as high as $8 million.

The publisher's only hope is to cut costs to the bone, cease soliciting any discounted subscriptions, fulfil the subscriptions with very thin, very cheap editions of the magazine – now a shadow of its former self in quality and number of pages – and thereby reduce what, in the jargon, we call the 'subs liability'. This can only be done if the poor beast is still technically alive.

In the meantime, the publishers hope that many staff will not wait to be fired but will seek other jobs and reduce closure costs by reducing redundancy payments. It took one of the largest magazine-publishing corporations in America over *five years* to bring about the closure of what was then still one of the best-known magazines in the world. It lost money for every one of those five years. Let's take a look at why.

Over five years, in our hypothetical example, losses would total $15 million – surely more than the cost of instantly shooting the brute? Yes, but that $15 million will have been *spread out* over those five years. The parent company can afford to carry such a burden. Profits will only be slightly affected each year and senior executives will still receive their precious annual bonuses. Even better, the share price will suffer mildly, if at all. On the other hand, if the full $8 million (or more) for sudden death was charged in a single year, not only would the senior management's bonuses evaporate (horror of horrors!), the share price would probably take a hit from negative publicity and profit-and-loss considerations.

But how can it be good for a company to waste the difference between $8 million and $15 million for an asset going nowhere? The medium- or long-term answer is that it isn't good. The company will have squandered $7 million (more, with inflation taken into consideration) and clogged up its managerial focus with a deadbeat property. But the short-term answer is that it's probably the best thing to do in the circumstances. Not to mention that in larger corporations, the short term is often the only term senior management, goaded on by share price 'analysts', can bring itself to care about.

I mention all this just to give you a sense of what failure tastes like and a glimpse at the hidden costs of closure. If there is any way at all you can play 'pass the parcel' with a venture you believe is destined to fail and in which you are a principal, then do not hesitate. Pass the damn parcel and move on to the next opportunity.

But how can you *know* when things are going to fail? You cannot. Nobody has 20/20 future vision. But if you are running the business, you will certainly know much earlier than anyone else, providing you are willing to stare reality in the face, that is, which many executives and entrepreneurs are not.

I'm now going to give you a piece of obvious advice. Listen closely to your bean-counters and accountants. Or seek one out you trust when the whiff of failure is in the air and get advice. They are a much-maligned group, bean-counters. It is true that they are risk averse to an extraordinary degree, and that if bean-counters ruled the world we would be permitted to produce nothing but beans, just to be on the safe side. But they also have professional training. And many of them have seen financial failure before and know that the light at the end of the tunnel is probably an oncoming train. If you listen very carefully and are careful, too, to mask your irritation at their litany of hard facts, you might save yourself a small fortune.

There are incompetent and even crooked bean-counters, of course, and I have, sadly, employed one or two of them. But on the whole, I wish I had listened more often and more carefully to their advice in my business life. When the going is getting tough, when there is a scent of rotting fish in the air, they are right more often than they are wrong. Curse them.

All very well, but how can you *know* when things are soon to collapse about your ears and what can you do if, having followed my instructions to the letter, you are the sole owner of your little company? Not a lot, but we'll take a shot at it.

Books on management theory at this point normally advise you not to panic. I don't agree with that. It's my belief that adrenaline and a touch of panic are tremendous motivators. Of course, you can't *stay* in a panic, but a dose of panic in a private place, with a bottle of malt whisky on one hand and a bean-counter on the other, can be a very motivational experience. Motivational and salutary.

But never despair. We are not engaged upon a serious business here. We are only talking about the getting of money, and, occasionally, the losing of money. You may despair when you have broken your neck; you may despair when your only child has predeceased you; you may despair when terrible wars, famines or plagues afflict millions of innocents. But you must not despair over a simple thing like money. Take a shot of comfort from poetry – here are three stanzas from Arthur Hugh Clough's poem, 'Say Not the Struggle Nought Availeth':

> *Say not the struggle nought availeth,*
> *The labour and the wounds are vain,*
> *The enemy faints not, nor faileth,*
> *And as things have been they remain.*

> *If hopes were dupes, fears may be liars;*
> *It may be, in yon smoke concealed,*
> *Your comrades chase e'en now the fliers,*
> *And, but for you, possess the field.*

> *And not by eastern windows only,*
> *When daylight comes, comes in the light,*
> *In front the sun climbs slow, how slowly,*
> *But westward, look, the land is bright.*

It may not be great poetry, but at least it's cheerful in a melancholy sort of way. And his point about the smoke of battle obscuring the landscape is well made. So what are we to do? Or, rather, what are *you* to do?

Firstly, you must see how much time is left. In the days of the dot com boom they used to call this your 'burn rate'. (At what rate were the dot com bandits and entrepreneurs burning through the money provided to them by misguided saps who trusted and believed in them? When would they go bust or need more money?)

Once you have established just how long you can continue to trade without falling into the technical trap of illegal trading (which you *must* not do, my friend), you should make an inventory. And I do not mean an inventory of your office furniture, computer systems (you will have spent far too much on those items, I will wager) or your piles of unused stationery.

You need to analyse the beast you had hoped would make you money. Just like those brilliant software designers, who invent software that solves no known problem and must then search for or invent a problem for their software to solve, so you must consider whether your beast would make money in another man's kennel.

Might it have uses that you have not yet considered? Might it be a money-maker if it was viewed in another light? This is more often the case than you might suppose.

Take the story of Ray Kroc, founder of the McDonald's fast-food chain. He bought McDonald's, an uninspiring, ho-hum burger business, because he realised, in a flash of astonishing intuition, that what Americans on the road needed was not fine cuisine or the best burger money could buy. What Americans wanted, as they travelled vast distances across interstate highways, was *consistency*, *cleanliness* and *fast service*.

They didn't care if the burger was a mediocre burger. All they cared about was being certain they would be served the *same* burger they consumed in the last McDonald's they visited, perhaps hundreds of miles away. Swift service, a clean environment and *consistency*. That was the secret of one of the most astonishing business success stories in American history. Kroc was viewing an existing product in a different light.

Kroc did not invent the hamburger. He saw that hamburger outlets could become a *different* beast from other fast-food outlets at the time. McDonald's is only called McDonald's today by an accident. It would not really have mattered *which* burger business Kroc had decided to purchase. His genius lay not in producing a burger, but in allaying Americans' fears that the next place they stopped at for fast food might poison them, or charge exorbitant prices, or make them wait an instant longer than was necessary. (This tale is simplified. The business of creating franchises also had a great deal to do with Kroc's success. But the analogy holds true.)

So look at your own, ailing beast. Can it be something else? Can you make it a tiger of a different stripe, or can somebody else? Is it really not a valid business? Would more capital help, or would that be throwing good money after bad? Your analysis must be ruthless. If there is anyone with business savvy in the world you trust, now is the time to seek them out, tell your story and *listen*.

Should you determine that the beast is worthless, both to you or anybody else, still do not give up. At least *try* to sell it. I once forgot to do so and lost a lot of money that already had my name on it. Money that was piled neatly in a bank waiting for me to collect it. Let me explain.

We once launched a magazine in Britain called *Stuff*. It was a big launch, too. The idea behind *Stuff* was that it would be like many other young men's magazines (zany humour, great photography of beautiful girls in swimsuits, articles stuffed with attitude), but it would also specialise in gadgets and new technology. The magazine would be a shop window for the kind of guy who always seems to have a new gadget before you've heard of it.

Stuff was launched with a great fanfare in the UK and promptly failed. It took us a while to cotton on (too long, to be honest) but the writing was on the wall.

Stuff had cost me a fortune to launch and I was angry about it. We should have done better and we all knew it. I demanded it be closed at a tension-packed board meeting. We began preparing the closure press release and readying ourselves to tell the staff of *Stuff* the bad news. Word of our decision leaked out around the British magazine industry. (Why is it that bad news travels faster than the speed of light?)

What happened next is the subject of dispute. I believe that I was already slated to have lunch with one of Britain's most amusing and canny magazine publishers, Michael Heseltine—that's the Lord Heseltine to you, chum. Michael had helped to found Haymarket Publishing many years before, after a career as a property developer. He then went into politics and very nearly reached the top of the greasy pole. Personally, I think Britain would be a better place today if he *had* reached it, but that's by the by.

Michael and I always lunch in a seafood restaurant called Wilton's. We've been doing so for years. Michael had heard that I was closing *Stuff*. And he had seen what I had not. That *Stuff* could be a tiger of a different stripe if it was published *solely* as a gadget magazine around the world. It didn't need too much zany humour or girls in swimsuits. They could be dispensed with.

He made me an offer. I was caught unawares, having gone to Wilton's to drown my sorrows. I was also massively embarrassed, not because we were going to close a magazine – we all have to do that from time to time in the publishing game – but because we had FORGOTTEN TO TRY TO SELL IT.

It was humiliating. I could have kicked myself. I tried damage limitation in our 'negotiations', but Michael has negotiated with the likes of the rulers of China and the USSR and he knew I was bluffing. I had no other potential buyer. I could not create an auction. Dennis Publishing had all bar announced *Stuff*'s closure. I was trapped and had nowhere to go.

To cut to the chase, Michael was very decent about it and paid me a fair sum for the brute. I cannot tell you how much, but I suspect it is more than most individuals have earned in the last decade. Even so, it was not exactly a fortune. I did manage to negotiate one concession, one 'rogue element'. Haymarket would buy the right to publish *Stuff* anywhere in the world except for North, Central and South America.

I duly launched *Stuff* later in the USA, where it has been a success and sells more than its rival, *FHM*. Haymarket, on the other hand, has launched *Stuff* in *many* countries around the world. I do not want to know how many countries, because I will only get cross again if someone remembers to tell me. I had broken two of my own cardinal rules and paid the price. I had *not* looked to see if the leopard could change its spots, and I had *not* instructed my managers at Dennis Publishing to quietly sound out the chances of selling *Stuff*.

So just before you dump your dream into the gutter, ensure you do the rounds of other companies in your neck of the woods. It only takes two of them to become interested and you have the chance of getting an auction going. That has to be better than throwing your toys out of the cot in a paddy, as I did with *Stuff*. But only a bit better. Failure is always a bitch.

FACING THE MUSIC

Behold, I have played the fool,
and erred exceedingly.
THE BIBLE, I SAMUEL 26:21

So here you are up to your neck in trouble. You have figured out your business isn't viable. You've tried to look at the beast another way. No joy there. You've made some humiliating telephone calls and paid some visits and tried to sell it or even give it away.

No interest. What now?

Of course, you can try cutting costs to the bone. But that is of little use if there are insufficient costs to cut. And firing people is never much fun.

Downsizing

The firm's alive with murmurs,
The thrum of gossip's din,
The shrugs of old long-termers –
Whoever's out – they're in.

No parachutes or rip-cords,
No lifebuoys as she dives,
Fat bastards with their clipboards
Are sharpening their knives.

Receptionists are tearful,
The Boss averts his eye,
'H.R.' is grimly cheerful –
But then – they're paid to lie.

It's meeting, every minute,
It's tackle, grapple, block!
It's 'keep yer 'ead down', innit?
It's in by eight o'clock!

It's straining blood and sinew
To keep abreast of moves:
'The hangings will continue –
Until morale improves!'

And if 'downsizing' and cutting costs won't do the trick, what then? You'll have to close the business. Be careful not to continue ordering goods or services you know you will not be able to pay for. That's not just ethically wrong, it's legally wrong and you can get into serious trouble if you do it.

If necessary, you might have to declare bankruptcy. Well, you won't be the first dreamer to do it, nor the first who came back from the experience for a second bite at the cherry. Besides, bankruptcy laws and rules have changed beyond recognition in recent years and have made the process far less onerous than it used to be. The authorities appear to bend over backwards to help people declare bankruptcy today.

I've never had to declare bankruptcy, thank goodness, but I sailed fairly close to the wind a few times in the early days. I expect most entrepreneurs do. It has always amazed me how kind many suppliers are if you speak to them on the level. It's the lying and ducking and diving, the wasting of their time calling you and never having their calls returned that really gets their goat. (They probably knew you were going to go belly up before you did.)

Don't play it like that. Play it straight. Be honest with them and show them you're doing your best. You can't do any more than that.

Especially don't forget to let the VAT and Inland Revenue boys know what's going on. The earlier you take them into your confidence, the more leniently you will be treated. Sure they can seem like ogres, but I've never found them to be so. They're human beings, just like you. Treat them like human beings, show them you are doing your best, and you may be very pleasantly surprised.

But don't try to cheat them, my friend. Don't even think about screwing the VAT man or the Inland Revenue. Your arm's too short to box with God.

And do your damnedest to see that the little people get paid, if you can. Your large suppliers will have built a bad-debt percentage into their budget for the year. You will become just another irritating percentage point in their annual accounts. But the lad you hired to answer the telephone doesn't have a bad-debt percentage built in, or an accountant to keep it all straight. He expects to be paid. And he *should* be paid, even if you have to sell that nice office furniture you foolishly ordered.

The more honest you are about your misfortune with those affected by it, the easier the comeback will be. There *is* going to be a comeback, isn't there? But the more you weasel and fib or tell outright lies or blame somebody else, the less likely it is that anyone will want to do business with you again.

Some people seem to think that out of sight is out of mind. That if they cheat you and a few months or years go by, you will forgive them, or, better still, forget about them. But we don't forget and forgive people who weasel.

I can remember the name of a man who stitched me up for only a thousand pounds twenty-five years ago. I've spent more than that on a fancy business lunch since, and yet if his name comes up I will still cheerfully traduce him to anyone who will listen. If he'd said sorry and been honest with me, I doubt I would remember the incident had occurred.

Screwing up isn't criminal or deliberate or malevolent. But *covering* up is, if you get caught. And you will get caught – ask the shade of Richard Nixon.

Closing down a business or going into bankruptcy is a miserable affair at any time. My advice is not to make it worse by omitting to apologise and shoulder the responsibility squarely. But don't take it too much to heart. There's always the chance of a comeback.

That sounds easy for me to say. But I came very, very close to having to declare bankruptcy back in the *Kung-Fu Monthly* days due to over-trading, and I went through many of the procedures I've just discussed. It's a rotten job, so get it done as fairly and as responsibly as you can. Experience is only a name we give to our failures.

You are now a more experienced person. And next time round you'll ensure that you do not duplicate your earlier mistakes. As old lags tell new inmates in the nick: 'You've done the crime, now do the time. No whingeing.' It's good advice.

KEEPING IT STRAIGHT

Once in the racket, you're always in it.
AL CAPONE, *PHILADELPHIA PUBLIC LEDGER*

Lastly in this section on business catastrophes, I'd like to talk a little about *company* money, *personal* money, and keeping on the straight and narrow. About dealing with temptation and avoiding a particular type of catastrophe for which there is not the remedy of a bankruptcy petition or a sincere apology.

When you start a business, you are taking a risk. Sometimes a huge risk, relatively speaking. This can have the effect, if you're lucky enough to have any success, of muddling in your mind just what money belongs to which party.

It seems simple. It's *your* company, and therefore *your* money. But it isn't, you know. That's not how the law sees it and not how your creditors see it and not how the tax authorities see it. It took me a while to get all this straightened out in my own mind and to learn from one or two unhappy experiences.

If you're game, I hope to be able to save you from the errors I made and that I've seen others make on the subject of what money belongs in which pot. It goes something like this.

A limited liability company is a legal entity. In theory, it is immortal. It has rights and duties just as you do. It cannot be used as a personal milk cow for you to plunder at will. You can certainly milk it, but only within reason, only when there is enough milk to do so, and only in certain ways. If you deviate from permitted methods, you can get yourself in a whole heap of trouble very quickly.

I have a friend, who must remain nameless. You'll see why in a minute. He is a lovely bloke with a fantastic wife and two great kids. He started with a little more capital than I did (that wouldn't have been hard) at about the same time I set out. His business is international in scope and must be worth tens of millions of pounds by now. The compilers of the Sunday Times Rich List certainly think so, and have placed him in the lower reaches of their list for years.

But he has a blind spot. He believes he *is* his company. He thinks he and his company are the same thing. Nothing will persuade him he is not. That's a huge, potentially catastrophic, misunderstanding.

He has a home in Spain, and what a home! He has equipped it with phones, fax and computers and stays there a couple of months every year, with his family. The company owns the house. He used his company's money to buy it. He claims he works from that house – and maybe he does, a little.

But there aren't many people like me. I can sit (I *am* sitting) in one of the loveliest houses on earth and work. I work eight to ten hours every day locked away in a purpose-built work area. And I can prove I work. I make sure I can prove it. I am not *pretending* my house is a place where I work for several months every year. It *is* a place where I work and all the records of telephone calls, computer usage, fax communications and the resulting paperwork proves it. More importantly, I bought my house with my own money, not the company's money.

That's not my friend's way. Not with a beautiful wife and children at an age when you want to spend time snorkelling and playing soccer with them on a Spanish beach. He doesn't really work in his Spanish house. He pretends to. For years, I have warned him he is running a huge risk. His company is paying for a 'benefit in kind' and that's just not on. He is breaking the rules and breaking the law by having the company pay for everything and not declaring a 'benefit in kind'.

And what's so bad about that? Rather a lot, I'm afraid.

If (and I pray it is not *when*) the Inland Revenue catch him, he will be for the high jump. If you use your company's money to buy yourself a fancy car or a house or a boat or anything at all of that nature without declaring it, you are a criminal. Full stop. And sometimes, the Inland Revenue and the VAT collectors put such criminals in jail. As well as fining them huge sums of money. So why does my friend do it? Because *he* founded the company. In his mind, *he* took all the risk and he thinks that whatever money the company has no use for belongs to him. But it doesn't. Not unless it is paid as salary, or a bonus or as a dividend. This is the thing to keep in the forefront of your mind.

It's the *company's* money. Believe it or not, despite the fact that my friend is the sole shareholder in the company, he is not only stealing from the Inland Revenue by his actions, he is *stealing from his own company*. It sounds bizarre. But it's true.

Now I hate taxes as much as the next man. We are ridiculously over-taxed in Britain and the clever-dick 'stealth' taxes that our current government loves to worm into the fine print of every budget are a moral disgrace, as well as counter-productive in raising total revenues. So are our inheritance taxes, our so-called death duties. So are capital gains taxes, in my opinion. But my opinion doesn't count. I do not have judges and police officers and Inland Revenue investigators and jails at my disposal.

The government does. It's crazy to take on an opponent with so much firepower and try to cheat it of what the law says is its due.

There are a thousand other ways sole owners can cheat the Revenue and bilk their company. There's no need for me to list them here – I'm sure you can imagine them easily enough. But listen to me. Don't go there. Just don't go there.

Pay your taxes, remembering that no less a person than a lord chief justice of England once said that an English citizen has not only the *right* but a *duty* to pay only the minimum tax applicable to him. You see, even high court judges aren't too keen on the Inland Revenue! Pay the least tax that is lawful. But pay it.

Because I own numerous companies, I have even set up a private office to ensure that one company isn't paying for me to make calls on behalf of another. It's a good system and has worked well over the years.

It needed to. When you are one of the richest people in the country, the Inland Revenue allots you a special 'watcher'. This experienced civil servant keeps his or her beady eyes on you and your private and corporate tax affairs. I know he's watching me – and he knows that I know he's watching.

Recently, I was investigated by the tax authorities. It was a long investigation and cost the Revenue a good deal of money, I should think. I had never been investigated before. The arguments were complex and related to what tax was owed at what time, as opposed to *whether* tax was owed or not, or how much it all came to.

I was able to settle for a fair sum. (You *always* seem to have to settle in a tax investigation, or so I'm told. The taxman rarely lets you off scot-free.) My advisors and accountants demonstrated that I had never knowingly robbed the Revenue of a penny.

It cost me a lot of money to prove it; some of which will be defrayed against my next tax bill. But I wasn't concerned during the investigation, because I knew I hadn't diddled anybody. That's another reason to keep on the straight and narrow. You don't waste a lot of time covering up and wondering if you will be found out.

The directors of my companies, too, know that I do not 'raid' those companies improperly for cash, or force them to buy me my Rolls-Royce Phantoms, Maybachs and Bentleys. Nor do I get the companies to send me abroad for vacations or ask them to purchase houses for me to live in.

This is not because I am a better man, or ethically and morally superior to my friend. It's because I have been in prison once, for a short while, and I have no intention of going back there again. (I wasn't sent to prison for anything to do with money – it was over a hippy magazine the government took exception to decades ago.)

My friend, however, has never been to prison. Let's hope he never does. But I don't fancy his chances much while he keeps up his idiotic belief that he *is* his company and he can do what he likes with his company's money and cheat the taxman while he's at it.

On a separate and happier subject, if you wind up investing and doing business in the USA, do make certain you become a part of 'the non-double-taxation treaty'. This ensures you are not taxed on profits you made in the States and then taxed on them all over again when you bring the money back to Britain. Or vice versa.

As for becoming a tax exile (leaving a country to avoid paying tax by exploiting loopholes in the law), I tried it once, twenty-odd years ago. It may work for some people, but I found it tiresome, oddly disturbing and counter-productive. (Mind you, the capital gains tax in those days was *astronomical* – something like 80 or 90 per cent, so it was understandable that many of us were on the same Concorde flight on 3 April 1983! You see? The date is engraved on my soul. Exile of any sort is never pleasant and rarely worth the bother.)

How to sum all this up? I'm not an accountant, but it goes like this, I think. If your company can afford to pay you money, then that's fine, as long as you declare that it has been paid and get ready to pay the tax on that payment. If you find other ways of moving the company's money into your own pocket without reporting the movement or using a company asset for your personal life, you're almost certainly milking the cow in a way that is not permitted.

It's that simple. And my advice is to keep it simple, and to hire competent tax advisors just as soon as you begin earning money over and above your salary.

After all, what's the point of getting rich and then sitting for a year or more behind bars in a nasty, dangerous environment while the authorities figure out just how much they are going to fine you and how long you are going to rot there? Prisons may have improved since the days of Newgate, but I can assure you they are not pleasant places to be.

There are a thousand professionals who will show you how to pay the minimum tax possible in return for a fee. I reckon that an investment in those services, extortionate as they may seem, is a far better one than fiddling what you should have paid the taxman in the first place.

Getting rich isn't so difficult. But if you want to *stay* rich, then pay your taxes and don't milk the cow without reporting it. End of lecture.

17

A RECAP
FOR IDLERS

Here we all are in no-man's land,
The lame and the halt, the sick and the damned;
Tunnelling dirt and shovelling sand,
Here we all are in no man's land ...
'NO-MAN'S LAND'

Most of us love short cuts, though they often lead us astray. Or magic bullets which we are told will solve an intractable problem, though we know they don't really exist. Not in the real world.

This desire to 'cut to the chase' is perfectly understandable. Our lives are short, and none of us is getting any younger. But if you've just picked up this book and have turned straight to this chapter, then I'm afraid you're probably in for a disappointment. 'A Recap for Idlers' is not a short cut or a magic bullet to save you reading the rest of the book. Instead, I am going to attempt to recap the 'important bits', or rather, the bits that I now believe were important when I was getting rich myself.

So please be warned: parts of what follow won't make much sense if you are unfamiliar with what came before.

THE QUEST FOR WEALTH: A HEALTH WARNING

There is no fortress so strong that money cannot take it.
CICERO, *IN VERREM*

Cicero was a subtle man. Money *can* reduce any fortress; but which fortress is he speaking of, do you think? The *enemy's* (whoever the 'enemy' may be) or your own? Let us assume it is the latter.

So what *is* your fortress? It is your inner core, your integrity, your belief in the worth of others and the love of those dear to you. Not to mention your own worth. It arises from belief in yourself. And, for a few, from a belief in their own destiny.

Excessive idolatry of money will 'take' all those. It will corrode both self-belief and love. It will stretch integrity on the rack. It will 'take' the fortress; and it will not be a pretty sight.

Seeking substantial wealth is almost always a fool's game. The statistics show that very few people ever succeed. Most of them should never have made the attempt in the first place. They aren't suited to it, and if that sounds defeatist, then consider the fact that the search will take up a great deal of your waking life for many, many years.

You cannot get rich without 'wasting' that time. Not unless you were born lucky – so lucky that luck has squatted on your shoulder virtually from birth. You would not need to get rich, then. You would already *be* rich, in one way or another.

Time is finite. Which is a fancy way of saying that you only have so much of it – then it will run out. When you are young, time seems to stretch into the distance for so far that surely it will always be on your side? When the young catch the old unawares, they may sometimes glimpse a look of naked envy, which is then instantly disguised.

And the old have reason to be envious. Truly, truly, they do. Ask me what I will give you if you could wave a magic wand

and give me my youth back. The answer would be everything I own and everything I will ever own. In *The Odyssey* we read:

> *And Achilles replied, 'Do not speak soothingly to me of death, glorious Odysseus. I would rather live on earth as a bondsman to the meanest peasant, than be king of all the shadows.'*

Homer, as always, is right.

If you are young and reading this then I ask you to remember just this: you are richer than anyone older than you, and far richer than those who are much older. What you choose to do with the time that stretches out before you is entirely a matter for you. But do not say you started the journey poor. If you are young, you are infinitely richer than I can ever be again.

Money is never owned. It is only in your custody for a while. Time is always running on, and the young have more of it in their pocket than the richest man or woman alive. That is not sentimentality speaking. That is sober fact.

And yet you wish to waste your youth in the getting of money? Really? Think hard, my young cub, think hard and think long before you embark on such a quest. The time spent attempting to acquire wealth will mount up and cannot be reclaimed, whether you succeed or whether you fail.

Even should you succeed in becoming rich, unlikely as that is, what will you have achieved? Independence of a kind? The luxury to choose what you wish to do with the rest of your life? Happiness? No, no and no. You will not achieve any of those things. Not when you have too much money.

As Francis Bacon, one of the greatest minds ever to grace England's corridors of power, warned in his *Essays*:

> *I cannot call Riches better than the baggage [hindrance] of virtue. The Roman word is better, impedimenta. For as the*

> *baggage is to an army, so riches to virtue. It cannot be*
> *spared or left behind, but it hindereth the march; yea, and*
> *the care of it sometime loseth or disturbeth the victory.*

It does indeed. Wealth makes many demands and, by the time you have acquired it, you will be prey to certain habits. You will fear to lose it and must spend a great deal more time to defend it. No one is 'independent' of the human race. 'No man is an island entire of *itself*; every man is a piece of the *continent*, a part of the *main*.' Heed the words of John Donne, finest of poets: 'And therefore never send to know for whom the bell tolls: it tolls for thee.' Aye, so it does.

No luxury of choices for rich little you. You will be too busy keeping the sea from washing away the sand you have spent so long collecting at such terrible cost to your health and your sanity and your relationships with others. It is always thus. There is no escape. You believe (I know you do) that it will be different for you. But it won't be. It never is.

Happiness? Do not make me laugh. The rich are not *happy*. I have yet to meet a single really rich happy man or woman – and I have met many rich people. The demands from others to share their wealth become so tiresome, and so insistent, they nearly always decide they must insulate themselves. Insulation breeds paranoia and arrogance. And loneliness. And rage that you have only so many years left to enjoy rolling in the sand you have piled up.

The only people the self-made rich can trust are those who knew them *before* they became wealthy. For many newly rich people, the world becomes a smaller, less generous and darker place. It sounds ridiculous, doesn't it? Ridiculous and gloomy.

But then, you are to consider that I have been very poor and I am now very rich. I am an optimist by nature. And I have the ability to write poetry and create the forest I am busy planting. Am I happy? No. Or, at least, only occasionally, when I am walking in the woods alone, or deeply ensconced in composing a difficult piece of verse, or sitting quietly with old friends over a bottle of wine. Or feeding a stray cat.

I could do all those things without wealth. So why do I not give it all away?

Because I worked too hard for it. Because I am tainted by it. Because I am afraid to. All those reasons and more. Perhaps, if I am lucky enough to become old, I will accumulate something else: the courage to give it all away before I die. That would be a good thing, I think.

(When I die, it is all going to a charity called 'The Forest of Dennis'. You see, even when I do a good thing with my money, my ego insists that I name it for myself. Not a good sign.)

Giving money away when you are dead takes no guts. No courage. But to divest yourself of hundreds of millions of dollars, or the greater part of your fortune, *before* your death? That would be something to be proud of, don't you think? It even makes logical sense.

For what is left afterwards but a few tears by a graveside and years of bickering and waste over a complex will? (The wills of the rich are always complex.) Bitter years, where lawyers count the number of fairies they believe you once thought danced upon the head of a pin – years in which they enrich themselves at your descendants' expense. A fine legacy, to be sure.

But you must make your own choice. I have said my piece and I meant every word of it. This small part of my book was composed in my mind years ago. It was easy to write. I knew all of it before my fingers touched the keyboard. It has troubled me for years and I thank you for allowing me to share it.

I suspect it will have little effect on you, though. You are probably young and are tired of being poor. And tired, from years of growing up and schooling, of being lectured. Very well. Let us return to a recap of the 'important bits' to help you on your journey. But just before we do, can I ask you to do me a small favour?

Please lodge one fact in your memory: that the last one thousand five hundred words *was* an 'important bit'. In my heart of hearts, I know it was *the* most important bit you will read in this book.

Mark it with a bookmark and write today's date upon it. Come back to it in twenty or thirty years, when new books printed on paper will be rare objects. Then cast your mind back to a time when you were young, and you first read this book, and to the thoughts of a fool, a rich poet, long dead, who once typed these words sitting in one of the most beautiful houses on earth, staring at a turquoise sea, sipping a glass of slightly chilled Chateau d'Yquem.

That will be enough for me.

Enough! Let's get on with getting rich!

CUT LOOSE

When all the world is young, lad,
And all the trees are green;
And every goose a swan, lad,
And every lass a queen;
Then hey for boot and horse, lad,
And round the world away;
Young blood must have its course, lad,
And every dog his day.

CHARLES KINGSLEY, FROM *THE WATER BABIES*

You have to cut loose to get rich. There isn't any other way.

Firstly, of course, you must break loose from your parents and family home. It's possible to get rich from your bedroom while your mother is ironing your shirt or blouse downstairs, I suppose. But it's unlikely.

I read in my magazine *The Week* (shameless plug) that hundreds of thousands of young men in Japan are isolating themselves in their bedrooms for months or even years at a time in a growing phenomenon known as *hikikomori*, or 'withdrawal'.

How ineffably sad. Modern society is breeding a race of New Age young hermits. The article goes on to report that many parents can support such children indefinitely, and they choose to do so. 'Japanese parents tell their children to fly,' one expert told *The New York Times*, 'while holding firmly to their ankles.'

Let's assume you have no wish to spend the next few years locked in your bedroom. What then? Perhaps you are already working. Perhaps you are living with someone, or are married, or have children. No matter. As long as you have cut the parental knot, you are in good shape.

Now you must cut yourself loose from naysayers and negative influences: the Jeremiahs. These wretches cover the face of the earth. They will tell you, if you listen, about the impossibility (not the foolishness) of trying to make yourself wealthy. In doing so, they drain confidence and optimism from you. Such people often include your parents, your lover, your husband or your wife, and your 'friends'. Which is not surprising. It's not that they do not care about you. They may well do so, in their own way. But two cardinal fears rule their concern.

Firstly, they fear that you are placing yourself in harm's way – and, to them, that cannot be a good thing. Secondly, they fear that if you should succeed, you will expose their own timidity to the light of day.

The order in the 'pack' from which you spring, the family grouping, will be shattered. Should you become rich you will become the number-one dog in the pack, and their own order will slip accordingly. Above all, they do not wish to be faced with the mess and chaos that accompanies strenuous effort. They want the familiarity and sense of false security that comes with things staying as they are.

Do not despise these people. Seek to calm them. Or hide from them what you are about for as long as you can. If that will not work, ignore them and move on. That is a hard thing to say and a harder thing to do, but it is necessary. You cannot spend your life assuaging the fear of failure (and success) that is the common lot of the risk averse.

Should you have parents who are *too* ambitious for your future, then much the same advice applies. The stereotype for this in the twentieth century was the American Jewish mother, determined that her sons should become doctors or lawyers. This is all very well, but it will not make you rich, because, in its way, it is yet another attempt to slot you into a preordained path. You must cut loose from it to become wealthy. Or to be happy, for that matter.

Fear of failure is a subject about which I have already written in this book, probably to excess. I repeat that it is the main stumbling block to getting rich for most people. You simply have to face up to it, stare it in the eye and cut loose from such thoughts. Here is Robert Johnson, perhaps the greatest blues guitarist who ever lived, singing about fear of failure:

> *I got stones in my passway and my road seems dark at night.*
> *I got stones in my passway and my road seems dark at night,*
> *I have pains in my heart, they have taken my appetite.*

No doubt. Johnson died of poison, administered by the lover or husband of a girl he was making eyes at in a juke joint. The story goes that he was *warned* that his drink had been poisoned. He smiled and drank it anyway. It took him a day or so to die, in agony one assumes.

I have often wondered why he did it. Perhaps it was because he already knew how great a musician he was. (When I say Johnson was the greatest blues guitarist who ever lived, I mean precisely that. He is worshipped by musicians such as Eric Clapton and Ry Cooder.) Such knowledge breeds the kind of recklessness you see when people walk right to the edge of a cliff and perform a handstand, just for the hell of it.

I used to do such things myself. I would run across a narrow waterpipe that spanned a canal and weir. If I had fallen, I would probably have drowned. The canal was near a pub where I used to play with an R&B band. Some nights, I would earn more money from bystanders by running backwards and forwards across that pipe than from my performance fee. It was stupid and dangerous. But somehow, I *knew* I wouldn't fall.

I'm not suggesting you begin doing handstands on clifftops or risking life and limb. But I *am* suggesting that you must cut loose, in your mind, from your previous life. Getting rich comes from an attitude of mind. It isn't going to happen if things drift on pretty much the way they are right now.

Cutting loose can be painful. I have heard of very few men or women who made a ton of money who did not leave, or divorce, their wives or husbands or lovers sooner or later. Or who were not estranged from family members, often their children. It comes with the territory. Even if you hand over large sums as a gift to those you had to cut loose from to get it, they will never really forgive you.

It isn't the money, you see. It is because you have humiliated them, in their minds anyway, both by succeeding and by valuing the time it took for you to succeed over their part in your life. And that, in a nutshell, is why it is so important to cut loose, especially in the early days.

Focus, determination and relentless drive are wearing in themselves – both to you and those around you. Any distraction whatever can cost you a chance that may not come again. And, for the purposes of this book, family, lovers and friends are distractions, plain and simple.

There are exceptions, of course, and perhaps you will be one of them. But don't count on it. Chances are that you will have to cut loose from your old life in more ways than you imagine and that the breach will never really be healed.

Lastly, it goes without saying that you must cut loose from

working for other people. If you have been gainfully employed since you left school or college, this is an oddly difficult thing to do.

It is dunned into our head that we should work. Western civilisation is based upon a work ethic that has propelled it into the front rank of the tribes and cultures we share this planet with. If you have ever stood, early in the morning, on a weekday in New York City and watched the countless tens of thousands of workers hurrying to their steel and glass towers, you can catch a scent of this ethic. It is frightening, but exhilarating, too. The air itself reeks of drive, and determination and focus. It is like a drug. And it has served America and her people well – at least in the sense of material wealth.

Now you must leave the safety of the ant colony and the hive. You are to become a loner, an outcast, cut off from the very thing that defines what many of us believe we are. What is the first question usually asked by strangers of each other? Right, it's 'What do you do?' In some cultures, the way of answering may be different; but it nearly always relates to work in the West: 'I'm a teacher; I'm in banking; I'm a dairy farmer; I'm an HR administrator; I'm a sound engineer.' Our job defines us.

But it cannot define you. Not any more. You are a wild pig rooting for truffles. You are a weasel about to rip the throat out of a rabbit. You are an entrepreneur. You are going to be rich, and you don't much care, within the law, how you are going to do it.

I recently attended a funeral. These days, I attend too many of them. The elderly mother of one of my girlfriends at school was there. Truth to tell, I had forgotten of her existence. I only dated her daughter once or twice.

The old lady looked me up and down in a disquieting way and I had a vision of a much younger woman cutting me a slice of cake and pouring me a cup of tea.

'So you did it,' she said, her thin lips half smiling, but compressed in a disapproving line.

'Uh-huh,' I replied, not knowing what the hell she was talking about.

'I hope it was worth it?'

'What was worth what, ma'am?'

'You used to frighten me, did you know that? Oh, I was frightened you would marry Sally. But I was frightened of *you*. I was a mother and thirty years older than you. But you scared the hell out of me. I told Sally to stay away from you.'

'Yes, I remember. Why?'

'Because when you first began coming around after Sally, I asked you what you were going to do when you left school. You looked me in the eye. Your eyes weren't like any teenager I ever knew. They were fierce, like a tiger's. You were insolent and arrogant and frightening. I told my husband so.'

'I'm sorry for that.'

'You told me you were going to get rich. Not that you were going to university or were after this or that job. Just that you were going to be rich. I never forgot it.'

I made some inane reply and tried to jolly her along. But she wasn't having any. The one advantage about being old is that you can say whatever the damn hell you please and younger people have to listen to it.

She'd said her piece. She had no more to say. I left the funeral with a double burden. Not just the death of an old friend, but the knowledge that I had frightened a woman who had tried to be kind to me when I was a boy. Not exactly an epitaph to be proud of, is it?

But she was right. I *was* like that. And so will you be. You will do anything it takes, short of larceny, fraud, blackmail and murder. You will cut yourself loose, but the tiger chained to your ankle will come right along with you. He will always be with you, until the day you turn him loose by an effort of will.

By cutting loose, you will be free to make a whopping great fortune while your tiger scares the hell out of little old ladies.

And old gentlemen for that matter. And if you do not have a tiger handy, I suggest you acquire one quickly if you wish to amass serious wealth.

No matter. We are not here to discuss the rag-and-bone shop of your heart or make metaphors about tigers.

Cut loose, my friend. Cut loose and get rich.

CHOOSE THE RIGHT MOUNTAIN

There stands a lady on a mountain,
Who she is I do not know,
All she wants is gold and silver;
I shall to the mountain go!

ANON. 'KISS IN THE RING'

The world is full of money. Some of that money has your name on it. All you have to do is collect it.

If you are not just reading this book for a bit of entertainment (nothing wrong with that), and if you seriously do wish to get rich, then I am going to ask you to memorise the words below, close the book and repeat the words again to yourself. Let's go:

THE WORLD IS FULL OF MONEY. SOME OF IT HAS MY NAME ON IT. ALL I HAVE TO DO IS COLLECT IT.

Done that? OK, now we're rockin' and rollin'. The first question to answer is where *is* the goddamn money? Let's imagine it is in a mine in a mountain. Fine. Which mountain? The mountain that is already making a lot of other people rich would be a good bet.

Gold rushes don't happen in old mines. There will be people making a good living out of old mines, but they won't be too keen to let you muscle in on their stake. Look for new mountains where gold is being mined; or will be mined soon.

Let us speak plainly. This is not the time to begin a chain of car dealerships. Car dealerships are great, but it's an old mine. Don't go there unless you have a brand new angle. Making and distributing beer is an old mine. Unless you have a new angle (like 'real ale'), then that's a mountain to avoid. Of course, if you're really imaginative, you can often come up with such an angle.

In St Vincent and the Grenadines, a small country of which I am a proud citizen, there is a beer company. They make a good beer called Hairoun. I expect the company makes decent money even though the entire country only has 120,000 citizens. Could I muscle in on this market?

Yes.

How?

I would invent a new beer. I would print a number inside each bottle cap. I would set up a lottery, with the agreement of the government. There would be a draw once a month. Whoever produced the beer cap with the winning number would win a substantial cash prize. Fifty per cent of the lottery money would go to the winner. Ten per cent would go to the government. Forty per cent would go to good causes – children in need, orphans, education, that kind of thing.

I would then launch my beer with the kind of advertising blitz that St Vincent and the Grenadines has never (mercifully) seen. I would make television commercials where a bartender asks a good-looking Vincentian man if he wants another beer. 'Sure,' he'll reply. 'I'll have one for the widows and orphans.' Big grin. Frothy beer slapped on the counter. Logos for the beer explode on screen surrounded by falling money.

My beer would wipe the floor with Hairoun. (Hey! this is a hypothetical example we're exploring here.) Everybody wants to get rich. Once a month people smiling and holding a big cheque would appear on television advertising my beer. I would begin exporting the beer to other islands and doing the same trick there. What would I call my beer? Let's see: the slang for a

Vincentian citizen is 'Vincy'. That's it! I'll call it Vincy Beer. The slogan will be: 'One for the Widows and Orphans'. Or: 'The Beer for Winners'.

(OK, OK, I'm not as good at making up marketing slogans as I am at brewing beer.) So why have I told you this, and thereby warned the brewers and distributors of Hairoun of my evil intentions concerning my (truly) great idea? Easy. Because I have about a hundred good ideas every day. Ideas are ten a penny. And because I have no intention of going into the beer business. (Or is that a double bluff?)

You see, you have to choose a new mine where you suspect there is money, or an old mine with a different angle to get rich. The right mountain. A great new mine right now is in telecommunications, or the internet, or legalised gambling. Property is always good. (You can start small in property and you can get lucky quickly. It's a crowded market, though, for that very reason.)

It's vital you choose a mountain which produces money that has your name on it. Your instinct should come into play here. Everything depends, just for once, on what you feel drawn towards and what repels you. I have always hated watching television. Paradoxically, I have always fancied being a producer or director of mindless garbage. I think I missed a trick by not going into television earlier – although one of my companies in Beverly Hills is busy at it right now.

One thing is for sure, you must avoid the trap of going into what you think will make you money if you have no empathy or feeling for what you are about to do. There's no future in that.

I know an editor and writer. He's a great editor and writer. But he feels he *has* to be a publisher and do all the stuff that publishers do – like wear suits, write cheques and hire and fire people. He's crazy. He will never be rich because he will not use his vast writing and editing talent to the full. He's always too busy being a lousy businessman.

Avoid that trap. Don't do anything because you feel you

have to. Go for what attracts you. Go for something that exploits your natural talents.

Go to the mountain which produces money. Money that has your name on it.

FEAR NOTHING

*No passion so effectually robs the mind of all its powers
of acting and reasoning as fear.*
EDMUND BURKE, *THE SUBLIME AND BEAUTIFUL*

Fear nothing. Another easy-to-say and impossible piece of advice. Tough luck, chum. Life's a bitch and then you die. Get used to it. It isn't going to change any time soon.

What is there to fear? Everything and nothing. Try looking at it through my eyes. I am an insignificant little worm on an insignificant planet which circles an insignificant star in a big (presumably) bad universe. A universe I will never comprehend, nor can ever hope to comprehend.

Just like everything that walks, breathes, grows, flies, crawls or swims, I am going to die. One day, my planet will die. Long, long after, the sun it still circles as a dead rock will die. Then there will be darkness on the face of the earth. That is, there *would* be darkness if there was any creature alive to view it.

Armies and governments fear men or women who know they are going to die soon; and they have good reason to. Such people have nothing to lose. They will commit any atrocity and take as many others with them as they can, if they are driven to it. *You* must now become that doomed man or woman. You are going to *die*. Nothing can alter the fact. It is immutable. Incomprehensible. Unfair. All those things.

But it sets you free, don't you see? It sets you *free*.

What does anything matter if you are going to die? Nothing matters. Nothing at all. Get that through your terrified mind and you will wake up in the morning ready to rip the throat out of the first gazelle unfortunate enough to cross your path. Why would you rip its throat out? Because you *can*. Not for breakfast. Not for the 'thrill of the chase'. But because you *can*.

If you want to be rich you must make a pact with yourself about fear of anything. You cannot banish fear, but you can face it down, stomp on it, crush it, bury it, padlock it into the deepest recesses of your heart and soul and leave it there to rot.

Just try. Try for just a single day, a whole day when you refuse to acknowledge fear of failure, fear of making yourself look like an idiot, fear of losing your lover, fear of losing your job, fear of your boss, fear of anything and of any kind. Fear will creep back, usually at three in the morning. Laugh at it and tell it to take a hike. Smash it in the teeth. Spit on it. Put your arms round it and make nicey-nicey. Then slip a sharp blade into its stinking throat just as you're French-kissing it.

Go on. I dare you. If you can do it, this will transform your life. Not for the better. I didn't promise you that. But you will instantly perceive (among many other things) just how much *money* there is in the world and how pitifully easy it is to *obtain* it. Money that already has your name on it.

All that is stopping you is fear. I do not know of what kind. It may even be fear of succeeding. But if you want to be rich, gentle reader, and if you can read these words, then all that is stopping you is fear of one kind or another. You have no one to blame but yourself. The world is full of gazelles with diamonds in their guts.

Look! There's one over there, right now! Let's go rip its throat out and take the diamond. Maybe there will be *two* diamonds. If there aren't, then *I'm* keeping the first diamond, you understand? Otherwise I'll rip *your* throat out, too. Come on! There's nothing to fear. Let's get rich!

That is what getting rich is going to be like. You will become a predator. A killer. You will cease to be prey. You will not succumb to fear. Others will fear you. Especially gazelles bearing diamonds.

This will make no difference to an insignificant worm on an insignificant planet circling an insignificant star. No difference whatever. Nothing can hold back the coming dark. Nothing can alter the fact that you will cease one day to breathe and think. Nothing can amend the truth that within a few million circlings of a rock around a dying sun, there will remain no trace of you, your tribe, your race or your diamonds. Nothing can alter that.

But just for a moment (just for *one* moment, you understand?) just for a heartbeat in the life of the planet, one little worm, who thinks he is a tiger, will be rich.

Much of what I have written in this book may be wrong. Misguided. 'Tosh' as we used to say in my school playground. I accept that. I am far from infallible on the subject of getting rich. But this last short essay concerning fear and its influence is, I think, wholly true. It *is* fear that rules us. Love and respect and other such emotions make it bearable, at a price. But fear rules us all, and always has.

Which is odd. Because what can there *be* for us to fear, when each of us knows we shall die eventually? Is it a definition of sentiency?

Fear is no bad thing, perhaps. I have been feeding a feral cat here on Mustique in my new cottage for the last few weeks while I wrote this book. She is a tabby I call Stringy because her tail is so thin. She comes to my porch when I call twice a day. Yesterday, she finally peeked, and then edged, into the cottage itself and padded across the Persian rugs. Within minutes, she was playing with the rug tassels like a kitten. Maybe she had no kittenhood, in the eat-or-be-eaten world of feral cats.

Yet she takes flight at the least sound or movement. If the refrigerator turns itself on, or if I rise from my chair or move suddenly, she scoots to the door. Why? She is safe here and must be beginning to sense the fact. She is eating better than she has ever eaten in her life. She has grown used to the delicious taste of cow's milk. Not to mention smoked salmon. So why does she flee?

Fear rules her life. That is why she flees. Fear keeps her safe from her enemies – though there are no predators on the island to trouble her, except man. Perhaps I should be careful not to cause her to lose her fear of humans completely, even if I could do such a thing. Perhaps she is better off running scared of her own shadow.

To be rich, if that is still your desire, you must somehow learn to harness fear to your own advantage. Is that what I have done in my own life? Was all that rage and fierceness and drive and stamina rooted in my own fear? Have I used fear as a fuel in the getting of money?

Perhaps I have, although I never thought of it that way before. In any case, I'm not certain I *want* to know. I have never trusted armchair psychiatry.

But I *do* know that you must make an accommodation with your fears if you are to succeed. At least, I know that to be true in my own case. As to how such a trick is to be accomplished, I cannot help you. We each, in turn, must face down our secret demons, if we can, whether we wish to be rich or not. To succeed in the game of piling up material wealth, it becomes a necessity.

In the words of the wisest of men, William Shakespeare: 'Present fears are less than horrible imaginings.'

Aye, that they are, William, that they are. 'Horrible imaginings' will rule all our lives if we are fools enough to let them.

GO! GO! GO!

He either fears his fate too much,
Or his deserts are small,
That puts it not unto the touch
To win or lose it all.

JAMES GRAHAM, MARQUESS OF MONTROSE, 'MY DEAR AND ONLY LOVE'

You have little time to waste, gentle reader. Even as you read these words, a clock is ticking and time is streaming by, governed by the speed of light, racing towards a point where you will have no more need of clocks, or light, or money.

So many hundreds of millions of dollars to make – so little time! What are you waiting for?

We used to have an expression in the England of my youth: 'On yer bike!' And that's what you must be about shortly. On your bicycle and pedalling for all you are worth against your only true enemy. Time. In four of the most memorable lines in English poetry, Andrew Marvell, attempting to persuade a young lass to come to his bed, put it thus:

> *Had we but world enough and time,*
> *This coyness, lady, were no crime.*
> *. . . . .*
> *The grave's a fine and private place,*
> *But none, I think, do there embrace.*

There's the nub of it. You have less time than you think. We all do. Why then are you waiting to fulfil your perfectly legitimate, if foolish, desire? If you do not start today, then when *will* you start? Tomorrow? Next year? The year after?

You will *never* start unless you start NOW!

That's right. Right now. Even as your eyes scan this page, your brain should be plotting and planning ideas and possibilities, weaving a web to ensnare what you *could* achieve, if only you will cease this endless prevarication and commit yourself.

Commit yourself heart and soul, mind. Heart and soul. No half measures or lukewarm approach is likely to succeed in what William Butler Yeats called 'this pragmatical, preposterous pig of a world'. Your quest is mad. What use to muddy the waters with logic and statistics – bugaboos that will only serve to discourage you from taking the plunge?

There is a place for impetuosity and leaps of faith. A place for belief. That place is here. And the time is now. You must take your first steps on the long, lonely road to wealth by beginning now, or you must hurl this book into the fire, or out the window, for all the good it will do you.

When opportunities come you must pounce. Whether you are just starting out or have been at it for a long while. If an opportunity should arrive just as you are taking your family on vacation, for example, do not weaken. Let the family go on without you or cancel the trip altogether. I can tell you a true story of a man who lost millions and millions of pounds that were his for the taking because he went on vacation.

The magazine that generated my first huge pile twenty-five years ago fell to me when the managing director of a large rival suspended negotiations with the founder of the magazine while he went abroad. He probably figured the deal was nearly done and the seller could cool his heels for a week or two. It wasn't important enough for him to change his travel plans.

Naturally enough, this angered the young man attempting to sell his prized asset. It was disrespectful. By the time that managing director returned from abroad, a majority interest in the magazine was mine, signed, sealed and delivered to Dennis Publishing.

My rival deserved to lose out. He prevaricated. He wasted his opportunity to purchase a magazine that has since generated way over $100,000,000 in gross revenues. You can forgive yourself for not doing something if you honestly got it wrong. But it is harder to forgive yourself when lack of impetus allows it to slip through your fingers.

Need will drive you, but you must not prevaricate. You must act at the slightest hint of a chance to make money. You must go, go, go!

My little feral cat, Stringy, crept into my cottage driven by desperate need. She was hungry. She was reckless to enter. I might have slammed the door, grabbed her and roasted her! How would she know otherwise? Yet in she came, driven by want and desire. Now she feasts on the finest meat, fish and milk money can buy – twice a day. She seized her opportunity.

You may have many reasons for caution and proceeding carefully. There always are such reasons. They creep about a fearful mind like Tolkien's Gollum, wearing spirit to a shadow and sapping optimism with dread. Cast them out, these 'reasons'. They are nothing. They are sprites and fancies of your imagination that will vanish if you so much as say boo! to their lickspittle goose.

If you wish to get rich, there are no reasons why you should not get rich. *None at all.*

For they are not 'reasons'; they are *excuses*. For the most part they are pitiful *alibis, half truths* and self-serving *evasions* you have erected to spare yourself from the quiet terror of taking your own financial life in your hands and making your dreams concrete reality. They are the children of fear and the parents of a thousand 'if onlys'.

It may well be true, should you succeed, that you will discover you are not as happy as you once believed wealth might make you. But is that a reason for not beginning? Perhaps I will be proved wrong and you will become rich *and* as happy as a lark in spring. Who knows? You will never find out if you do not try, and if you do not begin trying *now*.

Believe me, I have heard all the reasons. They have been laid out for my inspection on scores of occasions by people in a similar position to yourself. Even by several of my godchildren. On close examination, they have all proven to be bogus.

The only three valid reasons for not attempting to become rich are: 'I do not wish to be rich.' Or, 'I wish to be rich but I have other priorities.' Or, 'I am too stupid to try to get rich.'

These are valid reasons, especially the last. As for the second, what kind of a world would we live in if Vincent van Gogh had never painted, if Beethoven had had no time to compose symphonies, if Emily Dickinson had never written a poem or if Narcis Monturiol had not perfected the world's first, fully fledged, double-hulled submarine? All of them died relatively poor or flat broke. Nor have I ever read that giants of thought and philosophy fared much better.

And what of your family? Ah, yes; what kind of a childhood would you have had if your mother and father had abandoned you to a wet, dark cot while they scrabbled day and night to become wealthy? So, yes, there are valid reasons. But not many of us can lay claim to them. Most of us are ordinary Joes. We will never compose a symphony or invent the modern submarine. And a great many of us will not have children.

Which leads me to what, I suspect, will prove a controversial take on the subject of having children and getting rich. No one who has not had a child can know the depths of anguish and joy that parents endure. I accept that as a childless man. But so often, children are used as a bogus trump card in any debate on the central theme of this book.

'It's OK for you, but I have responsibilities. My family comes first.' Yes, yes, yes. I am sure you feel better having got that off your chest. But how much real truth is there in it?

I have many godchildren. I have watched, closely in some cases, as newborn babes become toddlers, as young tykes shoot through school and college and as body-pierced immortals launch themselves like demons of the pit upon an unsuspecting world. And I have seen the relationship between children and their parents alter. Close-up and personal.

It is my belief that children do not care if parents are rich or poor, providing there is enough money for basic essentials like food, clothing and shelter. What they care about is unconditional love. That is the only key, the only true priority, although they neither know it, nor say so, after five or six years old.

In my formative years, I was brought up in surroundings that our politically correct age would describe as 'modest'. For part of my early childhood we lived in my grandparents' tiny terraced house, two steps up from a slum (although kept spotlessly clean) with no electricity, no kitchen that you would recognise as one, and no indoor lavatory or bathroom. The tin bath hung in the coal shed to keep it from going rusty. There was no heating but a coal fire in the parlour. No light but gas and candles.

In the affluent West, that's poor, my friend, any way you cut it. If times were tight, the nasty, shiny Izal lavatory paper that came in a box would vanish from the outside lavatory to be replaced by neatly torn squares of newspaper hanging on a butcher's hook. Personally, I preferred the newspaper and always kept a secret stash in the garden shed.

Then my mother's career began to flourish and our lives changed. We became 'middle class' overnight. I got a bike. There was a smart bathroom in our new garden flat with a modern bath and hot water pouring out of the tap. The lavatory paper came in soft, comfy rolls. We were allowed pets and we had a lawn with a big tree to play cowboys and Indians in. Was I a mite happier?

I don't believe so. I had a *wonderful* time in my grandparents' house. All the other kids in the alley there were in the same boat. We didn't even *know* we were poor. Material surroundings are of far more importance to adults than to children.

Logically, then, the excuse 'I have got responsibilities' can only refer in most cases to the unconditional love part. Young children neither know nor care if their mummy and daddy are rich. It doesn't enter into the equation. But the unconditional love part, and especially its expression, are central to any child's well-being.

Now you can see, perhaps, why I have little time for what appears, at first, to be a Teflon-coated excuse. At least, in many cases. If you want to be rich and you have young children, then do not use them as your alibi for not making the attempt. Or, if you must use their existence as an alibi, then at least have the courtesy, the decency, to acknowledge that such reasoning is *nothing* but an alibi.

Of course, scrabbling to get rich is harder for those with than it is for those without children. I do not deny that. But it *has* been done, and done thousands of times, to boot. It is *not* a fatal impediment, merely another 'stone in your passway', as Robert Johnson would put it.

I happen to know a man, a relative of sorts, who has many of the character ingredients of an entrepreneur, and yet has remained poor all his life. He is a pain in the neck. For years I had to listen to his blowhard spouting about how many of his ideas would have changed the world, if only he had not had children and 'responsibilities'.

Finally, I went out and bought him a copy of a Louis Jordan CD and played it to him at full blast. Here's one of the verses:

> *I been hearin' all about all your big ideas*
> *Since you started. What's the hitch?*
> *You ain't never made ten dollars yet,*
> *Yet you say you can balance the national debt,*
> *If you're so smart,*
> *How come you ain't rich?*

He blustered as usual, so I gave him my 'alibi' speech, in front of his wife and children. Then I left the house, which was in uproar. I doubt I will ever be invited back – which is fine by me.

His kids, who are fully grown, were in secret ecstasy when I played that record. Fancy having to listen endlessly to a father who, between the lines, is blaming *you* for his and his wife's relative poverty. What a schmuck. What a silly man.

Watch out for blowhards. There are a lot of them out there and they are very negative influences. They can stop you from getting started, from getting going, from taking a massive running leap into the dark. Always remember that they *want* you to fail, just as they did. Ignore them.

That clock is still ticking. It's been travelling at the speed of light while you read all this. Now is the time. Now is the hour. Let's go. Come on, brother and sister, up off your idle butt. Let's find ourselves a gazelle with diamonds in its entrails.

Time to go. Let's GO! GO! GO!

Let's go and get *rich*!

THE UPSIDE-DOWN PYRAMID
FOR GETTING RICH

1. Commit or don't commit. No half-measures.
2. Cut loose from all negative influences.
3. Choose the right mountain.
4. Fear nothing.
5. Start now.
6. Go!

18

HOW TO
STAY RICH

So on we worked, and waited for the light,
And went without meat, and cursed the bread;
And Richard Cory, one dark summer night,
Went home and put a bullet through his head.

EDWARD ARLINGTON ROBINSON, 'RICHARD CORY'

You can skip this chapter if you want. It won't help you to get rich. But it might help you *stay* rich. Big difference.

It's been fun. Writing this book, I mean. It's taken me nearly eight weeks. But I have to get back to work now – planting trees, writing poetry, making money. That sort of thing. So this chapter is an 'extra', if you like. I'm writing it because I'm enjoying myself.

THE PERILS OF WEALTH

I'm no great prose writer (and no great philosopher, either) but I've read a lot and lived a lot and made a lot and spent a lot – and played the fool with it all to a highly satisfactory degree. Hundreds of millions of dollars have 'trickled down' (to use Margaret Thatcher's much-mocked, much-used phrase) from my leaky fingers into the general economy and the outstretched hands of various trades and professions and charities.

Wine and narcotic suppliers did exceptionally well out of me over the years. So did real-estate agents, book sellers, young ladies of easy virtue and upmarket British car manufacturers.

I spent a hell of a lot of what I made on sex and drugs and rock 'n' roll. The rest – as the footballer Georgie Best joked just before he died recently – I wasted. It's the usual old story. But whores have to make a living and so do purveyors of French wine and single malt whisky.

(To be serious for a moment, some of the smartest, nicest people I ever met in my life were whores. But only one of them, out of the hundreds I have known, ever got rich. A Saudi Prince picked her up in a nightclub. The rest is history. But she was one in a million. Whoring is a particularly dangerous and ineffective way of getting rich.)

I'm afraid that the crack dealers have had a pretty thin time over the last ten years from me because I gave it all up in a Damascene conversion. But I did more than my bit for them in my foolish forties. Drugs can be great, for a while, as I am forced to admit to my godchildren. Anyone who tells you otherwise is either lying or ignorant. But they will very often kill you and wreck your life. That is the problem. And, *while* they do it, they *stop* you from getting rich. Better to forget about drugs and move on.

As for the wine merchants, I've been keeping careful count. By my reckoning, I have bought £790,000 worth of French wine over the last twenty years. When I reach a million quid, I'm applying to the Frogs for a *Légion d'honneur* for services rendered. I won't get one, but the French wine trade, when they read about it in the newspapers, will probably send a certificate and a pretty ribbon for *le madman rosbif.* Maybe even a free crate or two of Chateau Petrus!

Who else have I 'trickled down' my dosh to? Thousands of people have earned their living working at companies I founded or co-founded and hundreds still continue to do so. Printers and paper manufacturers, of course – but that's a cost of doing business and doesn't really count.

Lawyers – they always do well. Accountants, and tax advisors, naturally. Charities have done very nicely. Farmers have sold me thousands and thousands of acres of land they no longer needed. And banks have made a pretty penny from yours truly over the years. And art dealers. And Persian rug dealers. And architects. And restaurant owners.

Oh, and the tax man. How could I forget him? One year I paid £10 million to the UK tax authorities – or maybe it was twenty million. I forget. And they *still* tried to make me pay interest because I was *one* day late with that cheque, the rotters. When the story got out, the newsreader Trevor McDonald used it on *News at Ten* in his signature 'And finally … ' slot. Hilarious stuff – even the Inland Revenue thought so – but I still had to pay them that one day's money.

By the way, I always pay the Inland Revenue by old-fashioned cheque rather than by electronic transfer whenever I can. That way, I have a Xerox copy of the cheque to pin up on my kitchen wall as a memento (there are a *lot* of them on that wall) and the Revenue tend to lose a day or so's interest to the clearing banks. Now two days' interest on £20 million would be, er … oh, eight or nine thousand pounds, give or take. That's how clearing banks get rich. I'd rather the banks got rich than the taxman.

So is it true that 'Whoever Dies with the Most Toys Wins'?

Naaah. That's rubbish. It's like 'Greed is Good', which came later. Greed ain't good. And toys are the last thing on your mind, lying on a bed of ice and fire while nonchalant young ticks in white coats pull a face like they're sucking a lemon before pronouncing your doom. You won't be worrying about toys and gadgets then, except perhaps the respirator.

Making a lot of money is like piloting a ship. You cease to be a person to many others. You become, instead, a freighter loaded to the gills with ingots. They want some of that gold and they will go to any ends to get it, the worst of them.

Here's John Donne, ostensibly writing about naval warfare, but he isn't, you know.

A Burnt Ship

Out of a fired ship, which, by no way
But drowning, could be rescued from the flames,
Some men leap'd forth, and ever as they came
Neere the foe's ships, did by their shot decay;
So all were lost, which in the ship were found,
They in the sea being burnt, they in the burnt ship drowned.

He was a clever dick, the preacher Donne. You'll have to watch you are neither burnt nor drowned when you're the master of your own laden galleon. Wait and see.

A lot of it I've given away. To friends, to good causes and charities and the arts and children's education and relatives and to anything that took my fancy in the newspaper that day. And to planting trees.

Seems daft, doesn't it? What was the point, then? Well, I can't tell you what the point of making all that money was. Just because I *could*, I suppose. And because I hated being poor all those years ago. Mind you, I'm still far from poor. And I'm not finished yet, either. Not by a long chalk.

But it will all go eventually. Where it belongs. Back into the hands of those who need it and, perhaps, to some who don't. But let's not get maudlin. Here's a poem to cheer you up.

Pitch and Toss

For thirty years, at pitch and toss,
    In Mammon's inky halls,
I hurled benighted dice across
    The stone of hazard's walls,
And little reckoned win or loss.
The game was all; the rest was dross.

As living ghosts, a world apart,
    We toiled in lucre's maze,
The sun shut out of each man's heart,
    The glittering lamps ablaze;
We little reckoned stop from start,
The Midas touch was all our art.

In frenzied play, at fever pitch,
    We sought to build our store,
While Lady Luck, that slattern bitch,
    Would taunt us from the door;
We little reckoned who was which:
The newly poor, the newly rich.

And there I built my dragon hoard
    Of silver and of gold,
And bound it with a miser's cord
    To gnaw when I grew old,
And little reckoned fire or sword,
And thought myself a mighty lord.

'Til, falling sick at last, I stepped
  To seek the open sky,
To bribe the guards with all I'd kept
  To lead me out to die.
I little reckoned as I wept
That joy into my soul had crept.

But joy in want, is joy deferred,
  And paupers' lives are short,
Fat worms are for the early bird
  And I was fit for nought;
A fool might reckon what occurred:
They took me back without a word.

So did I learn anything? Anything you might find useful when you become rich yourself? Yes, I did. Here are a few truths I discovered the hard way, some of them concerned with the immediate aftermath of getting rich, and some concerned with staying rich, not to mention relatively sane. *Relatively*, mind.

○ **Keep giving it away.** The faster you give it away, the more money will flow back to you. Not because of 'karma' or 'universal cosmic forces', but because you then spend less time defending it and more time making more of it. Investing in private companies you think can do well is another sensible ruse for staying rich, but giving it away on a continual basis is a surer route. By the way, when you do start giving it away, find someone to do it for you. Most of my money is given away by a lovely lady accountant called Catherine Bishop, and she does a far better job of it than I.

○ **As soon as you've spent it, gifted it, loaned it or invested it, forget it.** More angst and worry comes into the world from concern over past investments, loans or gifts than can be imagined.

It's gone. Forget it. If any of it returns to you, fine. But that should not be your primary concern, unless you invested for safety's sake. Which is a different matter. All you did with that type of 'investment' was take a punt or make a gift. Do not waste time playing the 'blame game' over investments, loans or outright gifts, however large. The blame, if there is any, is yours.

O **Never loan it to friends.** If you loan money to a friend, you will lose your friend as well as your money. Give them whatever you feel like giving. Then forget it. Ditto with relatives. If you diligently follow this one piece of advice, you will be saved a sackful of misery. Trust me. Broadcast your policy loudly. This will spare you from many embarrassing demands that will otherwise vex you.

O **Get 'first flush' barminess out of your system as fast as possible.** You're going to do it if you get rich. Yes, you are. You are going to buy a sodding great big house, then more houses abroad, then servants by any other name, then you are going to start misbehaving. Gambling. Credit-card abuse. Expensive clothes. Whores. Drugs. Drink. Fast cars. Private jets. Big parties. Interior designers. Gold taps. The lot. This probably can't be avoided. But the sooner you can work through this 'barmy' phase, the better your health will stand up, and the sooner you will get your second wind.

O **Your oldest friends are your only friends.** Sad. Very sad. But true. And not all those old friends will be comfortable with the new disparity in wealth between you and them. You'll have to wait and see which. And, surprisingly, you will have to work on those friendships for quite a while. They're important to you, believe me. Only your old, trusted mates can tell you when to get off. Will dare tell you that you're out of order. But why should you have to reach out to *them*? Because ...

O **Get used to being 'cut off'.** I do not carry a mobile phone or any communications device on my person. At least, not one anyone knows anything about. No one has my email address, because I refuse to register one. I never will. I am very hard to reach and that's deliberate. Only a very few trusted aides, business associates and my lover can reach me day or night. And sometimes, not even then. If you do not begin to isolate yourself pronto when you get rich, then you will be driven mad pretty swiftly. At least that's my experience. It isn't that *you* have changed so much, (although believe me, you have), it is simply that you are now a loaded galleon, a supertanker, and all the pirates have lookouts. There just isn't enough time in the world to deal with them all. Avoid them instead.

○ **Avoid developing 'plate-glass vision'.** It's true you want to be difficult to reach, but that doesn't mean you should allow yourself to develop what Bob Dylan called 'plate-glass vision'. No need for that. I often eat at the same small restaurants I always did in London and New York. They know I've done well, but the staff there have no idea *how* well. I drop by my companies without notice and chew the fat with employees and managers regularly. I invite many of them to visit me at my private office, one on one. Even with my poetry, I go on the road on long tours and let the audience tell me what they think, face to face. In Mustique, I often invite yachtie strangers I've met at the local bar up for a shower and a drink or a meal – to their astonishment, usually. 'Plate-glass vision' won't make you poor, but it will drive you crazy.

○ **Develop a passion outside of making money. Fast.** If I had made the time earlier to discover that I could write poetry that thousands of people would be kind enough to purchase and enjoy, I would have saved myself many torments of the pit. People who can make money are often easily bored. That is true of me. So when the day's work was finally done, I used to make my own entertainment. There's nothing intrinsically wrong with orgies, parties, narcotics and booze – but they *will* kill you in the end. If I had spent the thousands of nights writing poetry that I spent playing the fool to keep boredom at bay, I would be a happier, healthier man today. And a better poet to boot!

○ **Get your own private advisors.** The professionals who help run your company must be first class. The professionals who run your private wealth for you must be even classier. There is no substitute for a first-class lawyer, tax advisor, accountant, auditor, estate manager and business advisor. None. You will get into a ton of trouble if you don't search them out, appoint them, and make your peace with them at the earliest opportunity. Avoid the errors I made in my first few years of being rich. Do this earlier than you think is necessary. You'll understand why later.

○ **Watch out for fraud in the early days.** When you first hit pay dirt, you will not have the systems in place to detect fraud swiftly. That happened to me. A bent accountant siphoned off tens of thousands of pounds from my company before he was caught. That was a lot of money back then. Money I could not afford. (The scumbag's name was Ian F_____. You see, I haven't forgotten, Ian, you little toad.) How was he caught? He went on holiday and his deputy got suspicious of some stuff she found in the mail. Never trust a senior accountant who will not use their allotted vacation time! And install good accounting systems the second you can afford it.

○ **Do not try to be friends with your staff.** When you are worth several hundred or a thousand times what a member of your staff is worth financially (do the math), then trying to be friends with them or encouraging them to be friends with you is silly. *They* know it's phony and *you* know it's phony, and they *know* that you know. Not being friends comes with the territory. Being fair and friendly is always cool. Trying to be 'one of the boys' is pathetic.

○ **Do not sleep with your staff.** It's dumb. It's unfair. And it sucks. Period.

○ **Choose personal aides with enormous care.** You may spend more time with your PA, your chauffeur or your business manager than with your husband, wife or lover. Or even, sadly, than with your children. If a personal aide is not working out, then fire him or her just as soon as you know. But be very generous when you do so. Tell them it's your fault – it probably is. Close aides like these *can* become your friends, and usually do, over time. That's understandable. But try to keep a little distance 'just in case'. Ensure they are employed under a very different contract than employees of your company. They must work for *you*, not your company.

○ **Don't abuse it.** The maitre d' in your favourite restaurant doesn't mind being verbally abused. He's paid to be. He knows you will have to award him a huge tip next time if you want that 'special' table. Even your close aides will be prepared to put up with the odd temper tantrum and hissy fit. But your company's employees are not paid on that basis, and nor are the employees of other companies you come into contact with. They most certainly do *not* appreciate being verbally assaulted. Oddly, I could shout and rage a lot more easily in the old days with my company staff. We were all in it together, then. And anyway, they shouted right back. But not now. Unless you are a president, managing director or CEO of your company, keep your feelings about an employee's abilities to yourself in public. Being rich doesn't give you the right to abuse anyone.

○ **Be safe.** If you make a lot of money, then it's foolish not to look to your security. Even *speaking* to 'security advisors' is weird – you feel like a fraud or a B-movie actor. Get over that. Quickly. No need to get paranoid about it, but effective security for you and your family has to become a priority. If you get rich enough, you will end up with your own security force, as I have. It's a pain, and I still feel like a fraud, but the alternative isn't worth contemplating.

○ **Never stop looking for talent and promoting talent.** This single suggestion will keep anyone rich. Talent is all most companies consist of. Talented people are crucial to keeping your company humming right along and growing. As the owner, you have the right to seek out talent, both inside and outside of your company. You have the right to insist it is promoted or hired. Make use of that last right. If you get known for making use of it, the talent will start coming to you.

○ **No deal is a 'must-do' deal.** It's easy to get carried away when you are in pursuit of a sweet deal. But more entrepreneurs get themselves in trouble by overreaching than exercising discipline. No deal is a total make-or-break deal. Not one. If you cannot get the terms you know make sense, then walk away. This is one occasion when you have the right to overrule senior management in your company, if you feel strongly enough. Listen hard. But if you are not convinced, insist they walk away.

○ **Lead. Do not be led.** You have employed a bunch of talented boys and girls who are smarter than you. Great. But you are their leader. If you sniff an opportunity, then get them to consider it. If they prevaricate, call a meeting and brainstorm. If they still won't get excited, then take the project into your private office or somewhere else and begin it there. Do not leave the opportunity within the company to be sabotaged, focus-grouped and committeed to death – which is almost certainly what will happen to it. Your employees and advisors are just that: employees and advisors. You are the owner. You must follow your instincts. You must lead.

○ **Stay as healthy as you can.** I have no advice to offer on this subject – and no right to offer any. I'm rich, not a hypocrite. But staying healthy long enough to enjoy your wealth must make some kind of sense.

○ **If you're bored with a business, sell it.** You will not be able to disguise your lack of passion for a business if you fall out of love with it. Your lack of enthusiasm leaks out of you and infects those around you. They can sense it and they will find it hard to forgive and easy to emulate. Sell that particular business pronto. Then go and invest in something that doesn't bore you.

○ **Try to sell before you have to.** You're an entrepreneur. Your companies are not your 'babies', they are tools for acquiring wealth. Try to sell them before they peak. Buyers require what is called 'blue sky' (further growth) to get excited and offer a great price. I'm bad at this, sometimes. Fortunately, my American partners, Peter and Bob, are good at it. And, usually, they are right.

○ **Retirement will kill you.** It's official! Retirement kills the kind of people who make their own pile. I do know *one* couple, old friends called Don and Sue, who squirrelled away a million bucks or two (plus a house) and travel quite happily, and very modestly, for most of the year. They go to India and Indonesia and other such places. Or else stay with friends, like me. They love their life, and are content to live on the interest from their investments. But they are the only ones I know who ever really retired contented. Interestingly, Don always predicted he *would* retire early; long before he made any money. Still, for most men and women who have made a *lot* of money, retirement is usually a living death sentence.

○ **Remember you are only richer than them. Not smarter than them.** If you do not employ a great many people smarter than you in your company, you are either Albert Einstein reincarnated or a fool. Making money doesn't mean you are smart. Having a posh car, a fancy office and wearing a $5,000 suit doesn't make you smart. Being surrounded by technology, research and cool gadgets does not make you smart. Living in a big house does not make you smart. It makes you rich. The sun does not shine out of your backside. You are not infallible. You are neither the Pope nor Albert Einstein.

Here's my favourite story about the 'infallibility' of power. It concerns a man in charge of a billion dollars' worth of machinery who thinks he knows everything. The transcript was released (rather mischievously) by the chief of British Naval Operations in 1995, from a recorded radio conversation overheard at sea near the coast of British Columbia.

Navy voice: Please divert your course 15 degrees to the north to avoid a collision.

Civilian voice: Recommend you divert *your* course 15 degrees to the south to avoid a collision.

Navy voice: This is the captain of a US navy ship. I say again, divert your course.

Civilian voice: No. I say again, divert *your* course.

Navy voice: This is the aircraft carrier *Enterprise*. We are a large warship of the US navy. Divert your course now!

Civilian voice: This is a lighthouse. Your call.

Oh, boy. Naturally, that officer of the watch can never have lived it down. He will be nicknamed 'Your Call' or 'Lighthouse' until the day he retires. All those years of saluting and keeping his nose to the grindstone destroyed in moments, because he believed the sun shone out of his backside.

Can you imagine saluting such a man? You would be giggling uncontrollably in seconds. Screw 'infallibility' and bring on the Awkward Squad. These are the senior professionals and talent you have installed in your organisation. If they are paid and incentivised right, you will not be able to persuade them that the 'moon is made of Stilton cheese' or that you are infallible. That's what you employed them for in the first place, remember? So you could get rich and *stay* rich.

It's your call. Believe in your own bullshit and grow steadily poorer, or listen to the people you employ and get richer and richer. I tried it the first way in the early days. When that didn't work, I got sensible and started a policy of deliberately employing men and women who were smarter than I was – and listening to them. It works every time.

The trick to staying rich is balance. I guess Lao Tsu, or whoever it was wrote the *Tao Te Ching* back in the sixth century BC, would say that all of life, all of existence, is about balance. By seeking to make oneself richer than one's neighbour, that balance is destroyed.

And maybe Lao Tsu was right.

But it is amazing how many philosophers and academics and wise men I have ended up paying the restaurant bill for, over the years. Call me cynical. Call me whatever you like – I probably deserve it. But I just don't think I was put on this earth to wax philosophical too often, except occasionally in my poetry.

I was put on this earth to get rich. To collect money that already had my name on it.

And then to give it all away.

Now there's balance for you!

Stay rich!

19

THE EIGHT
SECRETS TO
GETTING RICH

Fear not. For fear itself is fed by fear,
And all fears pass. Did no one tell you so?
Come take my hand, my friend, and we will peer
Into this fear's abyss. And jump! And know.

There are secrets and mysteries in the world. I doubt, however, that many of them are of much consequence to the subject of this little book.

Looking for the 'secret' to getting rich is not a sensible exercise. If there are such secrets, then I have never discovered them.

But, as humans love lists and 'secrets', here is my best shot at a very short list. A kind of 'secret' recap. The essence, if you will, of what I have learned along the way. (Strangely, compiling such a list is rather like writing a poem. You have to strip out any word not absolutely essential. Like the word 'absolutely', for instance!)

THE EIGHT SECRETS TO GETTING RICH

1. Analyse your need. Desire is insufficient. Compulsion is mandatory.
2. Cut loose from negative influences. Never give in. Stay the course.
3. Ignore 'great ideas'. Concentrate on great execution.
4. Focus. Keep your eye on the ball marked 'The Money Is Here'.
5. Hire talent smarter than you. Delegate. Share the annual pie.
6. Ownership is the real 'secret'. Hold on to every percentage point you can.
7. Sell before you need to, or when bored. Empty your mind when negotiating.
8. Fear nothing and no one. Get rich. Remember to give it all away.

20
REMEMBER
TO DUCK!

And I dream of the days when work was scrappy,
And rare in our pocket the mark of the mint,
And we were angry, and poor and happy,
And proud of seeing our names in print.
G. K. CHESTERTON, 'A SONG OF DEFEAT'

So that's it. That's how I got rich and how you can, too. If you want to. I won't blame you if you don't. Far from it. There are far more important things in life than money. (Spoken like the rich, hypocritical beastie you are, Dennis!)

It may well be that I have unintentionally led you astray. The middle-aged and the old are always doing that to the young. Just as any system leads us astray. In the words of John Gall, writing about 'Systemantics' twenty years ago in *The Whole Earth Catalogue*:

Systems tend to oppose their own proper function. Systems tend to malfunction just after their greatest triumph. [We all] have a strong tendency to apply a previously successful strategy to the new challenge. The army is now fully prepared to fight the last war.

There is truth in that. My 'system' may prove useless to you. But much of what I have written about was true long before the birth of capitalism, or even the beginning of recorded history, let alone the birth of 'Systemantics', whatever that may be. Technology changes. Tools change. The social landscape changes. Human nature does not change.

If you wish to make any comments concerning this book you can do so via www.felixdennis.com. It's mainly an all-singing, all-dancing poetry site, but there's a section set aside specially for *How to Get Rich*. I do not promise to answer comments or enquiries, but I do promise to read them all.

While you are up on the site, check out my poetry and treat yourself to one of my poetry collections. There's plenty of advice about getting rich in those!

Good luck on your quest if you decide to undertake it. And remember the words of Benjamin Jowett: 'Never retreat. Never explain. Get it done and let them howl.'

The first step? Just do it
And bluff your way through it.
Remember to duck!
God speed …

and Good Luck!

ACKNOWLEDGEMENTS

This book was the result of a dinner conversation. I had written a review for the business magazine *Management Today* about a book called *Blink: The Power of Thinking Without Thinking* by Malcolm Gladwell. He's the same chap who wrote *The Tipping Point*.

One of the guests around the table had read it. He thought it was OK; not exactly sensational, but OK. 'Seems a bit silly to write a whole book about one observation, though. He's talking about intuition, although he won't use the word. What did you think, Felix?'

I told him I thought it was bunkum. Snake oil. Just like every other so-called self-help book I ever stumbled away from at an airport bookstall. 'What the world needs,' I thundered, 'is an *anti*-self-help book. A book that tells people how *hard* it is to be a great manager or a great anything. About how *hard* it is to get rich. Bugger the glib insights!'

'They'd never buy it,' my friend smiled. 'People buy dreams, they don't buy reality. They want it made easy. They want a promise a fool could keep.'

'We'll see,' I growled, an idea forming in my mind. 'Not one of those books was written by anyone who actually *got* rich – except by writing drivel for cretins. And I've got my godchildren to be thinking of. Pass me the wine, Marie-France. Hmmm, we'll see.' Marie-France rolled her eyes and passed me the wine.

So here we are with *How to Get Rich*. I want to thank Gail Rebuck, the boss of Random House UK, who invited me into her beautiful London home and locked me up in a cupboard until I agreed to write it. I want to thank Sue Freestone at

Hutchinson, to whom I originally sent my first synopsis. And to my old friend, the agent Ed Victor, who let slip a pearl of wisdom when I mentioned the project in passing.

And I especially need to thank my editor, Fiona MacIntyre, and her crew at Ebury. Perhaps they will all become very rich indeed after taking such care with my manuscript. They certainly deserve to.

I want to thank good friends, especially Don, Sue, Dick, Marion, Eric and Steve, who sat in my Mustique dining pavilion as I read them yet another a new chapter, hot off the laser writer. 'Under a wide and starry sky', while the tree frogs whistled and the cicadas hummed in staccato unison, we disputed points and chapters with all the vehemence and wit that only the blessing of good wine seems to provide – at least around *my* dinner table.

Suzen Murakoshi gently reminded me, as she always does, to be kind but ruthlessly honest in my book; otherwise there would be no point in it. This, among many others, is a particular talent of hers. Moni Mannings, too, brought her talents to play with many insightful observations.

I am grateful to Caroline Rush, my personal assistant, who shepherded the whole project through its various incarnations. As I am to my other assistants, Wendy, Amy, Sharon, Michael and Toby, for keeping the world at bay while I wrote and wrote. Not to mention the guys and girls who run my companies while I do such crazy things: Alistair Ramsay, Brett Reynolds, Stephen Colvin, John Lagana and James Tye.

Thanks, too, to Ian Leggett, Catherine Bishop and Rebecca Ho who look after my money, and to David Bliss who ensures the home fires, wherever they are, are *not* burning. Also to HSBC Private Bank, who allowed my publisher to use the dummy cheque as the front cover illustration. Don't try cashing it – it won't go through!

As to my long-time partners, Peter and Bob, they are the real heroes of this book. Because, in truth, they helped me *make* most of my money. The pair of them have never let me down. Not once in thirty years. Much of what I learned along the way, I learned from them.

Thanks are due, too, to my old friend, the writer Chris Rowley, who I asked to do some research. *Some* research? Hah! Chris waded through *fifty* of those airport self-improvement manuals with names like *Sleep Yourself into Making Millions* or *Become a Genghis Khan Wall Street Warrior.* Greater love hath no man …

And to the companion of my heart, Marie-France, as always, and to my mother, who will *not* be pleased to read about herself in this book. But hey! I'm fifty-nine years old. A man has to stand up to his mother sooner or later. Right?

And to a tiny feral cat called Stringy, who crept around my writer's cottage on Mustique while I wrote all this. I can never mend her broken tail. But she has allowed me to stroke her now. And soon, she will allow me to pick her up. Smart as paint, like all her tribe, she has already discovered that the vent from a refrigerator is the warmest place in an air-conditioned room. Not to mention that the very same refrigerator appears to contain an inexhaustible supply of smoked salmon, milk and roast ham.

Lastly, I wish to say thank you to my fellow homeowners on Mustique, and to the Mustique Company, run by my friend the Hon. Brian Alexander, and to the people of St Vincent and the Grenadines, a country of which I am now a proud citizen. Making money might be important, but so is getting away from it all. St Vincent and the Grenadines is the least spoilt group of islands in the whole of the Caribbean. They are stunningly, heart-breakingly beautiful.

My advice to you, gentle reader, is to come here and visit the rain forest, the volcano, the waterfalls, the empty, sun-kissed beaches and the quiet bays and keys. You will find a smiling face around each corner and a green flash in every sunset. This is as close to paradise as it gets. And you don't have to be *that* rich to come join us!

ABOUT THE AUTHOR

Felix Dennis is a poet, a publisher and a planter of trees. The Sunday Times Rich List ranks him in the top 100 of Britain's wealthiest individuals.

He is the author of three best-selling books of verse: *A Glass Half Full*, *Lone Wolf* and *When Jack Sued Jill: Nursery Rhymes for Modern Times*. His poetry has been performed on two continents by the Royal Shakespeare Company and he has toured extensively reading poetry to large audiences in Britain and America.

Dennis's other interests include commissioning bronze sculpture, breeding rare pigs (and occasionally eating them), drinking French wine, collecting first edition books and avoiding business meetings. His greatest ambition is to complete the planting of a native broadleaf forest in the Heart of England.

He has homes in Central London, Stratford-upon-Avon, Manhattan, Connecticut and the Caribbean island of Mustique.

Find our more on www.felixdennis.com